FROM SACRED TO PROFANE AMERICA

CLASSICS IN RELIGIOUS STUDIES
SCHOLARS PRESS
and
THE AMERICAN ACADEMY OF RELIGION
Number Two

FROM SACRED TO PROFANE AMERICA
The Role of Religion in American History
by
William A. Clebsch

FROM SACRED
TO
PROFANE AMERICA

The Role of Religion in American History

by

WILLIAM A. CLEBSCH

SCHOLARS PRESS

AMERICAN ACADEMY OF RELIGION

Distributed by
Scholars Press
101 Salem Street
PO Box 2268
Chico, CA 95927

FROM SACRED
TO
PROFANE AMERICA
The Role of Religion in American History

by

William A. Clebsch

Reprinted with the permission of Harper & Row

Clebsch, William A.
    From sacred to profane America

    (Classics in religious studies [S.P./AAR]; no. 2)
    Reprint. Originally published: 1st ed. New York:
Harper & Row, 1968
    Includes bibliographical references and index.
    1. United States—Church history. 2. United
States—Religion. I. American Academy of Religion.
II. Title.
BR515.C55   1981   209'.73   81-9142
ISBN 0-89130-517-3   AACR2

Printed in the United States of America
1   2   3   4   5   6
Edwards Brothers, Inc.
Ann Arbor, Michigan 48106

To Sarah and Bill

CONTENTS

PREFACE

This book contends that the chief features of the American dream were formed by people's religious concerns and that they came into realization outside the temple. In these senses the book finds the aspirations of Americans sacred in origin and their achievements profane in fruition. I use the term "sacred" to designate that which is religious in nature, use, or association, and "profane" to mean that which has discarded, superseded, or otherwise lost its religious nature, use, or association.

The pattern that I discern in the shaping of American history by religion appeared as I sought to gain historical perspective on the place of religion in American life. That subject commanded my attention first as a church historian and later as an intellectual historian. The former work involved identifying American religion and religious movements by looking primarily to the claims they advanced for themselves. The latter shifted attention to the function of religion and religious ideas in the common life of Americans. In somewhat technical terms, the quest for the ascriptive self-description of our religion was augmented by, and in a certain sense gave way to, a quest for its intention-action description.[1]

Since the ascriptive self-description of American religion is presented in a variety of available historical writings, it seemed appropriate to emphasize here the intention-action description, especially in order to demonstrate how religion appears in American history when we assume that, regardless of its self-presentation, it really is as it really does. While the two approaches are, in principle, ultimately complementary, the lines of interpretation that they yield with respect to American religion only converge, and, I think, cannot be made into a single line.

Many persons interpret American society today as a congeries of secular institutions which have broken every past bond between themselves and religion. Over that supposed breach some rejoice, others moan. Since the concept of the "secular" seems to stretch or shrink with every new application, I have preferred to state the relation of religion to American history in terms of the "sacred" and the "profane." I thus underscore my dissent from, and consequent refusal to take sides within, any theory of simple discontinuity. Moreover, current religious trends toward accommodation to the common hopes and achievements of Americans seem to alarm those who measure religion by its own claims. From the more pragmatic perspective, the same trends appear to be quite natural and normal.

The relation between religion and American society is, I think, undergoing a very interesting change. Since the detailed discussion of this change is held off until the final chapter, it may help the reader for me to state forthwith that it strikes me as the kind of change which ought not evince a summons to refurbish the more palpably religious aspects of our national tradition, nor yet a call to clear our religious institutions by theological purgatives. The older jeremiads and the newer lamentations will do far less, I think, than clear analyses and calm experimentation may do to understand the change and to discover how pluralistic religion can serve a pluralistic society.

The instances of my dependence upon teachers, colleagues, students, friends, and (by no means least) foes are so numerous that I cannot recall them all; I do, however, sense great indebtedness to many persons. Certain special help deserves acknowledgment. Hans W. Frei, Winthrop S. Hudson, Martin E. Marty, and Alfred Clebsch made valuable critiques of typescripts at various stages. Carey S. Bliss and his colleagues at the Huntington Library turned the trials of research into happy times. For encouragement and inspiration I am deeply obligated to John W. Dodds.

More than any others my wife Betsy and our daughter Sarah helped me over the humps.

WILLIAM A. CLEBSCH

Stanford University
October 1967

FROM SACRED TO PROFANE AMERICA:

The Role of Religion in American History

CHAPTER ONE

THE PARADOX OF SUCCESS
AND FAILURE

Since early colonial times, religion has been engaging American history in a special way. Instead of commanding that society conform to a preplanned City of God, the American way has been to marshal campaigns to inaugurate in this or that dimension of the common life a yearning to turn holy hopes into earthly fruition. This religion has been predominantly Christian and mainly Protestant during the three formative centuries of the Anglo-American experience, and to the extent that it saw obedience to God as attuning the common life to the divine will expressed to believers in Scripture, it has been Calvinistic as well. Yet only in those few utopian communities that arose far from the highways of historical flux has America seemed the place to build a permanent Eden under God's legislation.

What is remarkable is not the failure but the success of religious efforts to inspire hopes and summon energies for sanctifying the arenas of common life in America. Once won, however, the spoils of each such campaign belonged not to religious institutions but to society at large. In that sense the unintended but nevertheless salutary effect of religion on American history has been to make a nation profaned—a society standing *pro-fanum*,

1

outside of religion's temple. Being without land of its own, as it were, organized religion realized in frustration that the improvements it made belonged to all America. To cite but the case that comes readiest to mind, churches have built hundreds of schools and seminaries to train saints and ministers, only to find that those institutions which flourished became the society's colleges and universities for making good citizens and public servants. Nor is the turnabout a strictly Protestant phenomenon; if the pattern was established by Calvinistic religion, by it was cut the cloth of American Catholicism. "Education in Roman Catholic schools has been 'virtually wasted' on three-quarters of the students so far as influencing their religious behavior is concerned, a study financed by the Carnegie Corporation and the Federal Office of Education has found."[1] Instruction under religious auspices flourished when and where it served the common welfare.

The same pattern describes other instances of similar form but of quite different matter. This book tries to explain how religion stirred successive aspirations of the American dream, aspirations which when transformed into achievements belonged no longer to the saints but to the citizenry.

The pattern of initiation, success, "profaning" (in the literal sense), and sense of failure fits the theme of education rather neatly. Other instances of religious inspiration and worldly accomplishment introduce subtleties and complications into the general thesis without contradicting it. This first chapter names the instances and briefly illustrates them, in the order of their increasing complexity. Subsequent chapters discuss the religious impact on features of American history, each one in detail; these are arranged in general chronological order.

The introductory chapter, in a word, serves as a schematic statement of what will be developed more chronologically. Here it is convenient merely to mention these six contributions of religion to—better, these prominent functions of religion in—American history in chronological order: (1) a persistent sense of novelty as distinguishing the American experience from the rest of history, (2) the right and duty of participation in the American social and political enterprise by every person and the cause he advocates, (3) education as the means of increasing piety and personal improvement, (4) a prudential morality which became the basis of American manners and social welfare as the product of religious commitment, (5) a sense of distinctly American nationality unlike any precedent nationalism, and (6) pluralistic culture as the accompaniment to plural religion. In each instance religious yearnings became popular achievements whose profaneness elicited negative reactions on the part of official religion.

I. A MATTER OF APPROACH

Changing the figure, religion in America sought ceaselessly to call into being the City of God, and with striking consistency found itself having built instead the cities of man. That becomes the story-line of American religious history when we shelve the question of what American religion makes of its own past, in favor of asking to what uses American history has put its religion. The questions are significantly different. Answers to the former abound in both narration and description. The latter has been asked only of a few discrete episodes.

It is a truism that historical data yield answers which fit historians' curiosities. Until very recently it has been mostly church historians who posed questions to our abundant data about American religion, asking what can be said of the denominations in the terms and categories by which denominations make their claims: conversions, missionary work, doctrines, sermons, worship, and the like. From the magnificent *Magnalia Christi Americana* of Cotton Mather (1663–1728) to the recent flood of synoptic histories of American religion, the central questions have been whether, how, and which men and women were made into Christian virtuosi by (or, for theological propriety's sake, through) the churches and their ramified apparatus. The same data offer as eloquent testimony when asked whether, how, and in whom did religious hopes awaken dreams of a better America, and what happened when these dreams came true. The latter question is of chief interest here.

One need not claim a superior identification of religion by inquiring into its function in American history than may be gained by asking about its developing self-consciousness. It is just that autobiography differs from biography (to speak metaphorically). What America did for religion differs from what religion did for America. Surely a sharper identity comes from asking both questions than from asking the former alone. For religion in America, that reliable identity which historians gain by assessing convergences and divergences between "biography" and "autobiography" awaits much more "biographical" writing. These assertions may be explained by a brief review of the historiography of American religion.

Most early historical treatises on American religion as a whole, even down to the Civil War, were addressed mainly to European readers. That fact helps account for these histories' sensitivity to the *effect* of religion on English-speaking America, yet their overriding interest was in its *affect*. Mather's *Magnalia* showed how religion formed goodness in magistrates as well as in ministers because he courted English approval of New England's novelty. If Jonathan Edwards (1703–1758) is to be counted a historian of new-world religion, to the *Faithful Narrative* of the Connecticut Valley revivals must be coupled his posthumous *History of Redemption*; in both he invited readers—and at first he was most widely read in Scotland—to see in the Great Awakening a freshet of true spirituality, but one that would water the garden of civic harmony. Alexis de Tocqueville (1805–1859) blended his accounts of cultic religion with comments on civic religion, and the accounts are so widely anthologized that their attention to effect as well as affect may be filed by title. Both Robert Baird (1798–1863) and Philip Schaff (1819–1893) in the 1840's and 1850's wrote for Europeans, Baird for Englishmen and Schaff for Germans, and both insisted that there were connections between individual piety and civic prudence in America because both wanted to impress Europeans with the idea that pluralistic religion bore good fruit, not banality or barbarism.

But with Baird and Schaff we reach a turning point, for both also subjected specific denominations—or "families" of churches —to close discussion. Their historiographic beginnings coincided with romantic emphases on sectarian geniuses by polemical chroniclers, and that flint on that steel set fire to the really dry pasture of introverted denominationalism whose verdancy Baird and Schaff were painting. From this time forward the effect of religion on American life receded from historical interest and into its place flowed affective exploitations of the genius of each denomination; church history, partly delivered from its post-Reformation polemical use by Mather and Edwards and others, fell back, as far as America was concerned, into slavery. That is most plainly seen in collections made by denominational antiquarians from the 1820's to the 1870's.

Even as the universally acclaimed dean of American church historians, as the founder of the American Society of Church History, and as a noted ecumenist, Schaff in his later years helped commission and edit a series of purely denominational autobiographies known as the "American Church History Series." Of the thirteen volumes, only two—one mainly statistical and the other merely eclectic—tried to depict American religion entire, and neither of these paid much attention to religion's influence on national or private life. The series set the style for generations to come, a style that asked of religion in America only what it claimed to be, one that sought the identities of the denominations and of their joint enterprises as those identities manifested themselves in religious claims. Sectarian self-portraits need not be deceptively flattering but the danger is always present, and the histories of American religion written between 1890 and 1950 are rarely free of some brushstroke covering a blemish here, a wen there, on this or that denomination.

The wheel of scholarship's generations turns slowly; fads easily become fashions. The capstone volume of the American Church History Series summarized the many denominational volumes, just as it was commissioned to do. But it introduced a scissors-and-paste method of writing "general" as opposed to denominational histories of American religion, by clipping episodes from many denominational chronicles and gathering them into one chronological sequence.

The famous series' seeming endorsement made that method negotiable in universities, colleges, and divinity schools down through the career of the technique's most notable master, William Warren Sweet, who died after the middle of our century. Sweet made his original contribution, to be sure, by choosing a lattice of social history (in his case an exaggerated frontier thesis) on which to entwine denominational chronicles for the appearance of a unified arbor. By the time of Sweet's heyday in the 1940's, young scholars were already investigating relations between American religion and other facets of American life, such as religion and . . . progressive politics (Henry F. May), music (Leonard Ellinwood), literature (Nathan Scott), law (Wilber G. Katz), intellectual history (Perry Miller), and many another facet of the common or *hochkulturische* life. For the most part, these "copular" studies planted themselves firmly either in religion-study or in one of the respective correlates and leaned out toward the other side. Few were bridges with equally solid abutments and with strong spans. From the time since the 1940's one can find irenic copular essays on religion and almost all dimensions of American culture.[2]

To bridge the history of American religion and another shore of American studies is nevertheless to assume a chasm or dividing effluence between them. These copular studies have enabled a few ingenious interpreters to achieve "a view from the bridge"; one thinks of Edwin Gaustad, Sidney E. Mead, and (in a special sense) Perry Miller. But rather than show connections between religion and society, or even see religion and society from the vantage point of their conjunction, a genuinely functional history of religion in America would at once construe religion as integral to society and society as embracing religion—allowing, of course, for those unusual instances in American history in which sectarian

isolation was tolerated or respected, as for example in the case
of the Shakers.

The problem of understanding the action of religion upon the
American dream is not paucity of data but the fact that so
many important data already wear religious clothes in the
imagination of us all. Solomon Stoddard (1643–1729), for example, as a figure in colonial Massachusetts, is of course significant as the rather conservative Puritan that he was in a strictly
religious way, but his full historical dress must show him also
as the radical innovator that he became in proclaiming that all
of religion's ordinances were instrumental to the transformation
of personal and social life. Familiar data, then, need reinterpret-
ing. Moreover, an interpretation of religion's function in American history needs also new, raw data—raw in the sense that they
have been neither collected nor previously studied for their religious significance. For this study, these data seemed best available
in some extensive manuscript collection of Americana that was
broad enough to include all regions and epochs and to reflect
impressions of many social strata and denominations.[3]

II. SUCCESS AND FAILURE

From the beginning, American Christianity has been ambidextrous. The story of its right hand's labors is well known as
"American church history." The right hand summoned people
to church, inculcated spirituality, taught doctrine, praised God,
bought property, erected edifices, accumulated money, trained
and hired and used personnel, and served the religious needs of
members. But with its left hand religion strove to build certain
qualities of life in America. Not that it has ever had a blueprint
for the ideal America, nor even that it has ever been the real
glue of American society; rather, it has built within American
society several cultural cities by stimulating urgent desires for
education, for participation of diverse peoples in a common life,
for a sense of American novelty and nationality, for good and
acceptable morals and manners and the general welfare, and for

variety in American institutions—including religious institutions.

By devoting itself to the American dream, religion has been not only ambidextrous but ambivalent as well. While the left hand's work has been owned by society at large and not by the churches, the right hand has usually known what the left hand was doing. Just when common claim has been laid to achievements inspired by religion, the denominations have usually sought title or possession—at least long enough to take credit for the work. This ambivalence has never been clearer than it is today.

American religion at the middle third of the twentieth century presented a peculiar paradox of success and failure. By any measurable standard it had climbed very near its perennial goal of subscribing the nominal allegiance of a majority of Americans. Nearly two-thirds of the people in the nation had their names on the rosters of one (or more) formal religious organizations, and all but a tiny fraction professed their belief in God of some kind or another. By contrast, at the genesis of the nation's independent career, less than one-tenth of the people were enrolled in religious denominations, and opinions diverging sharply from all traditional varieties of Christian theism were not only respectable but seemed to be the wave of the future.

These figures, to be sure, give a distorted picture of the facts. For it seems likely that, between the Declaration of Independence and the Treaty of Paris, the professed members of the congregations comprised a third of the persons commonly attending their worship services, while after World War II that was indeed a thriving congregation which drew a third to a half of its enrollment to an average Sunday's services, excepting perhaps the vernal feasts of Easter and Mother's Day. Early Americans who doubted traditional Christianity's God nevertheless acted in general as though He existed, while modern Americans who so fervently profess belief in Him are hard pressed to know how or whether that belief makes any difference in the ordinary affairs of life. Most believe in no literal hell but are convinced that after death their own immortal souls will live in some vague heaven. It would be difficult to find a decade in all American history when religion wore a face more appealing to American culture than it did during the 1950's; it is impossible to find a decade when its leading interpreters so nearly approached unanimity of concern for religion's failure.

It is, of course, not unknown for critics to cry "failure" at moments of success. American religion has raised up a long line of sometimes lonely prophets to denounce the accommodations by which religion made its impact upon American life. Solomon Stoddard protested Massachusetts Puritanism's making the Lord's Supper an instrument for excluding seekers from the fellowship of full saints. His grandson Jonathan Edwards decried men's claims to their own agency in achieving the salvation that he preached to them and, ironically, urged them to accept. Horace Bushnell (1802–1876) rejected revivalism, that hallmark of early national religion in America, as an "artificial firework." Washington Gladden (1836–1918) substituted social salvation for individual piety. William Jennings Bryan (1860–1925) spent the last years of his bombastic life campaigning to reintroduce God into public education which in its infancy had nursed at the paps of religion. Reinhold Niebuhr denounced the Christian pacifism of the late 1930's for what he called theologically naïve optimism of the belief that the Prince of Peace was the real source of international peace. The list is long, and these are mere samples. These prophets cried that success of the church signaled failure of the gospel.

By turning the proposition around, a strong case can be made that when religion's spokesmen perceived a flowing gospel in America, church life and activity ebbed. Not that prophets usually rejoice in a faltering church, nor that they often acknowledge a flourishing gospel. Yet the same Reinhold Niebuhr once wrote, "It is no easy task to build up the faith of one generation and not destroy the supports of the religion of the other." His contrast between faith and religion correlates with that between gospel and church. Citing Niebuhr's incisive insight one writer concluded, "In a real sense the chief victims of fundamentalism were the fundamentalists themselves. Their insistence upon the literal truth of the Bible denied them not only the benefits of modern science but much of the beauty and spirit of the very religion they were attempting to preserve."[4] It seems hardly necessary here to enumerate examples which abound in the pages to follow. A vast literature, both scholarly and popular, predicting the effects of the Second Vatican Council on American Catholicism is almost gleeful over the prospect that reinvigorated faith will tumble or transform ecclesiastical institutions whose solidity made them seem grandly immune to historical change.[5] But this successful-gospel/failing-church attitude is not new, for it is not far distant in spirit from the attacks by Awakening preachers—in no case more vociferous than in that of the Reverend James Davenport (1716–1757)—on the ministers and congregations of mid-eighteenth-century Boston. Thus critics who noted that ecclesiastical flood tide coincides with low-water piety have been complemented by spokesmen who wanted rising piety to damage churchly shoreworks.

In the middle decades of the twentieth century this paradox of failure and success came to be polarized. Sweepingly put, the clientele of American religion, the laymen—the men, women, and children "in the pew"—gloried in a succeeding church while the religious professionals they acknowledged as their leaders adumbrated a gospel to check that success. Theologians pleaded the ministry of the laity while laymen urged the sanctity of the clergy. The churches waxed strong after World War II on traditionally sound American principles by accommodating themselves to a major new trend in society, specifically the trend of suburban living.

Meanwhile, the professional ideologues of the gospel had been learning their theology from German-speaking dogmaticians who, by working on traditionally sound European principles, were recovering the symbols of those ages in which continental Christianity was most self-confident. The European theologians were led by Karl Barth, but most of them either veered from his path or else ran out ahead of him; they adumbrated a new terminology for an old gospel to reawaken a church that had failed to protest nazism but not communism, alas, to the same extent—worse than that, a church that had failed to serve people. But when that renewed gospel for a failing European church found expression in American idioms, there was no failing church for it to challenge, because the church was succeeding without really trying—succeeding in protesting nazism and even more so communism, as well as in serving people.

The devotees of the so-called theological renaissance in America fell into a trap of their own manufacture, the trap of thinking that the best way to proclaim Christianity was to claim for it everything. Rather than saying which, if any, of modern man's questions Christianity answered, they insisted that moderns must learn from Christianity to ask antique questions, e.g., about the inner nature of God, in order to receive Christianity's answers to all human yearnings. What has been hailed as a renaissance of theology was more essentially a subtle return to dogmatism. Following its advice led many Americans to discover that the old questions are not our questions, that the ancient language is no longer our language, and that ex-Christians understand modernity better than Christians.[6] The so-called theological renaissance has largely bypassed the lay Christian of twentieth-century America, not because he failed to hear its message but because its message failed to encounter his life. In a sense, the man in the pew had to learn to sing his cherished "Nearer, My God, To Thee" as descant to the preacher's "neo-orthodoxology." The clientele of American religion believed in the church while the professional class of American religion concentrated on a particular statement of gospel. This statement emphasized that, experience to the contrary notwithstanding, man stood under adverse judgment of God in solving his social problems to his own liking, and that man individually was too spiritually paralyzed to hear (much less comprehend) the word God spoke to him, that only when God provided the hearing—or at least the hearing aid—could His own word be understood, that only when the word was understood might true obedience to God arise. The radical message became more plausible to middle-class Americans when they read the clauses backward: since, as they thought, they lived in true obedience to God, what better evidence could there be that they understood God's word? If they understood it, they must have heard it; the doctrine of sin seemed aimed at somebody else.

To be sure, certain intellectuals, who had absorbed the literature and philosophy of pessimism which has fascinated Western thinkers since Kierkegaard and Nietzsche, comprehended the first word of the neo-orthodox gospel, but these rarely felt a need for what followed. T. S. Eliot's *Wasteland* was their home, and they drank Niebuhr's anthropology, intended as apéritif for the gospel, without becoming hungry for the main course of his theology. If, as this gospel asserted, Christianity provided the answers to the human predicament, the ordinary man in the pew seems to have heard that, since he subscribed to Christianity, his personal predicaments were being solved.

In the middle of the twentieth century these conflicting features of religion became polarized in America: sophisticated preachers adopted the new version of old dogmatism while their parishioners clung to the more available tradition in which Christianity improved the lives of those who subscribed it. That polarization of the success/failure paradox both culminated and transformed the dominant tradition of American religion. Since colonial times religion has encountered our society in a series of campaigns which ran through similar (but not identical) patterns. Here the similarities are chiefly interesting, but variants must be remarked where appropriate. Religion commanded attention by revealing a certain flaw or lack in the society, for which religion held the remedy. But when victory was in sight the society claimed the endeavor as its own and in doing so "profaned" it. At that point religion judged its success to be somehow a failure and it turned against the very feature of life it had fervently advocated. Then religion sought another point of contact at which to confront a problem with proffered cure, waged another campaign that led to success, condemned society's claim over the success, and so through the cycle again.

There have been, in the history of American religion prior to the middle years of the twentieth century, six such religious campaigns waged, won, wedded, and rejected. This historical pattern in the social utility of American religion of course gives no warrant of future recurrence. The consensus of astute observers of religion and culture in America today indicates that the pattern has run a certain logical course to its own exhaustion, evidenced by the polarization we have been discussing. Professional religionists tend to insist that profane achievements pervert religious aspirations, while the public apparently rejoices in the achievements unperturbed by alterations of original hopes. But all this is not to say that profane America has become separated from or has lost interest in the sacral stimuli that helped elicit the dream. Perhaps the apparent stilling of interaction between the two promotes historical understanding of their patterned relation.

As Henry F. May noted in 1964, "For the study and understanding of American culture, the recovery of American religious history may well be the most important achievement of the last thirty years." He suggested that enough monographic studies of episodes in American religious history now exist from which "to build a convincing synthesis, a synthesis independent of political history, though never unrelated to it." May thought American history had been "brought . . . back into the great dialogue between secular and religious thought. It is to this dialogue, after all," he asserted, "that American culture itself owes much of its vigor and complexity."[7] During the 1950's American church historians outgrew the style of denominational chronicles, either taken one by one or else woven into "general" church histories of America, and began to view American religion in a genuinely synoptic way. Yet these explanations of the churches in their own language as belonging to a common religious movement fall short of "a convincing synthesis." American religious history as embodied in churches—or "the church," if the singular has a palpable referent—is, then, a far advanced field of study in our time. American religion is distinctive, however, precisely for the fact that the aspirations it nurtured have found profane embodiments.

If the "great dialogue between secular and religious thought" is really to be resumed, the stand-off of polarization which switches these patterns into one another's terms must be undercut by understanding historically the function of religion in America. In such an understanding the churches will be seen not as institutions owning distinct or composite histories. Rather it must be relearned that the American churches in most important ways undertook sacred programs which helped to make American history as they were profanely embodied by the society. For viewed as one of many strands (but a vigorous one) in the experience of the American people, religion repeatedly enriched, fashioned, and transformed—and having transformed also repeatedly blocked, truncated, and diverted—that people's aspirations and achievements. To identify the aspirations which religion in good measure elicited and to describe those achievements which at once fulfilled and terminated such aspirations would indeed be to enter a persistent dialogue between the religious and the worldly dimensions of the American experience. It would also be to discover that many proud accomplishments now encased and cherished in mundane form were once infused with religious zeal and, paradoxically, became true achievements only by shucking their religious husks, thereby inviting the enmity of the very religious forces by which they were earlier cultivated.

III. SIX CAMPAIGNS

The chronological story that yields this aspiration-achievement-adversity (or need-campaign-success-failure) morphology of religion's function in American society is best introduced by reviewing the campaigns in the order of their increasing refinement of the basic form. What remains in this chapter is a brief statement of the programs for (1) education, (2) pluralism, (3) social amelioration and personal morality, (4) novelty, (5) participation of diverse peoples in an open society, and (6) nationality.

1. Education

The most obvious of all accomplishments stimulated by American religion is our system for making education available (in varying quality) to all, and proffered in advancing stages to the limit (ideally) of every person's capacity or desire. If not the mother, religion was surely the midwife and wet nurse of that system. In all its forms, and not least in the Calvinistic form, Christianity stresses literacy. For if God's self-revelation, which Puritanism took as the charter for all human action, was recorded in a set of writings, those who would interpret it to others must read, write, understand. In the earliest American settlements schools were founded as a religious duty. By the early eighteenth century, Massachusetts, Connecticut, and Virginia had not only schools but colleges. Among their most important aims was the training of learned ministers. To higher education the Great Awakening provided strong stimulus. After independence, instruction in many states became a public function, and the Northwest Ordinance decreed that "means of education shall forever be encouraged." In the great westward movement schools and academies were founded by missionaries and often conducted by them or their wives. Before the Civil War the vast majority of college presidents were clergymen.

Willingly but a bit uncertainly, religious institutions gave over most of their educational programs to public or private sponsorship. The child put out for adoption gained a brash, adolescent independence when state systems of education began to respect religious freedom by adopting policies of neutrality toward religion and when universities judged that academic freedom entailed independence from religious tests and controls. To the mature adults of American education—the university and the state school system—religious leaders reacted jealously and zealously, attempting to reclaim parental prerogatives such as demands for compulsory devotions in public schools, school-time or released-time sectarian instruction, on-campus facilities for denominational activities (including worship), and even, in the form of more than one theologico-pedagogic theory, detailed plans to save the university from the pluralism which was its very lifeblood.

The success of the religiously inspired aspiration for universal education to the extent of each person's capacity became an embarrassment to religion because indoctrination, which from a religious viewpoint is an essential ingredient of instruction, conflicted with the worldly view of education as free inquiry. Catholicism first conceived its system of instruction because education in America seemed too wedded to the Protestant culture-religion, but the full development of this system came in opposition to the secular nature of American education. Recent studies expose, however, little correlation between Catholic education and devout adherence to Catholicism. Thus Catholicism is belatedly experiencing an embarrassment similar to the earlier Protestant quandary regarding education. For here is a sector of the common life exhibiting a pattern of religious sponsorship, relinquishment, attempted repossession, and partial opposition. The very success of religion in engendering appreciation for education made religious indoctrination suspect, whereupon success became failure.

2. Pluralism

American man[8] has lived within a religious "city" very unlike that of his European forebears and contemporary cousins. His religious city is unique both in itself and in its relation to his other cities. For his religious city has been only one of many cities he has chosen to occupy somehow both alternately and simultaneously. Therefore his other citizenships—economic, political, familial, intellectual, and (more lately) recreational— have formed the character of his religious citizenship quite as profoundly as his life in the religious city has affected his other activities and allegiances. Religion has been for him a *polis*, but it has rarely been either his *cosmo*polis or his *metro*polis. By some impulses derived from, and others expressed in, his religion, he has wanted and labored to be a "polypolitan" man. Liking a plurality of cities in which to celebrate his many achievements and to pursue his many aspirations, he has liked also a pluralism within each of these cities, the latter preference being particularly powerful in his arrangement of his religion. Nevertheless having a religious city, he has made for himself a religious history that is vastly more than the mere grand total of the institutional affairs of those multitudinous denominations he has chosen to bring into (and some of them, latterly, out of) being.

The danger of exaggerating the pluralism of life in the earliest colonies is more than offset by the folly of assuming that all seventeenth-century people in the Massachusetts Bay Colony, even before it suffered a royal governor, were saints dedicated to the original theological and religious errand. To all intents and purposes, each of the colonies save Virginia, Massachusetts, and Connecticut was founded on the principle of harboring peoples of diverse religions. In the seventeenth century that was still an important diversity insofar as people still received their identity from their religion. By a peculiar irony crown agents in America interpreted the Act of Toleration (1689), following hard on the Glorious Revolution, to mean that Anglicans were not only to be tolerated everywhere in the English plantations but that theirs should be the established church in dissent from which others might be tolerated. Only in Maryland was such a program actually put into effect—the Maryland where Cecil Lord Baltimore had created the previous irony of Roman Catholic proprietorship with broad guarantees of freedom for other Christians. But the Anglican establishment in all southern colonies had eroded into indefensible formalities at the outbreak of the Revolution. The sum total of the colonial experience proved denominational coexistence possible, fruitful, and liberating. Little wonder, then, that religious diversity unrestrained and unconstrained by central government (and implicitly also by the states) struck the early historians of religion in the United States as its unique, novel, and abiding genius.

In colonial times religious pluralism thrived on the general assumption that everybody would become Christian, or at least would sympathize with Christian values. The national Constitution undercut that assumption by protecting the right to be nonreligious or even antireligious, raising to official status a combination of Roger Williams' protest against magisterial constraint of religion and William Penn's objection to religious restraints. During the middle years Christian consensus ran strong on energy generated by the revivals and courts wavered in applying the guaranteed right of irreligion, but the twentieth century has seen a broad extension of this right even to the prohibition of compulsory prayers in public schools. By cultivating pluralism in its own garden, religion helped advance diversity in all sectors of American life.

In late colonial and early national times three themes of religious thought and practice enlarged that denominational fecundity which by the 1840's was the hallmark of America: the erosion of theological pessimism about man, the revivals, and new revelations.

Doctrines of man are always correlative to doctrines of God in Christian thought, and from the middle of the eighteenth century onward the notion spread that man was God's partner, not His dependent, in the enterprise of salvation. Whatever the point of departure, any new emphasis on man's agency or initiative in the saving process was labeled "Arminianism"—as shifting a term in American theology as "left" or "liberal" in politics. The *New England Primer* (1737), already in use by 1691, taught, "In Adam's Fall / We sinned all"; therefore only at God's behest might any man be delivered from sin. By the outbreak of the Revolution, Boston's Charles Chauncy (1705–1787) believed that the divine benevolence necessarily entailed universal salvation, which was to say that Christian regeneration was the appropriation of a God-given right never really withheld. By the end of the nineteenth century Lyman Abbott (1835–1922) was mocking the old orthodoxy outright by approving the gibe, "In falling, Adam did not represent me; I never voted for him." Religion as the expression of salvation became a voluntary option for Americans who felt little need of deliverance and thought themselves capable of choosing their preferred way, if any, of joining into partnership with the Almighty.

The history of revivalism from Theodore Frelinghuysen in the 1720's until today reflects the ever more voluntary nature of Americans' religious obligations and activities. Billy Graham is only an apparent exception, for he emulates the earlier revivalists who preceded Dwight Lyman Moody (1837–1899); Moody's logical successors are Norman Vincent Peale and other "help-yourself-to-self-help-religion" preachers. Like the doctrinal disputes, revivals begat denominational schisms.

By 1850 a United States citizen could belong to any of thirty-one states as far west as California simply by establishing himself as a resident. The same person could belong to any of three times as many denominations, as far out as the Mormons, by his own volition and action. For by then there were not only many rifts in the older churches but also a plethora of new sects, many of which departed radically from the old Protestant (or even Christian) consensus by basing themselves on new revelations.

American religion's fissiparousness was both reflecting and forming the social and cultural pluralism of national life. As one city among many, religion itself became a pluralistic city. Plural religion helped inspire American man to create his own universe as a congeries of parts—or, better, his "polypolitan" culture. The inconsistency which Ralph Waldo Emerson (1803–1882) extolled put such high premium on diversity that integrity, in the literal sense, became un-American. Once this pluralistic society was pragmatically justified, as in the philosophy of William James (1842–1910) whose pluralism was closely coupled with his philosophy of plural religious experience, the aspiration was achieved. Although the German historian Ernst Troeltsch credited James with making the only original contribution to philosophy of religion that America has produced, the pluralism of James's philosophy struck many American religionists as dangerously secular, especially as it found detailed expression in the thought of John Dewey (1859–1952). Dewey made pluralism the principle of Americanism in A *Common Faith* and pointed a plurally conceived venture of education toward producing good citizens. Thus the sacred aspiration for diversity became a profane accomplishment.

Religionists quickly pronounced the success of pluralism a failure of Christianity. The religious education movement, more profoundly under Dewey's influences than its supporters admitted, yet vigorously abjured pluralistic ideology. A *Common Faith* became the whipping boy of seminary courses in Christian apologetics. Reinhold Niebuhr nominated Dewey as the chief enemy of Biblical religion in America. Martin E. Marty recently scoffed at Mrs. Agnes Meyer as "a most eloquent spokesman" of "The Religion of Democracy" because she called Dewey " 'the most religious of contemporary thinkers.' " [9] Since World War II various professional religionists have sought to affirm modern America, even with its pluralism, as still under the providence of God and therefore not at absolute odds with Christianity. Most notable among Catholics of this opinion was the Jesuit, John Courtney Murray. Among Protestants, Gibson Winter in *The New Creation as Metropolis* and Harvey Cox in *The Secular City* found much good in modern culture but were hard put to approve its pluralism save as a tentatively beneficial means toward claiming urban-technological society for a revised but unified Christian ideology.

Cultural diversity in America is in part the reflection, in part the product, of religious diversity. When cultural diversity received theoretical and practical justification as a profane achievement, thus exchanging its religious origins for humanistic grounds, it at first evoked outright condemnation which then softened into attempts to reaffirm plurality as a cultural expression yearning for a unity that only the Christian vision of life can provide. The success of religious pluralism was judged a failure, but if the achievement could be reclaimed for religion the failure might be discounted as transitory. As an ingredient in the American dream, education is largely given over by religion to the common society. Pluralistic culture, many religionists are hoping, is not lost but only on loan.

3. Welfare and Morality

More difficult to classify under the success-failure syndrome is the relation between American religion and the struggle for social and economic justice, particularly as that struggle expressed itself in the movement known as the social gospel. Deciding whether the name fits the movement is less important than recognizing that while the Civil War was turning America into an urban and industrial society, Christian prophets arose in all the major denominations to preach that the gospel of repentance, conversion, and salvation applied to the whole society—not alone, as most revivalists urged, to individual persons.

From its inception, Anglo-American Christianity intended social submission to the divine will, and a common theme of colonial theology is the fruition of piety in benevolence. But before the Civil War, few theorists or practitioners of Christian ethics concerned themselves with political and economic structures—with the system instead of the person—as harboring evils which man could expunge from his garden in order to plant institutions yielding justice and welfare to all. Engaged though they were in politics, men like Cotton Mather and Jonathan Mayhew (1720–1766) and Benjamin Franklin (1706–1790) focused questions of good and evil on persons, not society. Both revivalism and romanticism before the Civil War strengthened this individualism, although the revivals did indeed spur attempts at social reforms such as temperance. Feeling that the war might have been avoided, Americans wanted to bend history to human advantage. Certainly it was the new, urban-industrial era opened by the war which gave early social gospelers their conviction that social systems must be harnessed to man's welfare.

Men like William Rainsford (1850–1933), Josiah Strong (1847–1916), Washington Gladden, Lyman Abbott, and Walter Rauschenbusch (1861–1918) are only a well-known quintet drawn from an entire orchestra of social gospelers who pricked the consciences of some early industrial barons, and whose programs for democratizing the economy and humanizing the social order struck alliances with the Progressive movement. In Theodore Roosevelt's administration some of their hopes took effect, but their entire vision of a society primarily concerned with justice remained a dream until they were in their graves and the great depression laid bare the twin follies of *laissez-faire* and *noblesse oblige*. Eventually, however, their vision became actual in the social-welfare legislation comprising Franklin D. Roosevelt's New Deal, Harry S. Truman's Fair Deal, and—after a pause that failed to refresh—John F. Kennedy's New Frontier. With familiar but telling irony the very successes of reforms proposed by the social gospel elicited theological and religious reactions appealing to older orthodoxies; these reactions denounced human progress as illusory, revivified the teaching of human depravity, italicized an eschatology which set low ceilings on historical possibilities, prompted a theological ethic that gloried more in describing the human predicament than in recommending ways to escape from or ameliorate it, and even refurbished the slogan that religion and politics must not mix.

It would be unjust to allow the inference that American Christianity's most prominent Jeremiah of the twentieth century was callous to social justice, for Reinhold Niebuhr paid attention equally to the necessity and to the impossibility of a moral society. Yet Niebuhr's "Christian realism" allowed no escape for "moral man" from "immoral society." It invited both its sympathizers and its exaggerators to enjoy a social pessimism whose only theological relief was the joy of knowing that the universality of sin pervaded even those small societies such as the family which Niebuhr held to be capable of replacing self-interest with some measure of love. The good news that all were evil salved many and may have saved some from the total dejection which nazism and World War II warranted, but that gospel seemed boringly repetitious as the country gained affluence to spend on relieving human misery at home and abroad and on avoiding nuclear Armageddon.

There were more cacophonous notes of religious opposition to the legislative success of the social gospel, sung by moralists who kept the individual person uppermost in their minds, by fundamentalists whose homiletical sallies against collectivism were broadcast by conservative millionaires, and by pietists who simply wanted to keep religion out of politics. Religious yearnings for the general welfare flinched at the realization that the common good often required breaches of an older moralism, such as the legitimation of divorce, population control, laws condoning abortion, and the cancellation of religious institutions' immunity from taxation. The social gospel's success in the welfare state, not in an ecclesiocratic kingdom of God on earth, tasted bad in many churchly mouths.

Religious forces, leaders, and institutions again became involved in social welfare when the Negro revolution gained national attention in the late 1950's and early 1960's. This movement demands careful consideration under the heading of participation by diverse peoples in an open society. But it has at least the appearance of the social gospel redivivus. The modern struggle for Negro rights, nevertheless, was inspired less by religious influences than by urbanization. By no means all Negro church leaders joined or approved the new demands. Predominantly white denominations pronounced nonviolent protests and certain court decrees morally righteous while condemning segregation as evil. Yet regional lines interrupt most of the general statements one attempts to adumbrate as touching the subject. Save for the Roman Catholics, the denominations that damned segregation were in 1965 hardly less monochrome in membership than they had been in 1945, Negro rights became a matter in which denominational and interchurch agencies issued guidelines for public policy which seldom jolted the normalcy of congregational affairs beyond eliciting differences of opinion and adjustments in contributions.

The churches' role in the Negro revolution is less a rebirth of the social gospel than an instance of religious effort to claim some credit for a profane achievement. Regarding racial affairs in the United States during the twentieth century, the credit due religion is for the steady attrition of positive theological sanctions for segregation and Negro inferiority; it was the social gospelers, notably Abbott and Strong, whose theological thrusts first effectively challenged racial superiority in American Protestantism. None of these statements accuses American religion of utterly neglecting social welfare, particularly of the obviously oppressed. But the campaign to apply salvation to society as well as to individuals was won in legislative halls and courtrooms, and the public character of the victory evinced resentment in the form of theological disavowals of utopianism and pious longings to keep religion and politics in separate pockets.

It is apparent that personal manners and morals were largely molded by religious sanctions, but the way that molding was done and the extent to which it was effective are elusive and widely misunderstood matters. The misunderstanding which must be set straight is that Puritanism developed a petty, hypocritical moralism under the aegis of religion. The elusive questions which must be answered are how and to what extent American religion let obedience to God's holy will become roughly equated with respectable manners. Neither of these tasks can be done well until the topic of morality is placed in its historical setting—the task of a later chapter. But to touch the points here may indicate that the theme of morality is crucial to a functional understanding of American religion.

The Puritan as moral prude is an image so deeply etched on the American mind that standard dictionaries confirm it. If the term is to apply either to the great majority of seventeenth-century Anglo-Americans or, more precisely, to New Englanders of the seventeenth and eighteenth centuries, denotations of restrictive precisianism must be laid aside. For the Puritan's genius was his use of the Bible as a reliable, yet flexible and varied, charter of the divine will for every human circumstance, personal and social. Obedience to that will brought palpable signs of approval, and disobedience resulted in calamity. In short, the good was the advantageous—even in a richly theological setting, morality was prudential. For New England Puritans the theological task was, as Perry Miller has put it, to show "that God's justice was for all intents and purposes the same as human justice, but they could not say that it was invariably the same."[10] The reservation arose from the distinction between God's secret will and His revealed will; he who read Scripture with faith learned the latter, but the ultimate mysteriousness of God included an overarching will which He kept to Himself. While no theological guarantee of identifying divine and human justice could be theorized, the self-consistency of a covenanting God made the identity practically reliable.

The revealed will was, however, flexible and varied as it impinged on human understanding. When calamity struck, behavior must be altered, and not simply by returning to the old ways; calamity meant God's disfavor, and to regain His favor involved searching Scripture anew to determine what lapses needed correcting. Thus the Biblical morality of the Puritans was both prudential and dynamic. If it lacked the spiritualistic immediacy of Quaker ethics, it also avoided the fixity that renders memorable the axioms of Benjamin Franklin—axioms which are prudential but which by forfeiting theological anchorage lost versatility. Thomas Jefferson like Franklin attempted to reduce Christianity to fixed moral principles. But such castings of Puritan prudence in rationalist molds did not yet profane the sacral authority of American morals. For the revivals extended the combination of prudence and flexibility, particularly in rural society.

Agrarian life, always economically precarious, required familial solidarity, personal alertness, and pecuniary frugality. Monogamy, the traditional Christian norm of relations between man and woman, became the prudential stabilizer of family life; philandering threatened the family as the basic producing and consuming unit of the economy, and revelries led to philandering, so preachers damned dancing. Calamity of fire or animal depredation could wipe out the pioneer's gains against the wilderness, and only the alertness of sobriety could guard against such threats; the preachers exhorted temperance toward liquor. Money was scarce but necessary to procure basic commodities unavailable by tillage or husbandry; therefore gambling was a sin. For sanction, the preachers searched—and indeed tortured—the Scripture.

When town and then city life replaced agrarian society's fragility with greater social and economic security, these particular goods were no longer advantageous. The ethos of the church, which had been forged for the pioneer's benefit by often rude but skillful revivalists, and the ethos of society were pulled apart by historical and sociological processes. The religious success in inculcating the practical identity of divine and human justice and in hallowing the classical equation of good with advantage permeated the life of towns and cities. But the avoidance of drinking and dancing and gambling became the specifics of Protestant morality in America, and when new circumstances robbed these specifics of their advantageousness, that morality lapsed into a moralism of respectability.

At the point of morals and manners, religion's interaction with American society is no simple instance of a success-failure pattern. Rather, considerable ingenuity had to be exercised in adapting the codes of nomadic or agrarian Biblical societies to the agrarian and pioneering phases of American history. The Puritan attachment to the Bible as God's charter for human action had as little purchase on American society when it became largely urban and industrial. Other forms of religion, e.g., Catholic, Lutheran, Jewish, more ably met the new American day because they had less experience with the old and because their morality had always been more cultic than covenantal. Cultic morality was less vulnerable to hypocrisy or to transformation into mere manners only by virtue of being less interested to cover all features of human affairs.

The American yearning to give prudential ethics theological sanction was generated by religious vigor that succeeded as long as America remained agrarian. Urban and industrial America clung to the axiom that the good was the advantageous, but in an increasingly profane way. While Christian ethics became manners and moralism, profane ethics identified the advantageous as the good.

4. Participation

Americans yearned to shift the denotation of the term "common" as applied to personhood from its European denotation of "lowly" to a new meaning of "equal." A commentator on the American dream put it with eloquence and fervor which beg lengthy citation:

But there has been also the *American dream*, that dream of a land in which life should be better and richer and fuller for every man, with opportunity for each according to his ability or achievement. It is a difficult dream for the European upper classes to interpret adequately, and too many of us ourselves have grown weary and mistrustful of it. It is not a dream of motor cars and high wages merely, but a dream of a social order in which each man and each woman shall be able to attain to the fullest stature of which they are innately capable, and be recognized by others for what they are, regardless of the fortuitous circumstances of birth or position. . . .

No, the American dream that has lured tens of millions of all nations to our shores in the past century has not been a dream of merely material plenty, though that has doubtless counted heavily. It has been much more than that. It has been a dream of being able to grow to fullest development as man and woman, unhampered by the barriers which had slowly been erected in older civilizations, unrepressed by social orders which had developed for the benefit of classes rather than for the simple human being of any and every class. And that dream has been realized more fully in actual life here than anywhere else, though very imperfectly even among ourselves.

It has been a great epic and a great dream.[11]

The great dream of the participation by all persons in an open society began as an application of Christian principles to new-world conditions. Its religious stimulus came less from Puritans than from Quakers. For the New Englander clung to an aris-

tocracy of religion and learning as firmly as the Virginian stratified his community along lines of breeding and property. But
once the two pervasive features of new-world Christianity—congregational polity and evangelical piety—merged into complementary instead of antagonistic impulses, religion became a
leveling force even in New England and tidewater Virginia.

Religion thereby became a powerful lever to pry open the
doors through which persons of every condition and estate—
rich and poor; men, women, and children; native and immigrant
—might participate fully in the social life, attain equal personal
identity before the law, and eventually be partners in politics.
The congregational pattern of religious organization was, to
extend the metaphor, the lever itself. It provided the primary
experience and repeated practice in social equality for a very
large number of Americans. American churches have always been
fundamentally congregational regardless of their theoretical
polities, and local religious societies gave generation after generation of persons their initial schooling in politics, in parliamentary
debate, and in that vaunted virtue of the mature American:
leadership. But the lever needs a fulcrum, and in this case the
fulcrum was evangelical zeal. Although typified by the Great
Awakening and the revivals, this zeal permeated American religion even in quarters stoutly opposing enthusiasm and excitement.
Discounting the few intentionally exclusive sects, each denomination has held in principle that every person might—and in
conscience every person ought!—join one of its congregations.

The statement that religion both practically and theoretically
initiated equality of personhood and openness of society is accurate only to the point where it was undercut by a strange irony.
For with few exceptions before the Civil War the statement
does not apply to the American Indian, and with few exceptions
after the Civil War it does not apply to Negro Americans. Thus
the remarkable success of religious stimuli toward equality of
persons, toward full participation of all in society, and even
toward the right to advocate any cause in the open forum of
politics seems to have been paid for by the heavy price of racial

exclusivism. Only in recent times have the denominations officially—and with obvious desperation—tried to reverse this exclusivism by decrees, by commissioning delegates to join in protests demanding full civil rights for Negroes, and, with less effect, by achieving integration of congregations in token or begrudging fashion depending on region.

Assignment of motive is rarely legitimated by historical data, but it suggests itself that the denominations' race to rectify their stands regarding Negroes has been impelled by shame for past neglect and perhaps also by envy; for it is the segregated Negro churches, not the white denominations, which have been directly relevant to the most notable social upheaval of mid-twentieth-century America, and that at a time when relevance was a chief desideratum of organized religion.

Participation as equals in an open society by all persons, although a goal religiously derived in large part, could be reckoned an achievement of free Americans by the 1850's. For a century thereafter the society as well as its religion acceded by design or default to racial exclusivism. Only when profane movements for guaranteeing Negroes full rights received judicial and then legislative approval did organized religion attempt to reclaim its campaign for equality of their personhood.

Here then is a subtle variation on the pattern of inspiration-achievement-resentment by which religion has functioned in American history. For the profane success of personal equality hurled no challenge at its religious sources until quite belatedly it became apparent that equality among the dominant white element of the society rested on indignities and inequalities immorally forced upon racially distinct minority groups. The tension between the sacral and the profane dimensions of American life in this instance arose from the fact that the latter awakened to this injustice before the former did so. Then embarrassment overwhelmed the guardians of the sacred, particularly because regional differences prevented a united religious front from forming to identify and oppose the injustice to which religion had been party.

5. Novelty

The characteristic of American common life that was earliest and most profoundly stamped by religion is the spirit of novelty. The lure of inaugurating a new era that drew early settlers to the colonies gradually melted into a conviction that the American experiment consummated the highest hopes of European history and broke down the walls that cabined man in traditional ways of thought and action. During the war for independence from England this innovating spirit jettisoned much of its religious content, but attempts were made to reenthrone God as guiding the nation into ever new endeavors. By 1840 the contest had been lost; American man ruled his own enterprise and he held open its future. Religious reaction to Jacksonian populism emphasized the traditionalizing force of religion, either by way of revivalism's presentation of "old-time religion" or through recovering the faith of European fathers by romantic theology.

Even as Englishmen and others enlisted in the colonizing enterprise, they were fashioning the theme of expectation—a theme latent in all Christian doctrine—into yearning for special newness of life in the new world. Turning their backs on enmities generated by appeals to divergent traditions on the part of each of Europe's post-Reformation churches meant facing westward for that new and, as some thought, final empire envisioned by the prophet Daniel as God's crowning work in history. Varying in form and intensity among settlers from New England to Virginia, colonists thought themselves to be both innovating and renovating as they set out to erect a new Zion in the American wilderness.

By the middle of the eighteenth century each region had established its own version of the new kingdom of God in America, when in the form of the Great Awakening there fell from heaven (some thought it arose from hell) yet another renewal, one which leaped over all colonial boundaries in the persons of men like George Whitefield (1714–1770). Conservative preachers more than their parishioners resisted enthusiasm by pleading the sufficiency—and sufficient novelty—of existing forms of piety and belief. Yet the Awakening captivated the colonists' imagination while raising up the first truly intercolonial heroes and offering the first generally American experience. The newness of the American experiment received from the Awakening a divine blessing in the shape of theological sanction. Jonathan Edwards among others interpreted the Awakening as demonstrating God's plan to save America for a new phase in the history of Christian redemption. The Awakening transformed "seekers" into what Oliver Cromwell had called "happy finders," and inaugurated, if not a Fifth Monarchy, a generally approved Joachimite "third age of the Spirit" in which men were to be free—under God, from King George, and for government by consent.

This religious basis for American novelty coalesced with political theories heralding a new era in human affairs, and the coalescence led most denominations to promote and, after the fact, all of them to approve, the war for independence. But as the new United States incarnated Christian as well as rationalistic novelty into a government friendly to France and the early phases of her Revolution, American religious leaders began to notice that the new age superseded Christendom; for most of them the success of this aspiration took on colorations of failure. Hundreds of pulpits hurled condemnations at the French Revolution; the blood baths and the guillotine seemed signs that providential wrath turned secular forms of the new era into chaos. The gist of the message was that a new Zion must indeed be a Zion if it were to be saved from new dimensions of human horror. For decades preachers all over America took up the cry, pointing the contrast between France and America. However they came by the knowledge, they were sure that God fostered the new era only in the new world, and there only if a renewed and renewing Christianity flourished without constraint or restraint.

The religious awakening in America at the turn of the century, commenced by Timothy Dwight (1752–1817) at Yale and then theologically grounded in the revised Calvinism of the New Haven school, proved the point. Theological reflection upon, and adjustment to, revivalism took historical events as proofs of God's "Nay" to irreligious France and "Aye" to pious America. In his famous *Concio ad Clerum* (1828), Nathaniel W. Taylor (1786–1858) modified for Connecticut clergy the old dogma of human depravity, relegating its applicability to the old world and claiming for the new nothing worse than the unavoidability —softer indeed than necessity—of sin. Revolutionary Paris, Taylor cried, "that city, the seat of art, of taste, of refinement, of every thing that can grace human nature short of religion," became overnight "a den of assassins, . . . her streets crowded with scaffolds raining blood on the gloomy processions of death, that pass beneath them." If one of the first true Calvinists to soften native depravity, Taylor was one of the last American Christians to claim the really novel power of religion in the new world. Conceding that not yet were *all* Americans friends of the Lord, he nevertheless found "this land" as the one "on which the Sun of Righteousness sheds his clearest, brightest day . . . ."[12]

Eventually the proponents of the old public sanctions for religion in Connecticut, New Hampshire, and Massachusetts joined the chorus calling, as had earlier Virginians and Marylanders, God's blessing on the novelty of the American experiment's free religion, unrestrained because unconstrained by governments. When the quest for an open future took form in the westward movement, however, the hope for an ever new start in life found goals that were spatial, temporal, and material rather than universal, eternal, and spiritual. First the popular churches—Methodists then Baptists then Presbyterians—went out to suffuse the pioneer with piety. As religious leaders measured the trek across the mountains they also took the temperature of Jacksonianism's hot blood; their answer to both was to develop stratagems and campaigns to tame novelty and to discipline freedom.

These tactics were modeled after the preachings of the Great Awakening, but when made into calculated devices with predictable results they became not awakenings of the spirit but resuscitations of the churches, not arousing courage and manly spirit for an unknown future but enlisting men into religious beliefs and behavior that leashed them to the traditions and stabilizing influences of the denominations. The spontaneity of a Francis Asbury (1745–1816) gave way to the competition of a Peter Cartwright (1785–1872), and the camp meeting became the revivalistic campaign. The surprising work of God which attended the preaching of an Edwards became the detailed plans for religious excitement and enlistment of Charles Grandison Finney's (1792–1875) "new measures." The new Zion in the wilderness became the temple of the old-time religion, and the force of American piety no longer sent man on toward the unknown heaven on earth but summoned him back to the well-known haven from the world that the denominations, each in its own way, claimed to be. Concurrently the main line of religious theory in America urged, under the spell of romanticism, a recovery of the grand antiquity of Christianity and a change in the function of religion from innovating to traditionalizing.

The sense of vigorous assent to novelty and innovation had by 1840 subtly but unmistakably changed to an attitude on the part of official religion that it must bind the American experience into the history of Christendom. The shift was subtle indeed, and those who brought it about seem only half aware of why they suspected the very novelty which their predecessors had urgently sanctified. The shift eventually elicited a "new theology," founded by Horace Bushnell, but this effort to recover religion's renewing power was so indebted to romanticism and so late in engaging the contest that in effect it became only a new theology, not a new religious stirring of the sense of novelty.

6. Nationality

The most complex of all American aspirations which were prompted by religious impulses is the sense of distinct nationhood. The Puritans' insistence that all who were covenanted with God also contracted with one another lies at the heart of this national consciousness, but it was awakened on a country-wide scale only by the early nineteenth-century revivals and was historically actualized by the Civil War. There and then was brought into being a nationhood independent of the religious ideas and experiences which gave it infant life. That self-substantiated nationality elicited religious possessiveness and resentment which, under guaranteed religious liberty, had to be borne in virtual silence.

Only in the seventeenth century and only in certain colonies was the cohesive principle of society in the new world religious uniformity. Yet throughout our history social cohesion has had a religious source in what is now called the "covenant theology" of English-speaking Puritanism. That vision of life, which received its earliest English expression in the writings of William Tyndale, is composed of three interlocking notions: that God revealed in Scripture everything man needs to know in order to live in holiness and die in hope; that God gave to believers in Christ the power to do what they knew would please God; and that God promised fulfillment here and in the hereafter to the faithful who kept the covenant with Him and with one another.[13] This covenant or "federal" theology enabled William Bradford (1590–1657) and his companions on the *Mayflower* to transform the congregational covenant of Scrooby Church into a written constitution for a civil body politic. The fellow believers of Massachusetts Bay Colony covenanted with one another in their meetinghouses, religiously on Sundays and politically on Mondays and other town-meeting days. In eighteenth-century New England less emphasis was placed on individuals' "owning" the covenant than on congregations' "renewing" the covenant.

Thus potentially any person might own the covenant, and therefore potentially all together might renew the covenant. By universalizing this candidacy for federal membership in a holy people, revivalism built in America what Perry Miller called "a religious nationalism which even the [Civil] war could not destroy."[14] Normative Christian interpreters of that war perceived that the covenant theory had early developed a nascent but proper sense of nationality, but that in the revolutionary and federal periods it was imperfectly applied as a mere compact between states and not as a covenant binding together a people. For these theologians of nationalism, perhaps best represented by Horace Bushnell, the Civil War brought the religious idea of nationality into full social expression. As influenced by religion, the idea capped a progression of awareness by Americans of themselves first as a people, then as a country, next as a government, and finally as a nation.

Nationality is of course more than an idea. It is also an experience by which modern Western man receives his historic and social identity, an experience conferring on men their commonness with one another as occupants of a place, as users of a language, as pursuers of identifiable cultural goals, as practicers of conventional mores, and as arrangers of internal and external political relations. The European nations whence America was mainly peopled had established their corporate identities on twin pillars of cross and crown. Royally sanctioned religious uniformity and religiously sanctioned royal authority were interlocking if not always smoothly connecting agents and symbols of nationhood in European Christendom. The older Augustinian theory of *homo religiosus* melted with the Machiavellian theory of *homo politicus* to empower each old-world nationality, large or small, enduring or transitory, with its historical and cultural genius.

The incipient United States of America presumed to brush aside most of this heritage in order to erect a certainly novel and perhaps pretentious nation built by *homo liberatus*, whose government and God were both placed in the service of the commonwealth. Samuel Hopkins (1721–1803), heir to Jonathan Edwards' library and system of doctrine, expressed the same idea more piously by making benevolence the chief content of holiness and nationalism the highest product of benevolence; it was a bold attempt to keep voluntary religion in intimate touch with the national sensitivity.

Former colonies became states with varying characteristics,

leaving unsettled the question whether sovereign states composed the union or the sovereign union comprised states. The vast continental territory invited occupation; with the statehood of Michigan in 1837 the number of new states admitted by the central government equaled the number of founding states. But few men could comprehend the reaches of a nation spanning the entire continent. As millions of foreign-tongued immigrants gradually acceded to a shared language, the national literature for which Emerson was pleading in his Phi Beta Kappa address of 1837 (the coincidence is notable) was long in coming into being. Liberty *from* traditions of Europe meant for many a loss of security in status, and only slowly were doors opened to liberty *for* national purpose. Aggregations of men able to believe and do much as they pleased, checked more by custom than by law and motivated more by opportunity than by order, became fellows one to another in the revival meeting more frequently and more profoundly than in common civic action. Within as well as to this country migrated men lured by rumors of fertile land, precious ore, and, later on, good jobs. A people of diverse language, ethnicity, custom, and religion were gradually to be absorbed by minimal political institutions, especially when the unitive forces of law and loyalty suffered vitiation by unexpected circumstances in unexplored regions.

A sense of national identity and unity was hard won because, before the beginning of military conscription, direct federal taxation, and general management of the economy, the central government rarely touched the lives of the people. Direct political participation was confined to state, district, or county for all but the most cosmopolitan citizens until the slavery controversy—exacerbated on both sides by moral and religious sanctions—galvanized attention more universally than anything else had done since the religious revivals.

Assuredly the Civil War brought a transfer of allegiance from statehouse to national capital for all Americans save the most unreconstructed states-righters. Between the Revolution and 1865 there fell heavily on the churches the related tasks of generating

a sense of nationalism and of raising an aspiration for real nationhood. After 1865 religious spokesmen interpreted the Civil
War not as disruption but as realization of genuine American
nationality. It was by then, however, a profane nationality:
ecclesiastically neutral, religiously optional, itself the attainment
of its own purposive act. By the end of Reconstruction the early
social gospelers were feeling resentment against this "profaneness" in their attacks on nationalism in the interest of a wider
brotherhood of man. In the 1920's the popular and populist hero
of many religious folk, William Jennings Bryan, tried to repossess
nationalism for religion by reconciling America and the Almighty, thus becoming the butt of Mencken's wit and Darrow's
realism. Nationality, the offspring of religion and history, had
made the first-named parent its lackey and held power of attorney
for the other.

Bryan's mentality tried to survive in tortured arguments that
God is humbly adored in the Constitution, in naïve exaggera-
tions of the meaning of such official phrases as "In God We
Trust" and "one Nation, under God," and in the utterances of
vestigial piety that often accompany major public ceremonies.
The ambivalence of these and other religious claims on American
nationalism appears prominently in pacifism, denominational
internationalism and ecumenism, American Zionism, and many
another instance of reluctance to hitch religion's wagon to
America's star.

In brief summary, American religion inspired universal education whose fulfillment in secular universities by and large has
been bitterly opposed by religion. Its own diversity demonstrated
the viability of a pluralistic society which it then yearned to
unify. It envisioned America as the site of a divine kingdom of
social and economic justice which, when politically inaugurated,
it chastened as blind utopianism. It conceived a prudential and
utile morality and conceded to a respectable code of manners.
It advocated the personhood of each human being but became
ensnared in a regnant racism from which it is only beginning

to escape. It engendered a sense of novelty which it eventually sought to stain with an antique finish. It mothered a nationality whose mature independence it deplored.

These several aspects of the American dream took prominent inspiration from religion. As dream became reality the source of inspiration receded far enough into the background to justify the conclusion that, on the whole, Americans did their planning within the temple of religion but did their building on profane ground. The priests who envisioned the kingdom of God as the habitat to which Americans should become accustomed in fact then derided the cities of man in which Americans began to live. For the actuality made religion one city among many and not the mother city at that.

What is now briefly introduced as the function of religion in American history must be scrutinized closely in order to identify the subtleties of the profaning process. That scrutiny exchanges schematic for chronological form, and reorders the themes in their overlapping but nevertheless significant sequence: novelty, participation, education, morality and welfare, nationality, and pluralism. Here the map; now to the terrain.

CHAPTER TWO

"AHEAD OF HISTORY"

Christianity's earliest stimulus to the American dream is also its most enduring influence on the American experience: the vision of the new world as locus for a new city. In theory the new city would not be entirely new because it would receive all that was good from the European heritage. In fact, it did inherit much of England's language, law, literature, and religion, but it gave the inheritance a new embodiment. Just as the City of God, as envisioned by Augustine of Hippo early in the fifth century, had rested on the Book of Daniel's apocalyptic theory that God planned a succession of kingdoms in progressively western regions, so the new world prompted Christians from the sixteenth century through the nineteenth to think of America as the last and best of human societies following the westward course of empire. Lincoln called it "the last, best hope of earth." As early as 1599 Samuel Daniel asked for the new city in Stanza 163 of his *Musophilus*: "What worlds in the yet unformed Occident / May come refin'd with th' accents that are ours?"

The answer, locating the final act of divine empire-building in Anglo-America, came with perfect agreement from such otherwise disagreeing voices as those of Bishop George Berkeley and Judge Samuel Sewall (1652–1730). The Bishop of Cloyne's poetic treatise *On the Prospect of Planting Arts and Learning in America* put it most memorably:

> Westward the Course of Empire takes its Way;
> The four first Acts already past,
> A fifth shall close the Drama with the Day;
> The world's great Effort is the Last.

The Massachusetts Judge was at once more prosaic and more Biblical in his *Phaenomena quaedam Apocalyptica* . . . : "May it not with more or equal strength be argued New Jerusalem is not the same with Jerusalem: but as Jerusalem was to the westward of Babylon, so New Jerusalem must be to the westward of Rome, to avoid disturbance in the order of mysteries."[1]

Through the pages of American (and sympathetic European) writings about America echoed the same theme; even so scholarly a historian as Philip Schaff sounded the note loudly when explaining the significance of the Civil War to German audiences.[2] In 1886 Josiah Strong was recalling with pride the enduring truth that John Adams said had been drilled into rock on the shore of Monument Bay in Massachusetts: "The Eastern nations sink, their glory ends, / And empire rises where the sun descends."[3]

I. SOMETHING OLD, SOMETHING NEW

Augustine applied Daniel's prophecy to western Europe's career by invoking a direct divine sanction for the City of God, a sanction claimed through the centuries equally by Holy Roman Empire and by Holy Roman Church. But before Samuel Daniel wrote his prophecy about America, the French political and economic theorist Jean Bodin (1530–1596) had interposed a jarring revelation: whether there would be four (or five) empires following the sun—the idea of a late Jewish mystic—was a question not of theology but of social enterprise. In this form the novelty proffered to the American experiment by Christianity was more the basis of a human dream than the assurance of a divine intention.

In the seventeenth century the proof of Scripture's pudding became history's eating. The Puritan founders of Anglo-America —and the founders of Virginia were in a sense as Puritan as those of Plymouth and Massachusetts Bay—knew that they must subject their errand to the severe test of historical endurance. They were no less insistent, no less determined than their successors to make novelty real, as they named places New England and New Haven. The same spirit led the Dutch to christen their colony New Netherlands and its capital New Amsterdam, and it prompted Scandinavians to found New Sweden. Both these settlements fell under control of the restored Stuart kings of England, and the former colony became New York. When the Jersey plantations united they did so as New Jersey. Even in William Penn's (1644–1718) woods the leading settlement bore the name of an old virtue newly embodied by people who had entered the new age of the spirit. Virginians named their colony for a reginal virtue, describing their hope for a pristine commonwealth; not so given to "New" in names, tidewater Virginia nevertheless offered New Alexandria, New Church, New Kent, New Point, and Newport News. Across the continent the more energetic Americans etched their determination to build New Harmony and New Hope, even after Franklin and Jefferson had placed on the new nation's Great Seal the motto, *Novus Ordo Seclorum.* Americans have continued their preoccupation with newness—however detached from Daniel's prophecy and Christianity's New Testament; the gazetteer in Webster's *New International Dictionary* (2nd ed., unabridged) listed 183 place names prefixed by "New," 117 of which are in the United States.

To the dream of American novelty Christianity made early and continuing contributions, despite the fact that organized religion by its nature is a traditionalizing institution given to celebrating the antique and seldom happy with innovations. As Winthrop S. Hudson noted, "The hope of all things being made new, in the course of time, was often subtly secularized and frequently restated in political terms. But the conviction remained that somehow this was God's country with a mission to perform."[4] In the process of becoming this-worldly, the hope of constant renewal, the pursuit of improvement over the old, and the quest for simultaneous fulfillment and transformation of the European past have not diminished, even when frontally opposed by religion.

To a considerable school of thought this restless innovating has made American society in all its parts ahistorical, antihistorical, or nonhistorical. Perhaps the most resounding of all such accusations is a typological but informative analysis of several major American historians, portraying Bancroft, Turner, Beard, Becker, Parrington, and Boorstin as theologians more than as historians. David W. Noble argued that the religious covenant which the Puritans intended as an escape from the complexities of history into the simplicity of nature became a national covenant with Jefferson—at least in the writings of our major historians since 1830. Only in Carl Becker's very late work could Noble find a "break from the Jeffersonian covenant" that might enable future historians "to find a way to relate American history both to its roots in the past and to its own fascinating record of development."[5]

Christianity's gift to the American dream has been, despite Noble's argument, to keep both a European and an American past in mind while seeking to transform those pasts by achieving their highest hopes. On close examination, the Puritans' covenant theology reveals a profound hope for novelty that is full of complexity, not simplicity. The profane version of that covenant hardly detached the American experience from its past, near or remote.

At once more strident and more speculative is a parallel view, according to which American historians have persistently failed to recognize "the *real* American tradition" which inheres "in the *assumed* disjunction . . . between the American mind and the American experience, between what America is and what it is thought to be, between 'this country' and the 'principles' or ideas that define that country." Here too Jefferson appears as the demon who, epitomizing the nation's founding fathers, thought "The work of the Revolution . . . had constantly to be done over again; the 'Old World' had to be destroyed anew; the

'New World' had to be reborn again as at the beginning." Thus "America's history, uncharacterized by the 'forms and principles' of the 'Old World', still resided 'in the future'." Roland Van Zandt argued that only in the twentieth century "America has achieved a history" by becoming "a 'new' society, thus giving it a 'past'—an 'old' society that has become historical." But it "is precisely the society that has always described the antithesis of American history, the society Jefferson had constantly destroyed as un-American . . . ."[6]

Such dichotomies between old and new, Europe and America, past and future, appear less to be cultural crevasses than polarities in tension when appropriate weight is given to the function of American religion as simultaneous stimulator of novelty and traditioner of the past. The trend of American history from religious inspiration toward profane achievement elicited an ironic religious opposition to the very innovations which in large measure were religiously inspired. If Jefferson secularized the Puritan religious covenant, in doing it he stirred enough New England antagonism to threaten the Union and a return to an American past of which Yankees were keenly conscious. Moreover, religion's feeding of novelties into the American diet was often interrupted by the traditioning force of religion which, although less prominent in America than its innovating force, demands careful attention.

Americans have rarely described the life they live and the character they manifest as convincingly as have foreign visitors. In every generation since the first settlements were secured, America attracted Europeans as something to observe and describe. It was not simply alien; it was new. A new commonwealth planted in a new continent, peopled by folk brave or brash enough to leave the familiar and embrace the unknown fascinated foreign observers no less than immigrants. Of course, the novelty was in many ways only the swift revision of traditions long refined in Western Christendom, especially in the "sceptered isle." English law and language forged the firmest links with old-world institutions. But law was early altered and ever administered by newly devised legislative and judicial systems which applied it to a host of new circumstances; language was both liberated and elaborated into something quite distinct. French political and social ideals flourished here once independence was achieved, but they became common property in the new world instead of the partisan programs they remained in the old.

All Europe from Scandinavia to Sicily contributed ethnic stock to the potpourri that was the American populace. All these miscellaneous folk brought their religion—for the most, various versions of Christianity—and to it they usually clung for at least a generation. This Christianity in one tongue or another sang of a God who, in Isaac Watt's words, was "our help in ages past" as well as "our hope for years to come." Religion was their anchor of identity, around which clustered hopes for the future as well as habitual sentiments that inoculated the spirit against virulences of mere innovation. It praised a God in whose sight a thousand ages were like an evening gone.

Europeans knew the traditioning power of Christianity, which had identified their families, unified their nations, sanctified their mores, justified their wars, and dignified their histories. It was indeed an "old-time religion" long before the rag-time song so named it. But it was also the religion that nursed apocalyptic visions of a heavenly city, the religion that by forgiving the past created new beginnings in this life and promised new bliss in the life to come. Its futurity enchanted Europeans by reference to the life after death. In America that futurity too underwent conversion as the kingdom of God became a hope for this earth and its time.

Almost a new Christianity—an American Christianity—came to imbue old holy words and sacred ways with novelty. Puritan Edward Johnson (1599–1672), at once a "foreign observer" and a founding father of New England, recounted the career of the first generation of Massachusetts Bay colonists, certain that "this is the place where the Lord will create a new Heaven, and a new Earth in, new Churches, and a new Common-wealth together."[7] Jonathan Edwards a century later thought a new phase of redemption was beginning with the "surprising work of God" not only in and around Northampton but also throughout Anglo-America. No wonder that de Tocqueville, nineteenth-century foreign observer *par excellence*, found himself baffled by American religion as something new and, above all, utile. "On my arrival in the United States the religious aspect of the country was the first thing that struck my attention," he wrote, "and the longer I stayed there, the more I perceived the great political consequences resulting from this new state of things." In his homeland religion and freedom were "almost always seen . . . marching in opposite directions. But in America I found they were intimately united and that they reigned in common over the same country." The Frenchman's curiosity was increasingly piqued by this new and salutary state of affairs; in describing the American character he literally could not let religion alone. The medieval Christian clergy, he well knew, "hardly cared to prove that a sincere Christian may be a happy man here below." But the preachers in America were of a different ilk, so concerned with religion's transformation of this world that "it is often difficult to ascertain from their discourses whether the principal object of religion is to procure eternal felicity in the other world or prosperity in this."[8]

A century later yet another French visitor similarly stressed the novelty of the American spirit, and captured its sense of novelty in a compelling phrase. Contrasting the reforming aspirations of Americans with a certain European apocalypticism, the philosopher Jacques Maritain noted that the Americans' "History is, in one sense, behind them. They walk, they march, they gambol ahead of history, as in those big processions with resounding bands and girls in fancy dress, which so often enliven American streets."[9] "Ahead of history," indeed, is where this-worldly Christianity had America marching. Without forfeiting its reverence for tradition, its remembrance of the old, saving acts, or its confidence that what is tried is true, American Christianity yet traduced (in both senses) its inheritance. If never precisely the majorette leading the great American parade, religion beat the bass drum to whose cadences men marched in front of their own times.

II. A NEW CHRISTIANITY

That religion like society in colonial America derived from Western Europe is a common truism. Precisely because this European Christianity moved to the new world—precisely because it went on an "Errand into the Wilderness," in the phrase Samuel Danforth propounded and Perry Miller developed—it was also transformed. Transference involved two phases. First, the wilderness turned the tables for the rival versions of English-speaking Christianity; Puritans dominated America in the seventeenth century as completely as they had failed to dominate England in the sixteenth. Second, the new-world settlements cast away old-world patterns of the relation between religion and society; churches became sects and sects became churches and eventually both churches and sects became denominations.

In England for a century before the planting of Massachusetts two prominent types of Christianity had vied for dominance. It may be less than helpful to label these recensions of Christian belief "Puritan" and "Anglican," but it is important to understand that for the one, personal life and social endeavor were regulated by the Bible, construed as a binding indenture between God and man, while for the other, the human enterprise was stratified vertically under royalty and episcopacy and nobility, all conceived as earthly analogues to heaven's hierarchy. In epitome, one conceived life constitutionally, the other monarchially. In sixteenth-century England the monarchial vision ruled. Its advocates beat down every proposal of a commonwealth chartered by the Bible, from that of William Tyndale in the 1530's to that of William Perkins at the end of the century. Some such proposal, greatly altered by subsequent events, won a brief day in English history under Oliver Cromwell, but by then the North American wilderness was already its main proving ground.

In Virginia as well as in New England the determinative religious aspiration of the seventeenth century was toward a society of proved—or approved—saints living under the covenant of grace which ramified into political and ecclesiastical compacts based on the Bible as source of the knowledge of God's revealed will. In both places that revealed will was taken to be reasonable and important. As God's covenanting made Him in effect a constitutional deity (although to have called Him that would have smacked of blasphemy), so His children's political and ecclesiastical compacting made kings and bishops constitutional rulers (although to have called them that would have smacked of treason). The Virginians were less scrupulous than the New Englanders over the formalities of monarchy and church, but the difference was one of degree, not of kind. In both these wildernesses distinctly Christian gardens were planted and cultivated; the southern one bore fruit political and the northern one fruit theological. But both were commonwealths chartered by God in Scripture. So was Rhode Island, although Roger Williams (ca. 1603–1683) discerned and emphasized aspects of God's will that frightened John Cotton and all the theologians of Massachusetts and Connecticut.

The American wilderness turned traditional English religion inside out: the essentially practical import of Christianity took ascendance over the essentially orderly element that reigned in England. Practicality became the essence of religion in America even for most Church of Englanders in the colonial period and their successors (Protestant Episcopalians) in the national period. The exceptions were the clergy and parishioners sponsored by the Society for the Propagation of the Gospel who tended to place higher premium on order, episcopacy, and monarchy than on morality, Bible, and saintliness. The Massachusetts Puritans arrived to build a new Zion in the strange wilderness, a wilderness unlike their old mother Church of England whose courts they thought cluttered with much unswept litter of popery. But they held in their hands an ancient blueprint for this Zion whenever they opened their Bibles. The novelty of their enterprise was foreshadowed by the old Israelites' experience—captivity which under King Charles I and Archbishop William Laud was worse than that under Pharaoh's Egypt, crossing the wider Red Sea of the Atlantic for their exodus and then occupying the promised land under the headship of their lawgiver Christ whom Moses prefigured. Their Zion would be new simply because they would follow all of God's intentions for the old; no previous generation of men had been so ready to heed the whole revealed will of God. For them the Old Testament recorded a model of aspirations for a godly, good society; out of this precedent they would correct history with the grace of Christ by achieving those aspirations.

For just this reason the polemical sword of Williams stabbed at the heart of Massachusetts Puritanism, whose John Cotton thought it both the providential blessing and the divine vocation of the colony to relive the history of Israel. In the seventh of its dozen novel proposals Williams' *Bloudy Tenent of Persecution* declared, "The *state* of the Land of *Israel,* the *Kings* and *people* thereof in *Peace* & *War,* is proved *figurative* and *ceremoniall,* and no *patterne* nor *president* for any *Kingdome* or *civill state* in the *world* to follow."[10] Williams was the first person on these shores to declare on Christian grounds an understanding of the past which freed Americans truly to bind their present to the future. Thus as early as 1644 came explicit newness as a Christian slogan for America. Williams saw in Christendom something crying for reformation root and branch; he would have none of religion as the unifying principle of society, no ritual conformity, no forcing of conscience. He made Christianity instead a matter of personal conviction and therefore a source of energy to reform and better society and the state. The prophet Williams, figuratively stoned and literally exiled by the priests of Massachusetts, remains the revered father of the multitudes of Baptists who swarm the whole of modern America. By contrast the priests of New England who expelled him became patriarchs of a regional sect.

Even the Massachusetts Bay Puritans found the raw, new world eroding their cherished traditions. Unlike their neighbors at Plymouth, they theoretically disavowed separatism and the congregational principle, but circumstances led them to practice both. Their closed church of pure saints opened itself to the not so pure children of saints with the Half-way Covenant of 1662. At the end of the century the Reverend Solomon Stoddard of Northampton, the redoubtable "Pope" of the Connecticut Valley who grandsired Jonathan Edwards, taught "The Lords Supper is Instituted to be a means of Regeneration"; indeed, "the end of all Ordinances is salvation," so that the church became not the hostel for saints that the old Puritans cherished but a clinic for sinners.[11] Eighteen years after Stoddard promulgated this doctrine Cotton Mather participated in the ordination of a Baptist minister; in 1722, several clergy leaders of conservative Yale College, dissatisfied with presbyterial orders, became Anglican priests. The new currents of religious diversity and toleration had swept most of the New Englanders' Bible commonwealth into the vortex of American Christianity that the prophetic Williams presaged.

Anglican ambitions to preserve the old church traditions in Virginia and other southern colonies also melted into adaptations not simply to the new world but particularly to its newness. Naturally enough, hierarchical Episcopalians *sans* bishops became lay-controlled congregationalists with the 1641 Vestry Act of Virginia. By the time the bishops of London began to appoint commissaries (James Blair for Virginia in 1689, Thomas Bray for Maryland in 1696, Gideon Johnston for the Carolinas in 1707) to exercise discipline over colonial ministers and congregations, laicism had won the day. After the Glorious Revolution at home, royal governors demanded the right to Church of England worship in northern colonies, and after Bray founded the Society for the Propagation of the Gospel in Foreign Parts (1701) the Anglicans waxed strong in Pennsylvania, the Jerseys, New York, and New England. North of Maryland, only in five southern New York counties did they enjoy establishment; even in Maryland its status was dubious. Thus the officially established religion of the crown learned to function as one denomination among many in the middle colonies. In New England where its clergy and adherents were most fervent, it was a dissenting, nonconformist religion existing at the reluctant sufferance of established Congregationalism. In these ways the two major representatives of English Christianity played roles in the American colonies opposite to their traditional intentions.

Later in the seventeenth century yet another element of English religion entered the American wilderness with its peculiar vision of the spiritual life. The Quakers did not so much differ from practical Puritanism as they carried it to extreme—some thought bizarre—lengths. Where the Puritan conception of the divine will appealed to the written word of Scripture, the Quakers learned what God would have them say and do, even where He would have them go, by the inner light of unmediated inspiration. But Quakers were certain that they knew God's will and were fully confident that no dark, hidden, secret Providence would upset the divine plans and wishes they apprehended. Not that they knew God entire; just that consistency, for God and themselves, was no virtue. Their resort in theory to direct, personal inspiration denied that social order was what God most wanted for creation. Anglicans were outraged; Puritans were shocked. But in the middle colonies of Pennsylvania and the Jerseys the Friends settled into patterns of piety which gave stability to personal, family, and community life. Far from being an exception to the advance of practicality in religion, American Quakers demonstrated that even inspiration and enthusiasm made a godly, tidy garden in the wilderness.

Thus in all these versions—Anglican, Puritan, Baptist, and Quaker—the Christianity of England operated on the seventeenth-century American scene more as the creator of new social forms than as the sanctifier of traditional forms. Southern Anglicans were sufficiently convinced of the covenant theology to employ its constitutional implications in representative government of colony and parishes. New England Puritans of the Massachusetts Bay Company domiciled their company in the colony itself and, despite John Winthrop's denunciations of democracy, joined themselves together in a commonwealth which set standards for Connecticut settlements as well. For Roger Williams the divine will precluded magistrates' exacting religious tests and oaths, and it flung open the door to religious pluralism. Friends ran their political and religious affairs on the basis of consensual inspiration, waiting for the sense of the meeting in religious matters and consenting to generous instruments of government in Pennsylvania and New Jersey.

English religion thereby assumed a formative rather than a normative function for the early generations of colonists. Religious types of continental origin also took on new colorations in America. While the initial Roman Catholic settlers were Englishmen occupying Lord Baltimore's proprietary colony of Maryland, their religion was counterreformation Catholicism rooted in Rome. That religion had learned to recoup many territories and loyalties lost during the Protestant revolt by increasing the authority of its doctrine and ministry, by reasserting its traditional insistence upon conformity under temporal penalties, by raising up an order of militant propagandists under absolute loyalty to the papacy, and by resort to military and diplomatic pressures.

The force of American circumstances shows in the fact that Maryland, the only colony under Catholic proprietorship and Jesuit chaplaincy, was the colony with the first explicit guarantees of religious liberty to all who professed Christ's divinity. Of course the majority of Maryland's settlers were Protestant; without official toleration Lord Baltimore's venture would have been in jeopardy. Nevertheless Catholic sponsorship brought about the greatest religious diversity known in any of the colonies during the seventeenth century. The Jesuits' militancy led to their brief expulsion, and they resumed the role of chaplains only after they assumed the unaccustomed duty of protecting the rights of Protestants. Thus from the very genesis of its experience in English-speaking North America, Catholicism accommodated itself to that religious and cultural pluralism which distinguished

America from Europe and American Catholicism from traditional Catholicism; the "Americanistic" attitude whose central points were to be condemned by Leo XIII in 1899 already cast its shadow in colonial Maryland, where Catholics and Protestants lived side by side as fellow believers in Christ's divinity.

Dutch Calvinism was the uniform religion of New Netherlands before it became New-York by conquest in 1664 and by treaty in 1667, just as Lutheranism was the religion of New Sweden until it was conquered by the Dutch in 1656 and taken by the English in 1664. In both instances the official religion of the conqueror introduced side-by-side duality of doctrine and worship. While this Swedish Lutheranism left little permanent impression on American religious life, some Swedes handily transferred religious allegiance when political control changed. The Dutch Reformed continued as a denomination in New York under English governors. In neither case did the European tradition of established, uniform religion transfer to America. German Lutheran and German Reformed religion in the middle colonies remained ethnic rallying points preserving certain old-world customs and beliefs, but during the eighteenth century these churches (which they had been in Germany) became ethnic sects newly set in the midst of communities with multiform religious expressions.

An experience similar to that of the continental religionists awaited Scottish Presbyterians who entered America, particularly through Pennsylvania and into the Appalachian valleys, during the second quarter of the eighteenth century. Replacing the centralized, rigorous kirk of the homeland were local congregations, presbyteries, and eventually synods based on representative ecclesiastical polity and claiming the rights and immunities of voluntary religious groups in such colonies as Virginia and Pennsylvania. Members of one of the most standardized national churches of Europe thus adjusted themselves to the American scene by forming not churches in the strict sense but voluntary religious groups ready to build up into denominations, designed less to continue old customs than to sanctify innovations in both church and society. Moreover, these Presbyterians found themselves linked in presbyteries and synods with Presbyterians sprung directly from New England Puritanism, first on Long Island and then in the middle colonies more generally. Outside their own magisterial protections in New England itself, Puritans adopted presbyterial forms of government, but they were doctrinally less rigorous and more given to enthusiasm than their Scottish or Scotch-Irish neighbors. Tensions between Puritan and Scottish Presbyterian elements arose often during the eighteenth century, with the result that certain characteristically new-world features such as voluntaryism prevailed eventually even among Scotch-Irish Presbyterians who at first stoutly resisted them.

In Connecticut and Massachusetts, Church of Englanders tasted the Americanizing process by which churches turned into denominations seeking the new more than saving the old. After missionaries of the Society for the Propagation of the Gospel placed Anglicanism in eighteenth-century New England on a more popular footing than was possible when Prayer Book worship was held at the insistence of royal governors, Anglicans protested their inequities under Congregational establishments much in the manner of Virginia Presbyterians and Baptists protesting similar inhibitions under the Anglican establishment. The official church of the crown to which all New Englanders owed allegiance thereby became a dissenting sect, tolerated but not locally approved, in that crown's own province.

In virtually all the expressions of Christianity in colonial America, new circumstances broke cherished patterns of English, continental, or Scottish origin. The balance always tipped to the side of practicality when Americans found little utility in religious conformity as guarantor of social order.

III. DIVINE INNOVATING

The religious movement that best manifested the spirit of American novelty and of independence was the Great Awakening. Critics like Charles Chauncy (not to say outright enemies like

Samuel Johnson) no less than leaders like Jonathan Edwards, who pondered its significance more carefully than anybody else, thought that the Awakening opened a new era in human history. The era was not, however, unpredicted. Massive evidences of outpourings by the divine spirit not only on the churches but on the Anglo-American colonists themselves from Savannah to Boston meant that the exodus was finished and the promised land occupied; it was time for God to give milk and honey to the people He chose to bear the meaning of human history. In every region of the seaboard, eighteenth-century jeremiads drew parallels between old Israel and new America, parallels intended to show not that history was chopped off from all previous ages but that history's promises were being fulfilled. William Bradford's *History* made the exodus story the guide to American destiny, but the idea caught the New England imagination neither as early nor as completely as many have supposed. It was between the Awakening's beginning and the Revolution's success that preachers habitually turned the exodus into an allegorical prefigurement of the American consummation. "The Revolutionary divines," wrote Perry Miller, "in their zeal for liberty, committed themselves unwittingly to the proposition that in this case expulsion of the British would automatically leave America a pure society."[12]

The sense of novelty generated by religion slipped its moorings to the churches and coasted to haven in the country. But since the Israelite promise was its prototype, the American dream blended with novelty a spirit of righteousness which connected with the past. Here was Europe corrected and completed. Preachers and founding fathers of the nation imputed to America all the values of old Christendom, reinterpreted as a society of enforced religious and intellectual uniformity—a uniformity increasingly epitomized by royalty. The effect was selective rewriting of the Israel myth to show that the real glories of the Hebrews preceded their royal era. Excision of the kingly tradition complemented the Puritans' habit of overlooking the cultic rules laid down in Leviticus. References to old Israel were thus genuinely allegorical; the covenants with patriarchs and the promises to lawgivers presaged the fact that America was becoming what God intended for His chosen people.

Americans were indeed a new people, whose new order of the ages lost no good things of the past, but who *ordered* them anew, purged them of dross, and renovated everything. Jefferson's 1816 declaration, "I like the dreams of the future better than the history of the past," [13] expresses a relative preference, not an absolute choice. The preference remained in force for a long time indeed; James Truslow Adams was still picturing the essence of the American dream as thrusting the best of the past into an open future. Adams illustrated the dream as ensconcing European virtue in a social order of freedom and equality marching "ahead of history." Adams retold how a young Russian immigrant, Mary Antin, responded to having tasted the riches of the Boston Public Library:

". . . This is my latest home, and it invites me to a glad new life. The endless ages have indeed throbbed through my blood, but a new rhythm dances in my veins. My spirit is not tied to the monumental past, any more than my feet were bound to my grandfather's house below the hill. The past was only my cradle, and now it cannot hold me, because I am grown too big; just as the little house in Polotzk, once my home, has now become a toy of memory, as I move about at will in the wide spaces of this splendid palace, whose shadow covers acres. No! It is not that I belong to the past, but the past that belongs to me. America is the youngest of the nations, and inherits all that went before in history. And I am the youngest of America's children, and into my hands is given all her priceless heritage, to the last white star espied through the telescope, to the last great thought of the philosopher. Mine is the whole majestic past, and mine is the shining future.[14]

In the Russian girl's rhetoric were sounding themes of Puritan patriotism that had rung in Bostonian ears a century before the Public Library was founded.

The Reverend Samuel Cooper (1725–1783) of Boston preached

his sermons well and often through the latter half of the eighteenth century and rivaled Charles Chauncy as a major theologian
of the Revolution. After General Edward Braddock's defeat at
Fort Duquesne, Cooper addressed himself to a public fast on
August 28, 1755, referring to "The invaluable Rights both civil
& religious w[hi]ch ye Britis[h] Nation & it's Dependencies have
so long injoy'd" as "Priviledges . . . peculiarly dear to our Fathers
ye Founders of this Country, who when they thought them in
Danger of being diminish't if not lost, in Europe, transplanted
them into these western Regions, where by ye Favor of divine
Providence, they have taken Root, and begun to flourish."[15]

Here was no Edmund Burke boasting that Englishmen fought
for English liberties even against England. Europe in the Enlightenment had its advocates of new orders of society: Rousseau
for equality, Leibniz for the bourgeoisie, Kant for thought and
morality—all proposed ways in which the good society might
generate forces to countervail evil and destruction. But Cooper,
and even more the founding fathers after him, called for pervasive innovation that at once summarized and outran these proposed renovations: the new *order* of the *ages*. Sanctioners of the
innovation included preachers and saints. Especially in moments
of apparently devastating jolts of reality such as Braddock's
failure, it was the preachers who saw in God's handling of the
old Israel as well as in the new covenant of grace the promise
that man could make a new beginning; in America man *was*
beginning anew.

There were, of course, Europeans who gloried in the American
innovation. From Naples in spring 1776 the Abbé Galiani
(1728–1787) wrote to Madame d'Épinay of the Phoenix character
of the American experiment; all which waned in Europe, "religion, laws, arts, sciences," came to resurrection in America. This
self-confident prophet advised, "do not buy your house in the
Chaussée d'Antin; you must buy it in Philadelphia," wistfully
regretting that "there are no abbeys in America."[16] The London
dissenting minister, Richard Price (1723–1791), saw in America
a "new era in future annals, and a new opening in human affairs

.... *A rising empire, extended over an immense continent, without bishops, without nobles, and without kings.*" Price thought the American Revolution a step in human progress second in importance only to "the introduction of Christianity among mankind."

If a preacher in the face of Braddock's defeat could offer solace by showing America to be the innovation of the true but prefigured Israel, by the same allegory and rhetoric he could solemnize success. Preaching before the legislature and governor of Massachusetts on the day the new Commonwealth's government began and its Constitution became effective, Cooper saw both Israel and America "chosen by God . . . for the display of some of the most astonishing dispensations of his Providence." Each nation "rose from oppression"; each was "led into a wilderness, as a refuge from tyranny"; each was "pursued through the sea, by the armed hand of power, which, but for the signal interpositions of Heaven, must before now have totally defeated the noble purpose of our emigration"; each had its moments of infidelity and ingratitude to God; each was corrected by God's judgment; each was blessed by His mercy. "This day, this memorable day," Cooper declaimed, "is a witness, that the Lord . . . 'hath not forsaken us . . . .' This day, which forms a new aera in our annals, exhibits a testimony to all the world, that contrary to our deserts, and amidst all our troubles, the blessing promised . . . to the afflicted seed of Abraham is come upon us; 'Their Nobles shall be of themselves, and their Governor shall proceed from the midst of them.' "[17] Cooper was sure the Hebrew nation was chartered as a free republic with three branches of government, that its apostasy came with the monarchy, and that God's will in the governing of men had not again been done until the American Revolution.[18]

If it took a Bostonian to conceive America as innovating a divinely blessed history reaching back to Abraham, only a Virginian might be expected to go the next step and compare America's new beginning with the very creation itself. The Reverend John Durbarrow Blair (1759–1823), a Presbyterian, for years after the Revolution led an interdenominational congregation with Episcopalian John Buchanan in Richmond. Preaching on February 19, 1795, "A Thanksgiving Sermon, in Consequence of the President's Proclamation" upon the suppression of the Whiskey Insurrection in western Pennsylvania, Blair seized the nettle. Old Europe, even where parties tried to imitate America's Revolution, was the place of "dreadful Havock of the human Race," and monarchy was most to blame. By contrast Americans "enjoy by the signal Blessing of God, a quiet, prosperous, & peaceful State." Scripture taught Blair as it did Cooper "that Kings were given in his [God's] Displeasure, as a Curse & a Plague to the Earth," from which America was separated "by the dissociable Ocean." History provided the evidence, Scripture the clue: "Surely the God of Heaven did care for this Land, he resided in our Councils, & gave us a wise & sober Mind: He united us together, & therefore we stand firm. Our Constitution is the Wonder & Envy of all Nations; & considering the Materials out of which it was made, we may with Submission compare it to the Work of God himself at the first Creation, when from a dark & confused Chaos, he produced the splendid & regular System of the Universe."[19]

In this preacher's view America was no renovation of Old Israel (novel as that might be) but new like the original creation itself, innovation pure and simple—*creatio ex nihilo*. He was of course not the only Virginian for whom independence and the Constitution—especially the latter—made a new beginning for mankind; James Madison (1751–1836) reckoned the novelty but the episode's religious dimension was notably absent from his consciousness. Himself a nominal Episcopalian who worked for full religious liberty in Virginia, Madison judged his own denomination dead and awaiting decent burial. But so ardent a student of the Reverend John Witherspoon at the College of New Jersey could hardly hold religion in contempt. What Madison intended was that Christianity should benefit man and that man should have the credit for the novelty of America. Nowhere more eloquently than in the fourteenth Federalist Paper did he praise Americans' "manly spirit" for "innovations"—and both phrases were meant literally. Not lacking either "decent regard to the opinions of former times and other nations" or a "knowledge of their own situation, and the lessons of their own experience," the Americans nevertheless made "posterity . . . indebted for the possession, and the world for the example of the numerous innovations displayed on the American theatre, in favor of private rights and public happiness." This was America's "new and more noble course"—"They accomplished a revolution which has no parallel in the annals of human society: They reared the fabrics of governments which have no model on the face of the globe."[20]

IV. ANCIENT OF DAYS

The novelty which religion helped to stamp upon the American self-consciousness prompted Madison to praise not God but the Revolution's leaders and the Constitution's framers. From the time of his—and Jay's and Hamilton's—propagandizing down to the time of Jefferson's presidency, preachers contested just this point with politicians and other public men who made Independence Day orations: was the new order of the ages ushered in by God for the happiness of subservient man, or was it achieved by man while a remote Providence approvingly smiled? By the time Old Hickory returned from the White House to the Hermitage (1837), the politicians had won; Jackson "Let the people rule" not only the federal government but American history. Yet the theological advocates were formidable; whether revivalists or rationalists, they spoke eloquently for God as the innovator, and they yielded only after long debate—the former by turning to moralism and the latter by fleeing to romanticism.

Perhaps the device readiest to the preachers' hands in defending God as America's innovator was attributing the failure of the French Revolution to its atheistic ideology and, by contrast

implied or asserted, crediting the endurance of American independence to the revivals of religion which followed hard upon
the accomplishment of federal union.

Perry Miller has put it well; religious leaders in the early
decades of the national period looked back on the revolutionary
epoch as "accompanied by a spiritual deterioration hardly to be
equaled in the darkest chapters of Christian history." Indeed,
"In all the land, no voice was to be heard, from 1800 to 1860,
to salute—and mourn—America's momentary chance to escape
its Christian specificity; no spokesman, whether Finney or William Ellery Channing, to deny that around 1800 the community
had been rescued, just in the nick of time, from descent into
atheism." Miller is also correct in writing, "There survives out
of the years 1790 to 1815 an immense . . . American literature of
denunciation of the French Revolution . . . ."[21] The revivalists of
the second awakening from Timothy Dwight to Lyman Beecher
(1775-1863) and Charles Grandison Finney thought their work
to be that of restoring God to His rightful place in the popular
affection as dispenser of vision and energy to make the American
experiment herald a new era in human affairs. In successive waves
the great revivals recurred frequently enough between 1800 and
1837 to warrant the confidence displayed in Finney's famous
Lectures on Revivals of Religion (1835), which Miller called
"indisputably the most powerful theoretical statement of the
significance of the titanic experience" which revivalism represented.[22] But increasingly after 1820 the enterprise shifted its
attention from total America to single Americans, from the
renewal of history by the nation under God to the renovation
of godly living by individual persons—in a word, from novelty
to morality.

In the summer of 1812 John F. Schermerhorn and Samuel
J. Mills toured the west to perform missionary services and to
study religion and morals; in 1814, they reported their findings
to the sponsoring Massachusetts Missionary Society and the
Missionary Society of Connecticut, giving what they entitled
A Correct View of that Part of the United States which Lies

West of the Allegany Mountains, with Regard to Religion and Morals.[23] Lax morals were their criteria for spotting fields of missionary promise, yet these observers wanted to lift western society from barbarism by instilling religious affections that would help people hold religiously to their Americanness, that would keep God enthroned over the kingdom of which the United States was the new colony on earth. The old east, by now debating whether God gave the novelty as well as the increase of America, meant to save the west from relying purely upon what Madison had called "this manly spirit." The danger of a profane American dream showed itself as clearly to these measurers of the pioneer spirit as it did to the revivalists who were to carry out their recommendations. But by 1815 both the proposers and the disposers of religious renewal were turning more to personal morals and withdrawing from the theme of the kingdom of God in America. In two decades, morality and even moralism won the revivalists' attention. Finney hardly mentioned a public event of his own time in his memoirs, and it may be added that save for allusions to the specific forms of immorality which Americans then indulged the *Lectures on Revivals* have no historical setting.[24]

Although revivalists and missionary-minded Christians dominated the era sufficiently to stamp on American religion a hallmark that would endure the terrible erosion of the Civil War, they held no monopoly; to portray their shift from innovating to moralizing (in a traditional way) is to omit the picture's background. During the Great Awakening a stern protest against enthusiasm arose from many voices; between the Revolution and the Civil War loud cries derided what Finney liked to call "religious excitements." Before yielding to romanticism, these rationalistic "old-lights" at first worked—in their own way—to retain the sanctity of American innovation by manufacturing halos for revolutionary heroes. They managed so to crown the wigged head of Washington and they etched on the popular imagination a picture of him at prayer. Jefferson was not so easily made a saint, although some tried. Jackson presented an impossible candidacy for canonization. In the 1830's this enterprise for extolling American novelty as God-given also folded—again in its own way—not by emphasizing personal morals but by glorifying denominational traditions. If, as it were, revivalists individualistically sang "Give me that old-time religion," the rationalists romantically chorused "Faith of our fathers, holy faith / We will be true to thee till death."

The piousness credited to Washington by "Parson" Mason Locke Weems (1759-1825) is too well known for any retelling to avoid condescension and banality. But Weems was neither the only nor the first canonizer of the father of his country. John Durbarrow Blair's sermon heralding the suppression of the Whiskey Rebellion argued that God and not man governed America, and that Washington knew it: "It must also afford the greatest Pleasure, & the most happy Presage to every reflecting Mind, to see the chief Magistrate of united America, acknowledging on all Occasions, the superintending Providence of Almighty God. Many a Heart was glad to hear him invoking the Favour of God, when entering upon his Administration; and it is with no less Pleasure that we join with him today, according to his Request, in acknowledging with thankful Hearts, the various & great Blessings with which it has pleased Heaven to distinguish our happy Land."[25] Blair conscientiously imputed President Washington's public nods toward religion and God to the man's private convictions—a procedure that is recurrently tempting but methodologically dangerous (a lesson easily learned by studying the voluminous literature on Lincoln's religion).

Jefferson presented a more difficult problem, for on many occasions he was outspokenly anticlerical and had harsh things to say about organized religion itself. He was suspect to Yankee Congregationalists, to southern Episcopalians, and generally to Presbyterians. The Baptist pamphleteer John Leland (1754–1841) lauded him primarily because their minds met on the question of religious liberty. Massachusetts-born Leland moved to Virginia in 1776 for fifteen years; fearing that the federal Constitution fell short of granting full religious liberty, he entered the lists for the Virginian Convention to oppose ratifying the Constitution and withdrew only when his rival, James Madison, allayed his fears. On returning home Leland was elected to the Massachusetts House of Representatives in 1811 and worked for religious liberty there. He was more a spokesman for civil and religious rights than for religion as such, which largely explains his dictum that America "was founded by Columbus, delivered by Washington, and taught by Jefferson . . . ."[26] The trinity of creator, savior, and comforter is notable for the patent humanity of each of the persons.

Leland blended Christian pietism with federalist rationalism as thoroughly as did anybody, uniting in himself "that strange coalition of rationalist and pietist" which achieved "religious freedom and separation of church and state." But at his best he welcomed American novelty as it impinged on religion, a novelty religiously inspired but profanely embodied. Sidney E. Mead, whose phrases have just been quoted, noted the frustration of religion over the alliance of pietism and rationalism. "Only *after* this momentous achievement" of religious freedom and separation of church and state "did pietism discover its latent incompatibility with rationalism and arrange a hasty divorce in order to remarry traditional orthodoxy," Mead wrote. "American denominational Protestantism is the offspring of this second marriage living in the house of religious freedom which was built during the first marriage. The child has always accepted and defended the house with fervor, if not always with intelligence. But it has commonly exhibited great reluctance to own up to its rationalist architect and builder."[27]

Jeffersonianism is a good name for that "architect and builder." What forced the divorce and new marriage was Jacksonianism. If Madison had seemed ambiguous in crediting American novelty to "this manly spirit," leaving room to interpret that spirit as derived from God, Jackson's motto, "Let the people rule," left God out of the American quest for novelty and made the achievement of that novelty man's alone.

A thousand political celebrations of the new profane epoch

rang in the fulsome rhetoric of Independence Day speeches. Americans were working out a new thing under the sun, and they were doing it on behalf of everybody under the sun. A paean to man for America's pioneering the liberty of humanity came in a Fourth of July oration in Petersburg, Virginia, where the horseman and legislator, William Ransom Johnson (1782–1849), traced the history of the United States until 1833, the year of his address. It was the endeavor of "laying the corner stone of the great work of universal emancipation; for . . . [the fidelity of Americans] has awakened our fellow men to a sense of their thraldom and nerved their hearts in a universal effort to become free; the world has known no rest since the great struggle of American liberty terminated in its blaze of victory, and the world will know rest no more till the great lessons of freedom which the American Constitution enforces 'have been listened to and embodied in action', in whatever form, by every people of the globe."[28]

Hardly had Jackson's administration ended when Emerson eloquently conceded that religion had yielded itself to the past, lamenting that the true Christianity which bound present to future had vanished from America. In his famous lecture to the senior students of Harvard Divinity School on July 15, 1838, Emerson defined "The stationariness of religion" as "the assumption that the age of inspiration is past, that the Bible is closed"; this assumption and "the fear of degrading the character of Jesus by representing him as a man indicate with sufficient clearness the falsehood of our theology." Conceding the death of true Christianity and the purely traditioning force of organized religion, Emerson asked for a transcendentalist modernness: "It is the office of a true teacher to show us that God is, not was; that He speaketh, not spake. The true Christianity,—a faith like Christ's in the infinitude of man,—is lost."[29]

If Emerson did not entirely describe contemporaneous American religion, he bespoke its immediate future. The year 1837 closed the great period of revivalism; after new but brief flurries in 1857–1858 and during the Civil War, Moody transformed it into a different, citified movement. The 1840's and 1850's were decades dominated on the practical side by religious moralism, and on the theoretical by a romanticism which would turn attention from future or even present to the old faith of the fathers. John Williamson Nevin (1803–1886) in 1843 decried all revivalistic techniques and effects in his famous attack on Finney, entitled *The Anxious Bench*. Catechism and Eucharist were the heart and soul of religion, according to Nevin. That Swiss historical theologian who did so much to lift American religious scholarship to new heights, Philip Schaff, joined in the retraditionalizing of Christianity as soon as he began his long American career in 1844. Old German Lutheranism gave America a romantic leader in the person of Samuel S. Schmucker (1789–1873), who as early as 1838 proposed to the American denominations ". . . *a Plan for Catholic Union on Apostolic Principles*." Saxon Lutheranism recently immigrated to mid-America had its spokesman for the old days in Carl F. W. Walther (1811–1887), and still another Lutheran, Charles Philip Krauth (1797–1867), extolled "the faith of former days."[30] By mid-century the leading Episcopalian voice was that of William Augustus Muhlenberg (1796–1877), who revived medieval liturgy and monasticism in his denomination, blending interests of evangelicals with those of traditionalists attracted to Tractarianism or Anglo-Catholicism.

In 1837 the Plan of Union between Congregationalists and Presbyterians to evangelize the west fell apart. In the same year different interpretations of the true denominational tradition split the Presbyterian Church into Old School and New School—a schism which lasted until the Civil War. The Methodists and the Baptists remained the popular denominations, but their evangelism turned from national innovation to individual morality as the goal of religion. Roman Catholicism became a "foreign" church again with the massive Irish immigration.

When American novelty with its powerfully religious inspiration became a profane reality, a strong effort by pietistic and

rationalistic Christians to reclaim it for religion produced immediately mixed and eventually vain results. Revivalists, epitomized
by Finney, became individualistic moralizers, and rationalists,
well represented by Blair, fell off toward romanticism. The
shift of religion from a rejuvenating to an archaizing element
in American life was noted by Emerson and other keen
observers. But the most convincing evidence of the new traditioning work of religion comes from believers. Diaries and letters
from hundreds of pioneers between 1830 and the Civil War—
and indeed after the war—ring repeatedly the twin peals
of religion and nostalgia.

Young Jefferson Martenet (1828–?) had known the gay life
of Belmont plantation in Loudoun County, Virginia, before
setting off for gold in California. From Harbaugh Mining Camp
near Jacksonville in Tuolumne County he wrote in 1853 of
good health—in body at least: "My spirits at times indifferent,
particularly on Sundays. I dont know why it is, but Sunday
morning seems to revive my every home feeling, and if ever
I get home-sick it is on Sunday."[31] George Sherman went to
Oregon in 1849 from the east; "Soon after arrival in Portland,
I attended a good homelike Methodist prayer meeting, at which
all were made welcome."[32] Charles G. Gray hired out as guide
and factotum for an overland wagon-train journey from Independence, Missouri, to San Francisco via Salt Lake City and
Lassen's Cutoff in the summer of the great Gold Rush. He
caustically ridiculed the piety of several persons in the company, and scoffed that Sabbath rest on June 10 was for washing
clothes and repairing wagons; at camp number 57 on July 1
"we intended laying up for the day to recruit man & beast,
but more particularly the *latter.*" Yet grumpy Gray for all
his disdain toward religion had been touched by it. On May
17, "We passed . . . a grave with a common wooden head board
& 2 large logs of wood on the sides of it. [I]t was of a young
man of 26—& killed by being crushed under the wheels of
his wagon—I was alone, ahead of our train 2 miles & as I
suddenly came upon it, my mind was never so powerfully im-

pressed with the idea of that all powerful King, to whom all shall bow—as at this time."[33]

By nature religion is more potent in evoking nostalgia than novelty, and so it came to be in America. Home—here or hereafter—became its effective melody; ages past, its harmony. It had been so for Loring Hodge in the 1820's. From his home in Buffalo, New York, he went to Mackinaw, Michigan, and later to Ohio. In Mackinaw and in Green Bay, Wisconsin, this layman helped establish "a Sabbath scool [and] Bible & Tract Society . . . as I am the only leader of religious exercises in this place . . . [where] Judge Abbott is my assistant or His . . . which assiste me mutch[.] . . . We feel that religion and Morality will soon flourish in these regions." Then in Jefferson, Ohio, Hodge was class leader "and think it a great help to me in guarding against many wiles of this world." In both places, Hodge saw and used religion as a domesticating, traditioning, ordering, moralizing instrument pointing always back to Buffalo.[34] So was nostalgia the product of religion for James Edward Glazier (1834–1922?), a Salem, Massachusetts, lad with General Burnside's expedition at New Bern, North Carolina, in summer 1862; he described camp life to his sweetheart: "The best of all is we have a chance to go to Church on Sundays while here in the city. The Chaplains preach & on Sundays it seems like home the bells ring—the stores are closed & every thing is in order."[35]

With such lay sentiments preachers agreed. Religion for the Reverend George Henry Atkinson (1819–1889), Congregationalist missionary in the Pacific northwest, established firm connections with his native New England and its history: "While working here I desire to do as well as I can what was done by our fathers in New England & what Christian friends there desire to have done, and what above all our Lord & Saviour desires to have done."[36] That the three might not coincide seems never to have crossed his mind.

From later in the century comes an eloquent description of the stewards of religion; the preachers stood for the past, the

unchanging, the abiding, all that was secure. George Wythe
Munford allowed no hint of innovation in approving this appreciation of them:

They are our friends. They stand by us; they are always faithful.
In our happiest moments they are with us to rejoice, to laugh, to
be happy, too. When sorrow comes they are faithful still.

They are the conservatives. They are good citizens, and set us
a good example. They are the balance-wheels of society, the scotch
to the wagon, air brakes to the train, the pendulum to the clock.
They are like the Sabbath, that gives us rest and peace. They are
to society what the judge is to the law. We love them all, and
when they are blotted out, which God forbid, we want to go too.
In sickness, in trouble, in affliction, yea, in the last agonies, they
are with us and comfort us, while the busy world wags on. God
bless the preachers of this land, the preachers of every creed that
teaches love for our Creator, and love and kindness for one another.[37]

V. THE CITY OF MAN

Slowly it sank into the mind of Americans that the new
order of the ages would never again be the new Zion in the
wilderness. Christianity's innovating and renovating force impelled colonial and early national America surely and swiftly.
Once novelty became a national trait, once Americans really
marched "ahead of history," man took the glory, leaving to
God and religion the accumulation of yesterdays while placing
in human hands today and tomorrow. Man and polity could
manage what had in good measure been generated by God
and theology. Were we to speak of the development in simple
terms of success and failure, then religion's innovating succeeded
all too well but the effort failed to credit religion permanently
for this success. In fact, the Gestalt of religion's historic relation
to American novelty is more subtle than that, but the subtleties
refine the simple terms without contradicting them.

The new era presaged by Puritan theology for the new world
was at first a new chapter in religious history; it became a new
day for mankind. That this newness could leave religion itself

several laps behind in the race against history was apparent to nobody until the Revolution had achieved more than anybody proposed for it: to outrun history indeed by building a city of man, a city without walls, a city ringed by gates inviting mankind to enter, a city of horizontal dimensions, a city which would nod in perfunctory gratitude to the Creator as its founder while rejoicing that its real builders were its inhabitants. In that city the very religious toleration for which the most prophetic innnovators (e.g., Roger Williams) had striven silently transformed itself into a tolerating of religion and its traditioning function. Yet the novelty which religion had generated grew of itself even as it relegated religion to the minor roles of moralizing and traditionalizing.

The last word on this matter may be given, as was the first, to another "foreign" observer, George Santayana: "A flood of barbarism from below may soon level all the fair works of our Christian ancestors . . . . Romantic Christendom—picturesque, passionate, unhappy episode—may be coming to an end. Such a catastrophe would be no reason for despair . . . . Under the deluge, and watered by it, seeds of all sorts would survive against the time to come, even if what might eventually spring from them, under the new circumstances, should wear a strange aspect. In a certain measure, and unintentionally, both this destruction and this restoration have already occurred in America."[38]

CHAPTER THREE

EQUALS—AND SOME
MORE EQUAL

Every society bases itself on a premise, a certain principle of participation, a certain understanding of the capacity of men to live together at least peaceably and at most creatively. American society based its possibility on a human brotherhood far broader than the religious uniformity that glued European Christendom together. Its principle of participation was a concept of personhood more elastic than the natural-law rationality that gave cohesion to the Roman Empire from Augustus to Diocletian, and its understanding of human potential arose out of a voluntaryism less confining than that of modern European nationalism. Americans dreamed of a society open to every man who was willing to participate in the quest for common advantage. Willingness to take part earned the right to advocate a cause and exercise a personhood. That principle freed participants—men, women, and children, but not Negro slaves and not Indians—to find their own way, and it also restrained those who had found their way from freezing the process of change into a closed social hierarchy. So stanch an advocate of the ideal of Christendom as Jacques Maritain loved America for the fact that its "body politic is the only one which was fully and explicitly born of freedom, of the free determination of men to live together and work together at a common task."[1]

I. CONGREGATIONS AND REVIVALS

The religious agent and expression of this voluntary freedom has been the congregation, which only in America became the primary, dominant unit of religious life. American religion deep in its heart is congregational in form and force, regardless of its varying theories of church polity and frames of church administration. This congregational feature resulted when certain sectarian impulses from Europe combined with certain social preferences that fit the American situation. Having manifested itself in early colonial days, it wore well. Its lasting power is attested by the fact that earnest, recent attempts to centralize the denominations into executive agencies under strong leaders met meager success. For the congregation has been to America what the family has been to society or the local store to commerce—the place where basic business is done.

Initial settlers were far from unanimous in specifying the true church and what they believed to be the true form of organized Christianity. Among them were Catholics for whom the pope headed a hierarchical church, Anglicans for whom king and bishop were twin pontifices, Puritans who would refashion the church into what they thought Scripture chartered, and Separatists who adhered to the local congregation's independence. Only the last of these found their condition fitting their conviction. For the first generation of Anglo-Americans lived in settlements each of which supported but a single congregation, and only after their experiences had formed their doctrines did they need to determine proper relations between several congregations. Even then American peculiarities altered European models.

In Europe the rule, *cuius regio eius religio*, made church coterminous with canton or duchy if not with kingdom or empire, and all within the ruler's realm at least nominally took the church for what it claimed to be, a social organism of divine origin and organization. In American colonies that rule was quite tentatively applied. Regions were vast and sparsely peopled, while rulers were distant in person and faintly represented by proxy. Insofar as the colonies provided places for religious experimentation, the dictum laid down for Europe at the Peace of Augsburg (1555) was obverted into *cuius religio eius regio*. During the national period, the coexistence of denominations took the matter to its logical conclusion, *cuius congregatio eius religio*. Although local, social pressures for religious conformity ran high in most colonies, it was usual for all but the Quakers to locate where one did not mind conforming. Moreover, the church was something the settlers brought with them from Europe. It belonged to them at least as much as they belonged to it. Thus long before the revivals—whose apparent enmity to the congregational principle calls for later comment—explicitly enunciated the voluntary principle in religion, the church was what its members made it. That, always in the first instance, was a congregation.

Conditions in the colonies thrust the typical forms of English religion into strange predicaments. Establishmentarian Anglicans in Connecticut and Massachusetts, where congregational separatism was established (the paradox does not alter the fact), were dissenting nonconformists. Here where Anglicans were a sect, they flourished in the eighteenth century while their established church in Virginia wilted. The most sectarian Christians in seventeenth-century England were the Quakers, whose spirited and spiritistic protest against all externals in religion led to a compactness of fellow feeling that generated power sufficient to fashion the societies of colonial Pennsylvania and the Jerseys as though the Quakers were established. But both Anglicans and Quakers were congregational in the primary form of their church life—the former despite allegiance to the episcopal principle since the nearest bishop sat across the ocean, the latter despite allegiance to yearly meetings, first in London and then in America.

At the outset of the national period establishmentarianism in religion was placed beyond the pale of the central government, and was set on a course of ultimate extinction in the states.

After disestablishment in Connecticut the Episcopalians there were no more dissenters than were the Congregationalists. Both were rival denominations, and both still based their church life on the congregation. Because the various religious groups in the United States took their distinctive modern forms in this disestablishmentarian milieu, they all became more or less congregational in polity and quite congregational in the self-understanding of their lay constituents. Had any denomination been exempt from this tendency it would have been the highly centralized, strictly disciplined Roman Catholic Church. But from the first organization of an American hierarchy in the 1780's, Catholic congregations claimed through their trustees the right to manage themselves and choose their priests. Probably the most nearly standard function of Catholic bishops in the United States to about 1840, when the Irish immigration changed the whole tenor of the church, was to protect their own canonical prerogatives against incursions by laymen waving the banner of trusteeism. And by no means was the congregational impulse eliminated by the impact of immigration, for as European Catholics arrived they employed their congregations as agents of ethnic identification. While each parish bore the name of its patron saint, it also spoke until very recently a distinct old-world dialect.

Called by whatever name—parish, society, meeting—"the church" of whatever denomination was to its American members the local congregation, bound to other similar units under a brand name personified, if at all, by a supervisory agent. Even in the middle of the twentieth century the trend remained strong to speak of the denomination—Presbyterian, Baptist, or whatever— as representing a "faith," for "the church" meant not the entire denomination but the meetinghouse, gathering place of minister and members. In America it has made more sense commonly to ask "Where is your church?" than it has made to ask "What is your church?" The answer may be that it is a modest building off the beaten track, marked by the inevitable sign displaying name, minister, and hours of service. The more affluent the members, the more likely the answer would allude to spacious lands adorned by distinct buildings for worship and fellowship and education, staffed by ministers and assistant ministers and secretaries—a very large congregation; the sign and steeple will be lighted at night, and the passerby can learn the topic of next Sunday's sermon. Even the mid-twentieth-century success of religion has not fundamentally altered the congregational impulse.

Big religion fits with big business and big government in big society. In America adherents to the various types of religion increase faster than the fast-increasing population. The denominations, like other articulations of mass society, have thrown up centralized bureaucracies in national headquarters populated by executives. But these bureaucracies represent far more clearly the professional religionists in the field—the priests and ministers and rabbis—than they speak for the lay constituency, for whom the church remains the congregation. The latter frequently protest against headquarters, and, however nettlesome to church executives and theoreticians, the protest has history on its side. For lay constituency has been the historically stable element in American religion, and very recently did the population become as mobile as ministers have long been. By and large, professional religionists in America, most notably among Methodists, lived like butterflies. One lit upon a congregation, adorned it for a year or two, perhaps pollinated it with spiritual fervor or theological rectitude, then fluttered off to the "larger field of labor." While ministers came and went the congregation's elders—as potent by any other name, vestrymen, stewards, or deacons—provided continuity and identity. If these men and women in the private parlance of the clergy were "lay popes," they seemed more like pillars of the church to their fellow believers. To the extent that continuity and stability is the stuff religion is made of, these lay symbols of continuity and stability became the means of identifying the congregation. In a way he never intended, Luther's dictum that congregations are to judge whether ministers rightly preach the word of God has characterized, even governed, religion in America. No doubt this congregational impulse, lodging power in leading laymen, has spurred ministerial mobility, for the congregation and not the minister is the "given" of religious activity.

Even with increased centralization in recent times, no national religious denomination in America is actually governed by its executive head. The term "denominational executive" is loosely applied to ranking members of headquarters staffs or to titular leaders, while these headquarters staffs of the denominations have been at worst bureaucrats and at best administrators of consensual policy. As the basic, constituent unit of the denomination, the congregation has in its pastor or leading layman the true denominational *executive*.

This stubborn congregationalism of American religion—Protestant, Catholic, or Jewish—may be camouflaged but hardly checked by theories of church polity espoused in the varying religious traditions. Centralization in religion has amplified more than it has strengthened headquarters operations, and for the most part they remained service organizations designed to assist congregations and local ministers. Denominational administrators understandably lamented the gap between their extensive portfolios of work and their minuscule authority. Sometimes their frustration was compensated by referring to the headquarters staff as "the national church" and by turning it into a congregation of administrators with its own ministerial executive. But no such central body, possibly excepting Mormon and Christian Science bureaucracies, has actually become the executive agency which preserved and regulated the life of the church.

If the day comes when the localism and laicism of American religion must be forfeited for the sake of self-preservation, it will be a day not of mere adjustment but of portentous upheaval. One minister with long experience as a denominational administrator predicted that in a world of rapid social change and swift governmental action, "the Church of Christ dare not wait on a slow-moving, out-moded, occasional gathering of its top leaders to cope with the gigantic problems and opportunities which mankind faces."[2] But there are few indications that the congregations, much less their lay leaders, expect the churches to cope with these great problems and opportunities.

Notwithstanding talk of clericalism and ministerial superprofessionalism. American religion remained at the middle of the twentieth century essentially a lay movement organized in congregations. As such, religion was expected to address itself to the needs and aspirations of the congregation's members and to leave to them the great problems and potentialities of mankind. Such has been the great tradition of American religion. One minister whose feet remained in the congregation even when his head reached into the world of theory has written: "In most of the changes surely ahead, the bureaucracy of the religious institution will *not* be able to lead. It seldom if ever can."[3]

Over the long term, congregational laicism has served as religion's chief buttress to the American ideal of equality of persons. This egalitarianism is itself complex and often ill understood, always piecemeal enough in actuality to earn criticism as empty hypocrisy. As a typical American aspiration the equality of persons has rarely meant arbitrary leveling so that everybody might start the race of life from the same place at the same time. It has been instead a negative protest against any general authority's dictating the terms of membership in local community enterprises. The American sense of fair play, prior to the civil rights movement of the 1950's and 1960's, has guarded the prerogative of a voluntary group to recruit its own members, with the implication that every person is a potential candidate for membership in every group. This equality of participation found religious expression through, not despite, the congregational impulse. For that reason the most pervasive feature of American religion, revivalism, has worked hand in glove with congregationalism, even though the two apparently conflict.

A stereotyped view of revivalism emphasizes its rugged individualism, its determined otherworldliness, and its rampant anti-ecclesiasticism. But T. Scott Miyakawa's partly historical and partly sociological study of revivalism in the old northwest improves our understanding of the movement by showing its many contributions to social conformity. Since "The Dissenting denominations" which Miyakawa studied—the Methodists, Presbyterians, and Baptists—"were formed primarily to satisfy the religious aspirations of their followers," these revivalistic groups aided their members by "using voluntary association to promote aims and mutual welfare not attainable by separate individuals." In particular, these denominations helped frontiersmen "to establish close personal relations quickly" with strangers, "to maintain high standards of personal and social behavior," and to exert forces for "preserving group unity." They fostered fellowship and encouraged members "to improve such personal and social skills as speaking . . ., reading, conducting meetings and committee sessions, and even some social etiquette."[4] An earlier and broader study found in American revivalism the main motive power of this-worldly social reform in the nineteenth century, thus linking the revival movement with the social gospelers' application of religion to the attainment of social welfare.[5]

In its true light revivalism becomes the means by which American religion foiled congregationalism's inherent tendency to exclusiveness. Either singly or cooperatively, congregations sponsored the campaigns of revival preachers from Jonathan Edwards down to Billy Graham, arranged for their appearances, peopled their meetings, and nurtured their converts. As the prime expression of American religion the congregation has guaranteed laicism; as a major mode of congregational religion, stamping its mark on routine worship and preaching and hymnody, the revival in a wide variety of forms has guaranteed inclusiveness by endorsing the equality of persons and the right of every man to inherit the benefits of heaven.

It is well known that in many localities, European and American, Western Christianity during the eighteenth century generated a quite unprecedented epidemic of affective piety. Whereas in Germany this pietism issued in quietistic inwardness (as well as good works) and whereas in England this evangelicalism gave the working classes a religious identity shared by the rising bourgeoisie, it was notably in America that religion of the heart

—dubbed "enthusiasm" and "emotionalism" by its deriders—determined principal developments in theology and church life as well as personal devotion. Earlier we referred to Solomon Stoddard's judgment that all ordinances given to the Christian church were means of regeneration. Although Jonathan Edwards eventually repudiated this dictum with respect to the Lord's Supper, Edwards built his theological work as well as his own career on the foundation of "religious affections." The bleakness of Edwards' view of man apart from God was but the counterpart of his resolute theocentrism; if human depravity and divine sovereignty were the poles around which his thought revolved, the thought itself was permeated everywhere by the universalizing presupposition that every man might expect to experience that regeneration which God bestowed and which fully incorporated him into the church.

The Great Awakening swept through all colonial denominations except the Roman Catholic Church and the Church of England, both of which were already "open" and universalizing churches by virtue of their conviction that any might and all should become their members. In fact, the reports to his ecclesiastical superiors by the Reverend Samuel Johnson, D.D. (1696–1772), renegade Puritan and stanch Anglican divine, asserted that the Church of England actually gained members in the northern colonies during the Great Awakening because the opponents of enthusiasm could trust that church's reasonableness to prevail over emotionalism. Yet even while Johnson so reported, the Reverend Devereux Jarratt (1733–1801) of Virginia, renegade Presbyterian turned Anglican priest, self-consciously patterned his revivalistic preaching after the work of George Whitefield. Early in the national period Roman Catholics and Episcopalians generally were attracted to variant forms of the revival movement. Few denominations were exclusivist enough to withstand the flood of evangelizing and proselytizing which engulfed American religion in the nineteenth century. For very good reasons the late Perry Miller found in this revivalism the basic and abiding influence on the American experience, and named Charles Grandison Finney the representative person of the movement.[6]

By casting itself in the sociological form of intimate but open fellowships—local, laic, and inclusive—religion in America engendered and partly realized the aspiration that every man be granted his place in the world. What family life because of its inherent exclusiveness and what national politics because of its vastness could never have done, religion undertook: to teach and practice the doctrine that every person may become a member and every member does become an equal partner in a common enterprise of utmost seriousness.

At the time of the settlement of Anglo-America, the Christian societies of Europe commonly regarded women and children, servants and savages, even apprentices and peasants as subjects of their adult male masters. These attitudes, to say nothing of the laws and customs embodying them, crossed the ocean with the colonists. In the new world, religion that was both congregational and evangelical tended to replace these attitudes with dreams of full personhood and full participation by every human being, to the extent of his ability, in a common society. The leveling force of economic and geographic factors in this new world is generally acknowledged to be of basic importance. Our concern is to show how religion functioned to inspire personal equality and social inclusiveness for women, for children, for Negro slaves, and for American Indians. In no case has absolute equality been achieved both legally and actually, but in all cases religious campaigns for ameliorated status and circumstances won partial success.

II. WOMEN AND CHILDREN

Women's rights were asserted hesitatingly in America by feminists before the Civil War and stridently thereafter, and became effectively as extensive as those of men only when the political franchise was extended to them in 1920 by the Nineteenth

Amendment to the United States Constitution. Since the achievement of this religiously engendered aspiration, women have swept on to occupy virtually every social function accorded to men except paternity. By 1922 the Cable Act granted married women citizenship independently of their husbands'. Children remained the wards and virtual properties of their fathers—notably not their mothers—until American interest in the personhood of children took specific form in laws restricting child labor; but these laws also were passed in the twentieth century.

Although the story of American religion's relation to the Negro and the Indian is a tale with two endings, both women and children found in and through religion an early, formative arena of participation in a transfamilial society. In general, religion has accented the aspiration of women to occupy the full sanctity of selfhood in society, in spite of widespread reluctance to admit clergywomen as religious professionals. Also religion has devised forms of membership for American young people as a mark of their maturity at ages far earlier than those set by law or custom for the attainment of majority.

Excepting a few sectarian groups with extreme doctrines and practices concerning women, American religion in thought and action received persons into complete membership regardless of sex. In the colonies' agrarian and town life the man was *paterfamilias*, and in the established churches of north and south his status as such in the civil body politic became the model for his role in managing church business. But the Quakers in all periods and the Baptists in colonial and early national times guaranteed women's participation in governing the congregations. For the Quaker the matter was theological: the inner light of God's spirit that came to every person who would attend it sang soprano as well as bass. Moreover, the Quakers resisted those distinctions between worship and government which characterized other denominations. Early Baptists practiced ministries of reconciliation and discipline in firm adherence to the teaching that every believer was a priest in the sight of God; when the church met after worship to do business, sisters as well as brothers were involved, both as discipliners and disciplined.[7]

In the middle period of American history, as a prominent interpreter noted, "Women as well as men experienced the emotions and aspirations of the religious revivals and were imbued with perfectionist ideas."[8] Not until the 1840's did an American woman become a professionally trained and officially ordained denominational minister, and a hundred years later the more conservative denominations still barred women from full sacerdotal functions. In Roman Catholicism the prominence of professed women monastics is of course no American phenomenon, but it underscores the tendency of all major American churches to confer titles of respect and functions of importance on women. More recently, Protestant churches in America, even those with policies against ordaining women, have opened to them careers as deaconesses, nuns, directors of religious education, choristers, and other remunerative careers, as well as innumerable volunteer services of institutional import and spiritual dignity.

The interest of American Christianity in the equality of women found cryptic expression by the Reverend George S. Phillips (?–1865), a young Methodist circuit rider of the North Ohio Conference. On December 17, 1844, Phillips "Spent a considerable [part] of the day in writing" and then "At night attended a discussion of the following resolution[:] Resolved that the female intellect is susceptible of as high a state of culture as that of the male." Although "A discussion was carried on to some extent," finally the matter was "decided in favour of the Ladies."[9]

It is not trite to point out that the early leaders of movements for securing women's rights were ladies actively engaged in church affairs. There they developed skills of leadership, practiced arts of persuasion, and learned techniques of turning voluntary organizations into social and political pressure groups. The organizing genius of the feminist movement in America, honored by her biographer as "The Greatest American Woman," was the

Quaker, Lucretia Coffin Mott (1793–1880), a woman experienced in advocating her convictions in the open forum of the Society of Friends.[10] The movement these persons fostered drew down the wrath of conservative clergymen, even of those who made common cause with feminists in crusades against slavery and demon rum. Perhaps most nineteenth-century Americans and probably all ministers of the time in one way or another were "higher law men," but it mattered greatly where the principle fell in application. Few clergymen sympathized with or even fully understood the cogency of Susan B. Anthony's parallels between the Fugitive Slave Law and laws repressing women.

Here as in many of its other social functions, religion's practices outran ministers' preachments. While doctrine exhorted the daughters of Adam's rib to cherish their dependence, deed made them equals in redemption if not in sin. The amazing Negro woman, Sojourner Truth, flung her namesake at a footdragging preacher during the Ohio Women's Convention meeting in Akron in 1851: "Den dat little little man in black dar, he say women can't have as much rights as men, 'cause Christ wan't a woman! Whar did your Christ come from? What did your Christ come from? From God and a woman! Man had nothin' to do wid Him!"[11]

The point is not to applaud Christianity for delivering women from bondage to inferiority; that was done by women. But the women who did it were, like most of their sisters in America, persons whose primary and major experience in practical equality and participation came through the congregations in which their souls were at least as good as the men's, in which "Amazing grace . . . saved a wretch like me" without regard to sex. To take part in American religion as a woman was, excepting ordination, no less full than to take part as a man. Both were dealt the same shame and proffered the same love from the same God by the same savior. The ladies' auxiliary or missionary society or sewing circle draped Christianity's cloth of gold not only on personhood but on womanhood. Before the law a chattel, in the frontier cabin a beast of birthing, in the plantation home a doll, in the eastern city a figure of finery, in economy and government a nonentity, in the professions an imposter, in learning and letters a luxury—woman in nineteenth-century America was all this, but in church she was all that man was: a sinner saved by grace.

Women's status in American religion has been described categorically; that is not so easy in the case of children. For there runs through post-Reformation Christianity a deep theological rift between churches which regard infants as candidates for membership and those which teach that only an adult profession of faith can win entrance into the company of believers. Because the Baptists—the term is used now to cover the entire latter group—have flourished in the American disestablishmentarian atmosphere, the rift is more notable here than in Europe. Yet even here the gulf that seems theologically absolute is in effect spanned by lines of communication if not by bridges of actual practice. On one side the Baptists, insisting on experiential faith as *sine qua non* of Christian initiation, have tended to lower the theological age of discretion to early adolescence and have allowed even newborn infants a relation to the church through services of dedication. On the other side the Roman Catholics, insisting that the sacrament of Baptism be administered to children of a Catholic parent at the earliest moment possible, have employed confirmation (with the subjectively more important "first Communion") as a second initiation ceremony at the age of puberty or adolescence. Since these opposite theological conceptions of initiation issue in somewhat parallel practices, generalizations about the attitudes of American Christianity toward children are legitimate.

The colonial Anglicans followed tradition in presenting their children for christening, but the absence of bishops cast confirmation into desuetude until the reorganized Episcopal Church obtained bishops in the early national period. Similarly colonial Catholicism made no provision for episcopal confirmation of persons reared in the colonies. Data regarding later campaigns for American bishops in both these denominations manifest no keen sense of lack with respect to this sacrament, although when there were American bishops they of course administered confirmation. Hitherto these two churches had identical practices respecting children: infant baptism as the rite of full initiation, the receiving of Communion from puberty or adolescence onward as the means of full participation, and matrimony as the usual entry into fully responsible adulthood. Normally the candidate for "first Communion" was prepared by catechetical or other instruction. The addition of confirmation in the national period did little to change this pattern, although in more recent times both churches have stressed instruction of candidates for matrimony.

Among the more ecclesiastical traditions in America it was the Lutherans whose doctrines best equipped them to adapt the inherited sacramental system to congregational church life for the participation of young persons in religion at their own level of psychological development. For in American Lutheran teaching the pastor, receiving his entitlement to minister from his congregation, baptizes, instructs, confirms, and admits persons to Communion. On the American scene the Lutherans made the pastor so self-sufficient that the office of bishop lapsed. Thus the Lutherans provided within the congregational framework the functionary and the occasions on which children were brought into participation: categorically for infants at baptism, experientially for school-age children through catechetical and other forms of religious education, ritually at confirmation for adolescents, repeatedly for youth and adults at Communion. All these instrumentalities lay within the ministerial competence of the local pastor.

New England Puritans initially assumed that every adult might become a proved saint and own the covenant of grace for himself, although in fact probably no more than one-fifth of the settlers of Massachusetts Bay Colony during the early decades were such saints. Originally the covenanting adult automatically brought his children into church membership with him, earning for them the right to the seal of baptism at birth. Having repudiated confirmation as popish, the Puritan expected his children to gain full standing as recipients of the Lord's Supper by confessing their own experience of regeneration. By the middle of the seventeenth century the inevitable problem arose: failing of such an experience, can the baptized noncommunicant present his own children for baptism? Some ministers were baptizing children of parents neither of whom was a professed Christian communicant. In the famous Half-way Covenant, approved in 1662, that practice was authorized. The urgency of the question was increased by subtle but intimate connections between church membership and full citizenship. But for our present purpose, the Half-way Covenant struck a happy *via media* between the historic opposites of Catholic and Baptist doctrine regarding children. However nominal the parents' ties to the church, every child of noninfidels might be baptized. But full membership, sealed by admission to the Communion, awaited the candidate's own experience of regeneration. Knotty implications of this compromise, without precedent in Christian history, beset Congregationalism in New England for more than a century, because it became centrally important for the church —congregation, believing parents, and minister—so to deal with children as to bring them eventually to an experience of regeneration. Out of this compromise arose the twin (and only later inimical) endeavors: religious education that would enlist as well as inform, and evangelistic preaching and pastoring designed to stir the affections of half-way Christians.

Nowhere in New England were these evangelizing efforts more fruitful than in Northhampton, where Solomon Stoddard employed the Lord's Supper "not only for the strengthening of Saints, but a means also to work saving Regeneration."[12] That doctrine began the eighteenth century in Northampton religion. By 1750 the congregation had removed Jonathan Edwards from the pulpit for attempting to reverse it by refusing Communion to all but proved saints. But Edwards himself as a young child had observed "a time of remarkable awakening in my father's congregation" at East Windsor, and experienced "a variety of concerns and exercises about my soul," including "two more remarkable seasons of awakening." The first of these occurred before he was twelve years old when he "experienced I know not what kind of delight in religion. . . . My affections seemed to be lively and easily moved, and I seemed to be in my element when engaged in religious duties."[13] Childhood as well as early apprenticeship to Grandfather Stoddard prepared Edwards for leadership of the Great Awakening in New England. That episode was touched off by Edwards' work with young people of Northampton, in which he invented the favorite device of American religion for encountering and encouraging adolescents: the youth group.

In his own narrative of the revival, written in 1735, Edwards recalled a diminution of "a party spirit, & a contentious disposition, which before had Prevail'd for many years between two Parties in the Town," young people and their parents. In urging youth to forsake their frolicking and night-walking, Edwards awakened in them a sense of need to reform their lives. After they were brought up short by the conversions and deaths of certain townspeople, Edwards "moved to the young People that they should set up Religious meetings, on Evenings after Lectures," where there began an earnest seeking and "a Concern about the Great things of Religion . . . ." The most notable feature of Edwards' arresting story of the early revival is that "many Little Children were affected Remarkeably"; his detailed account of one of them made four-year-old Phebe Bartlett almost legendary.[14] Thus at the outset the American religious revival sought conversion and religious participation of young people, not only youths but children as well. Although later revivalism in the early decades of the nineteenth century overemphasized, according to Horace Bushnell, the episodic and occasional to the neglect of routine, ordinary ministrations, it is a mistake to infer into Bushnell's critique the notion that the revivalist movement paid no attention to the young.

Bushnell proposed in 1847 a genuinely new effort on the part of evangelical religion in America when he stressed that children of Christian parents should be reared never to think of themselves as other than Christian. As a frank (though not uncautious) believer in the inheritance of acquired characteristics, Bushnell thought the only way the deleterious effect of sin on humankind might be reduced was to leave off teaching children what sinners they were in hope of cataclysmic conversion, and instead to take up nurturing their capacity for the good things of the spirit. Understood in the context of the function of American religion, what Bushnell wanted was that children, from birth and at their own developmental level, should be regarded as full participants in the churches without need for discontinuities engendered or implied by conversion, confirmation, or admission to Communion.

In making this proposal Bushnell drew on two sources: the expectation of New England's founding fathers that children of saints would normally and naturally become saints in their own right, and the romantic conception of family life that reckoned the home as the earliest and most determinative influence on personality and character. He wanted parents to regard their children as fellow Christians. Insofar as the religious education movement in America has remained true to him as its rightful founder, it has claimed genuine personhood for the baby, infant, child, youth, and adult, and has subtly but powerfully eroded their subjugation as virtual property of the *paterfamilias* in American life. Thereby American religion resorted to a "higher law" respecting familiality and personhood than either the law of nature or the law of society, and injected into the popular conception of the "natural family" and into the positive law a respect for individuality of persons regardless of age or sex. Whether psychologically salutary or not is quite beside the point that the achievement is itself very remarkable.

While religious education in the tradition of Bushnell affirmed the personhood of children without reserve, it nevertheless conceived of the family as the primary arena in which such personhood was to realize itself. Arising contemporaneously with that endeavor and pursuing a career parallel to it has been another affirmation of the child's individuality, but in this case the personhood was to realize itself in arenas furnished by the churches. For thousands upon thousands of American children the earliest sorties beyond the family into a social group (leaving aside the familylike birthday party) has been enrollment in the church nursery, kindergarten, Sunday School, or the parish day school. Through the Sunday School's orientation to character-building the child became an integer in an extrafamilial group that elicited rudimentary political, social, and even economic activities. Thus religious education sought not so much to teach as to enlist, not so much to impart information about Christianity as to evoke loyalty to the church or to the Sunday School class. The success and "profaning" of the enterprise are marked by the shift in general education, under the influence of John Dewey's theories, away from the three R's toward the provision of extrafamilial arenas for interpersonal relations and toward the evocation of loyalty to the democratically based community.

If the churches gave children their first experience as individual members of nonfamilial groups, the churches also devised means for continuing such experiences during puberty and adolescence. A plethora of young people's organizations—guilds, clubs, societies, fellowships, fraternities, with varying degrees of directly religious interest—has provided American youth basic and primary political experiences. How many Americans held their first elective or appointive office as president, secretary, or program-committee chairman of the Baptist Young People's Fellowship, the Catholic Youth Organization, or a similar club in another denomination? Perhaps indicative of religion's prowess in sponsoring organizations for youth is the fact that in recent decades the Boy Scouts of America sought to have each unit of organization sponsored by a local religious group.

III. NEGROES AND INDIANS

American religion always pressed the principle of every man's participation in human affairs to more universal application than the common social structures allowed, but with one cardinal exception, the Negro, and one minor exception, the American Indian. While fostering the aspiration that all men become brothers one to another, religion with few exceptions (most notably that of the Quakers) was racially exclusive. It is as though religion's right to insist that the noncitizen, the uneducated, the nonpropertied, the female, and the young be drawn into the body politic was bought by pledging—sometimes covertly, sometimes stridently, but always earnestly—that persons of color would be marked down for such participation only with one another.

Negroes were Christianized into fellowship with Christian Negroes. From the first posing of the issue in colonial times down to the day before yesterday, American Christianity erected separate (but in certain respects equal) religious institutions for white and for black, while American Jewry avoided bringing the Negro into close range by defining Judaism now as a race and now as a religion, and by remaining nonmissionary. The success of American Christianity as an equalizing influence on society was purchased by acceding to the inferiority of blacks.

Although several denominations had their own ways of dealing with Negroes both before and after emancipation, these distinctions can without distortion be composed into a general trend, provided the Quakers are reserved for separate comment. After initial quandary all denominations undertook the evangelization of Negroes. The manner of the quandary's solution determined things for a long time to come. The question arose already in the seventeenth century whether or not, under English law, the baptizing of a slave made him so nearly a person that no Christian could hold him in slavery. If the negative answer allowed the Christianization of Negroes to go forward, it also opened the way to a variety of Christian defenses of slavery. That masters owned not the persons but only the labor of their Negroes and that this employment blessed Negroes with civilization unavailable in Africa were points argued by Virginians, for example, for two centuries. Christianization during slavery in America was an interim stage in God's plan to Christianize

Africa, according to theologians urging manumissions, deportations, and missions. More hardheaded religionists took chattel slavery for what it was and argued that Ham's accursed progeny deserved no better. Still others viewed slavery as sin and emancipation as good, but few white abolitionists were colorblind egalitarians. Whether the Christians' plan for Negroes was evangelization or education, amelioration or colonization, slavery's abolition or extension, immigration to the north or segregation within the south—and it has included all of these—Negroes were stigmatized as inherently inferior and by exclusion from full participation in American life within and without the churches. Perhaps the intensity with which major denominations in the middle of the twentieth century identified the Negro protest for full civil rights with the will of God reflects the guilt they feel for this virtually unrelieved historical record.

Once it was clear that the slaves' legal status was immune to baptism's lustration and regeneration, church agencies both at home and in the colonies undertook evangelization of Negroes. The founding charter of the Society for the Propagation of the Gospel in Foreign Parts stipulated special care for Negroes; Frank J. Klingberg showed how the S. P. G. mitigated the exploitation of Negroes in America by promoting humanitarianism.[15] Quaker missionaries strove to convert Negroes for their betterment, and by refusing all traffic with slaveowners the courageous John Woolman (1720–1772) taught American Quakers to denounce and oppose the institution itself as wrong. The Friends alone among American denominations saw the Negroes as equal to the whites in the eyes of God, and therefore they were equals in the church. Quakers regarded all Negroes as persons, wrongfully abused by the wicked institution of slavery.

It seems impossible to know accurately the numbers of Negroes who were Christians at the time of American independence. But two things are apparent: the Methodists and Baptists had by then led the way in evangelization, and wholly Negro denominations were being formed—the African Methodist Episcopal Church from 1787 onward, the African Methodist Episcopal

Zion Church in 1796, and many others throughout the nineteenth century. Southern revivals at the turn of the century engulfed Negroes and Negro churches and stamped them with the marks of emotional fervor and evangelical zeal which these revivals left on most white denominations. Other denominations were not callous to the Negro. Episcopalians numbered large groups of blacks among their members by 1820, although as a rule (especially in the south) they were seated in special sections of the church building and received Communion after the whites. It was Episcopalians, notably the Reverend William Holland Wilmer (1782–1827) of Alexandria, Virginia, who led in the formation of the American Colonization Society in 1817, uniting previous movements in New England, New Jersey, and Virginia to repatriate manumitted slaves in a section of Africa where, according to plan, they would erect a Christian nation and undertake the conversion of Africa. By the end of the Civil War this society had received contributions totaling more than two million dollars to promote its goal and to found the nation of Liberia.[16] Its plan at the time was hardly as naïve as it seems in retrospect, but on explicitly Christian grounds the Colonization Society sought the elimination of slavery's ills via the elimination of Negroes' presence in America, not by assimilation.

The bolder solution, miscegenation, escaped the imagination even of abolitionists. Indeed abolitionists focused the Negro issue so sharply on the institution of slavery as to draw attention away from the question of the freedman's participation in American society. Among the most convincing of all the diffuse arguments put forward by defenders of "the peculiar institution" is that for a Negro to be slave under a beneficent master was far better for him than being a manumitted but oppressed citizen. But if abolition overspecified the issue, so did colonization. So also did Christian efforts at education and amelioration, both before and after emancipation.

It is estimated that at the outbreak of the Civil War no less than one-eighth of American Negroes were church members, and that by the time of the Emancipation Proclamation, according to DuBois, "one adult in six was a nominal Christian."[17] But after 1840 the number of Negroes, theretofore decreasing, rose sharply as slave labor in cotton fields proved lucrative to planters. During the Civil War itself and even after the defeat of the Confederate forces seemed inevitable, sincere southern church-men eagerly missionized slaves and laid on masters the Christian duty of encouraging their slaves' evangelization and instruction. "The [Protestant Episcopal] diocese of South Carolina, despite the depredations of war and the liberation of slaves by invading armies, in 1865 counted 3,404 white and 2,142 Negro adult members. . . . [Between 1862 and 1865] twice as many Negroes as whites were baptized [as Episcopalians] in South Carolina."[18]

But neither the fervid attempt to show that Christianity could flourish among Negroes in slavery nor the opposite effort to abolish slavery as unchristian brought about inclusion of Negroes in church life or, indeed, religious encouragement that they should be included in the common life. Northern churches and churchmen devised various strategies by which Negroes could become separate but equal Christians. Independent denomina-tions with exclusively Negro constituencies multiplied; seven Negro Methodist bodies were formed between 1840 and 1897. Separate associations of Negro Baptist churches arose in the north after the 1830's, and with whites' assistance a Negro national convention gathered in 1866. Splits produced the Na-tional Baptist Convention (1880), the American National Baptist Convention (1886), and the National Baptist Convention of the U.S.A. (1895).[19] Where Negro congregations were held within regional or national denominational frames, ways were found to prevent their administrative mixing with white congre-gations. Although some urban Episcopal parishes in the north received Negro members, that denomination normally formed all-Negro parishes, often under Negro priests; but when Negro bishops were consecrated their jurisdictions were so devised that they never supervised white communicants or white clergy.[20] As late as 1939 the Methodist Church's scheme to reunite northern and southern branches provided a "Central Jurisdiction" for

Negroes while all other jurisdictions were geographical; the palpably segregating device was debated until 1964 when the General Conference voted to abolish the Central Jurisdiction by 1968.

There were of course exceptions to the rule that Negroes were shunted off into their own congregations or denominations or sections of church buildings. An early settler of San Francisco reported to his wife in 1858 that the Methodist Sabbath School in the northern part of the city was a melting pot for children of various backgrounds: "The scholars are mostly American children, though in the school there are Spanish, Negro, and Digger Indian children. A sort of amalgamation. But all things went on orderly, prefitably and interestingly."[21] Yet it was the exceptional aspect of the experience which prompted Muzzy to remark it.

Down to the 1830's religious Americans generally conceded that Negro slavery deserved gradual extinction, but scarce indeed were efforts to lead Negroes into full participation in the common society by granting them equal membership in congregations. From the 1830's until the end of Reconstruction the issues of Negro personhood and participation were smothered by sectional controversies over slavery and by problems that followed emancipation. Although tangential to our main concern, the varieties of religiously based attitudes toward Negroes expressed by clergy and laity from 1830 to 1877 merit illustration and may illumine an important consideration—the effect of congregational participation and evangelical zeal upon Negro members of Negro churches.

1. Religious Attitudes Toward Negroes

When on December 6, 1833 William Lloyd Garrison (1805–1879) and his fellow abolitionists organized the American Anti-Slavery Society, they carefully made their "Declaration of Sentiments" more a renewal of the nation's founding principles than an appeal to religion and Scripture. They never doubted that the Almighty smiled on their endeavor to labor as Americans for the liberation of slaves as fellow Americans. The national ideal supplied their principles; religion generated sanctions and provided slogans. Southerners had a point in blaming the northern pulpit for promoting the abolitionist crusade, but that pulpit was never unanimous in this respect. The southerners equated any opposition to slavery with abolitionism, yet Horace Bushnell opposed both slavery and the abolitionists' techniques. John Henry Hopkins (1792–1868), Episcopal bishop of Vermont and presiding officer of his denomination, wrote a forceful defense of slavery on Biblical grounds.

Many denominations north and south slithered through the antebellum era without condemning or condoning slavery, but the issue rent Methodists and Baptists regionally long before Fort Sumter, and the war itself split churches, some temporarily, some for a century. It was a rare church judicatory that did not learn where its members stood on the issue. If the Civil War did not force the denominations to enunciate a Christian conception of the place of Negroes in American life, it drove persons, including church members, to take their stands. That they did so as persons and not as denominations cohered with the great tradition of laicism in American religion, and forms an ironic contrast to the circumstances of a century later, when every denomination spoke its official mind but the members reserved judgment on the issues of racial justice.

Men and women strove to apply their religious principles to the situation. Some fought for slavery; some, for freedom. The same Bible that both sides read and the same God to whom both prayed gave ambiguous answers to the question of slavery. A few learned from Bible and God the equality of Negroes and whites. In North Carolina in 1862 Union Private James Edward Glazier, pious Methodist lad and son of a storekeeper in Salem, Massachusetts, wrote of sympathy for contraband Negroes around New Bern, North Carolina, sympathy that developed into genuine identification with them as persons. He told his sweetheart that the freed slaves' religion provided them with hope and happiness and proved their spiritual equality with whites: "And to look at those happy faces while they sing and [to] witness the earnestness and devotion pictured there is enough to make one sorry he is not in one of their black skins, and, (in some cases) blacker circumstances." Superior only in education and well-being, he thought every encounter enriched not the Negroes but him. He broke regulations in order to attend and address a Negro prayer meeting. Not that Glazier was indiscriminate or undiscriminating; he had little or no fellow feeling with coarse or immoral soldiers, but oppressed blacks and misled southern whites who lived Christian lives were his brothers.[22]

Glazier's contemporary and fellow Yankee, Lyman Abbott, was a more representative abolitionist Christian noted for his advocacy of Negro equality. At the age of thirty Abbott was managing the American Union Commission from its New York offices, and he responded to a suggestion by the Reverend Jacob R. Shipherd, secretary of the American Freedmen's Aid Committee in Washington, that the two organizations merge. Shipherd thought Abbott's Commission aided poor whites only; Abbott replied by attacking any charitable organization that perpetuated discrimination between persons on the basis of caste or color. Abbott wished "there were but one organization, which, ignoring all distinctions of race and color should undertake to provide relilef [for 'relief'] for the needy and education for the ignorant, not because they were black or white, but upon the broad ground of a universal humanity alone."[23]

During Reconstruction, sentiments of equality were expressed by leaders of religious agencies working in the south, but it is not easy to find telling examples of practiced equality in the north. Southerners' insistence on handling the Negro "problem" their own way finally eclipsed egalitarianism. Northern Presbyterians admitted Negroes during Reconstruction to the college they established and maintained at Maryville, Tennessee. The Southern Presbyterian minister in Maryville asked his uncle, William Brown (1811–1894) of Richmond, editor of The Central Presbyterian, "to get the fact prominently before the country that this College here is mixed." He complained: "The men here have lied & do lie about it. I know students came here under the impression no negroes were in it. . . . You cant find a thing in any one of their Catalogues or advertisements to show there is a negro student there. It was denied even that there were any there last year, when there were more negroes than at any other time. The truth is they seek for negro students & avow here that *cast* is all wrong & anti Christian & all they want is time to inculcate the truth & all will be right." The minister vowed to fight the issue through, and if he failed, "I will quit this country. . . . If matters progress as they have done for 12 months color will be at a premium."[24]

2. *Negro Religion Itself*

After Reconstruction, encouraged by northern and southern denominations and cast loose by southern churchmen, Negro religion like Negro education became an isolated entity in American life. The white preachers and observers of antebellum days vanished, leaving the Negro minister as preacher, counselor, leader, negotiator, and latter-day "Uncle Tom." As Gunnar Myrdal and his associates noted, "Both the strength and the weakness of the Negro church as a power agency for the Negro people is related to the facts that the Negro church is a segregated church and that there is astonishingly little interracial cooperation between the white and Negro churches. In both respects the South is extreme, but the situation in the North is not very different."[25] Discounting the few Negro members of some liberal, urban, white congregations in the north and some uneasily interracial congregations in a few cities, the situation did not change importantly in the two decades following Myrdal's 1944 depiction.

But Myrdal failed to note one major if unmeasurable shift in white religionists' attitude toward Negroes. Since the beginning of World War II, positive sanctions for segregation and Negro inferiority by white ministers have seldom issued from southern pulpits even during racial crises. Mid-twentieth-century ministers were generally expected to acknowledge the contradiction between Christian teaching and racial inequality, even where their parishioners' segregationist convictions made direct action toward equality unwise, impolitic, or dangerous. By 1965 every major white denomination in the United States had spread on the minutes of its meetings resolutions favoring Negro equality. However, application of those resolutions to congregational life remained a matter of local option influenced but not determined by local clergy and regional church superiors.

Negro religion in America imitated white religion. Congregational form and revivalistic content found no finer expression among agrarian whites than they did among Negroes, slave and free. Myrdal noticed that throughout American history the Negro church had been a carbon copy of the white church. But the carbon paper somehow sharpened the characters, emphasizing contrast between line and space. In Negro religion the yearning for heaven that pervades all Christianity was heightened just as the gap between paradise and earthly vale was widened. The Negro American's church more clearly reflected his community life than did the white man's and, touching his life at every point, became, as the white American's rarely did, intimately bound with his destiny and hope. "Especially after Emancipation," according to Nelson Burr, "the church became the clearing house of the Negro community, with the pastor as secretary. No longer appealing to the master for guidance, the freedman sought counsel from his minister."[26]

While white America's pilgrimage toward success drove religion either to erode its gospel or forfeit its relevance, the Negro's woe at once vivified the meanings of the Christian message of bondage and deliverance, and made the church central to his mundane affairs. His minister knelt down as the Negro's consoler and stood up as his prophet of a better day. The church buildings—however heavily mortgaged, usually the only real property the freedman owned—served as site for worship and education, recreation and social protest, relief of suffering and redress of grievances. In it, usually only in it, he could be himself among his own, expressing his feelings as he saw fit by the skills of his choice. As Baptist or Methodist, Catholic or Pentecostalist, his denomination gave him a name and identity shared and respected by other citizens. Ecclesiastical gatherings, controversies, and schisms provided occasions for debating and voting, deciding and organizing, clarifying ideas and adopting courses of action. Since the Civil War and after the white minister disappeared from Negro churches and the Negro members left white churches, religious meetings became many Negroes' primary opportunity to be and to act free from surveillance by the racial majority.

In the decades between the two World Wars it appeared that Negro clergy were lagging behind some of their constituents in education and in reforming zeal, and that the Negro church confronted a time of severe testing. In the 1960's there loomed prospect of victory in the campaign for Negro equality in public education, voting rights, and public accommodations, and while the National Association for the Advancement of Colored People sought judicial relief, the churches, sparked by the Montgomery, Alabama, bus boycott and the leadership of Martin Luther King, realized their capacity to stir direct social action under ideological nonviolence. Religion, whether King's Gandhian Christianity or the Black Muslims' racist Islam, sprang to life because it inculcated a sense of personal dignity and promoted (in different ways) the full participation of persons in society. The Negro American's cruel fate was that religious inspiration for these facets of the American dream came to him late and lopsided. His personhood and participation were racially circumscribed until he demanded, on grounds of civil rights and secular justice, what the dream lied in promising him as an inalienable gift of God.

3. Indians

If religion functioned ambivalently toward extension of personhood and social participation to Negroes, its effect in these matters was almost totally negative with respect to the American Indian. Early missionary and educational plans were trimmed when controversy and hostility over lands set the early invaders' interests against those of the indigenous inhabitants. Soon the former drew sharp distinctions between submissive Indians and those who arose to protect their own customs and grounds. As increasing waves of Americans flooded westward, general enmity toward Indians sought their confinement on poor reservations or, if they resisted, their extinction. A story of disregard and depredation is punctuated by occasional episodes of heroic missionary work and of courageous attempts to guard Indian rights or to assimilate Indians into the dominant society. The same story is always moderated by characteristics of primitiveness and innocency which whites imputed to Indians—characteristics which almost any provocation could obvert into imputed savagery and devilishness. For the relation between American settlers and Indians, religion can hardly be held accountable because even slight strains pushed that relation into the arena of public interest. If the irony of American religious history, viewed functionally, shows the Negro imitating white religion to the point of outpacing it, then the same irony shows the Indian repeatedly confined, subjugated, coerced into submitting to the ways of the white, including his religion, but in a manner that never reversed the undertow of reluctance.

The Macedonian cry of the Indian depicted on Massachusetts Colony's first seal nicely illustrates what American Christians wanted to convince themselves was their attitude toward the red man. There was comfort in thinking of the white Christians' presence in the Indians' land as response to the latter's entreaty. A sense of virtue accompanied the white's self-persuasion that he encountered the Indian as helper. The earliest American settlers were no hypocrites, for indeed they sensed (among other things) a divine imperative to extend the Protestant faith among natives of North America quite as intensely as Hispanic Americans meant to enlarge the Catholic world. But those Protestants were exceptional whose missionary zeal and fellow feeling for the Indians endured the red man's resist-

ing dispossession by massacre or warfare. Virginia Anglicans'
desire to convert the natives cooled with the Henrico Massacre
of 1622, just as New England Puritans' evangelistic ardor waned
during King Philip's War of 1675–1676. Roger Williams in
Rhode Island thought Indians deserved recompense for their
land, and William Penn assured equable relations with them
by the terms of his treaty of 1683. Nevertheless, seventeenth-
century Indian missionaries are famous because they were few;
the storied Mayhews of Martha's Vineyard, the pioneering trans-
lator John Eliot, the Virginia promoter of Indian education
James Blair, the Dutch evangelist Johannes Megapolensis hero-
ically encountered the Indians with measures as unusual as
they were idealistic. Very few colonists possessed such sagacity
as did Penn, who wanted the Indians not only Christianized
but absorbed into the community life of Pennsylvania.

The Great Awakening brought new bursts of enthusiasm for
Indian evangelism in the mid-eighteenth century, exemplified
by David Brainerd, Jonathan Edwards, and Moravians in Georgia.
But by the end of the century the young nation's Northwest
Ordinance struck into law what had been the underlying attitude: white occupation of Indian lands was the fortune of one
and the fate of the other. Indian submissiveness was desirable;
Indian resistance would be overcome. If Americans had not yet
devised the cynical slogan that "the only good Indian is a dead
Indian," they were already convinced that no Indian was good
enough to hold the land he claimed, and he who tried it would
be a dead Indian. Six months before the Declaration of Independence one Gideon Hawley of Mashpee on Cape Cod
described good Indians in a letter to Samuel Cooper at Boston:
"I will only say that my Indians are the people whose ancestors
hospitably received our Fathers; who were their first converts
to Christianity and for whom the fund was collected & Corporation formed in London—These Indians never at any time
contended with us or deceived us. But they have fought for
us and assisted us in every expedition and particularly in Philips
war. And in our former attempts against Canada . . . [and]

against Norridgwork . . . [and] against Carthagena . . . [and] against Lewisburgh. . . . and all the last war had their warriors out upon every quarter and have now some, and if the war continues will have many more, in the service of the country."[27] By implication a bad Indian was one who had contended with or deceived or fought against or refused to assist and serve the whites.

Attitudes formed during the occupation of the old northwest served American expansionists right across the great river, the great plains, and the great mountains to the coast. The Whitman massacre in 1847 once more "proved" Indian treachery. There were few good Indians left after successive encounters by pioneers with various tribes, especially in the west. Orville A. Nixon recorded his opinion of the Indians he met journeying in 1855 from his home in Centerville, Tennessee, to Bent's Fort, Colorado: "A party of Kiowas came in to day; reports the Aropahoes, Sheyennes, and Kiowas a long ways off; gone to war, probably to join the Sioux. The Kiowas are a mean Indian; the Aropahoes a poor, filthy, lazy set. The Comanche, thiefs and Robbers. The Sheyens impudent, rougish, and lazy." A few days earlier Nixon had noted, "I never look upon these indians out here but what my blood boils for their depredations and rascality to the passing emigrants on this road. It is a sin and disgrace to the American name to tolerate such vilenys as they have frome such mean, blood thirsty people. They are [a] lazy, filthy race of mankind. Sic transit die."[28] These of course were Indians already subjected to a reservation policy which, with much abusive administration, often failed to protect as well as it confined. When white Americans swept into the western half of the continental territory under the Homestead Act of 1862, the least desirable tracts were saved for Indians. The peaceful were dispossessed and the hostile decimated.

Yet the almost unrelievedly sad tale of white Americans' relations with Indians does not want for some self-sacrificing endeavors by a few to Christianize, educate, ameliorate, and even absorb these native Americans into the mainstream of the commonwealth. Missionary activities in the national period were largely confined to the reservations, and only after the beginning of World War I did there arise a missionary policy designed to equip Indians to move from reservations into normal American communities. Despite points to its credit, American religion has on the whole been complicit to the official policy of dispossession and exclusion, and its protests against extermination have been faint. If the Indians' story of exclusion from American life lacks the poignancy of the Negroes', perhaps the reason is that whites' acquaintance with Indians has been too sparse to generate sympathy. If opportunity for symbolic revision of the record arises anywhere it is in Alaska, where benevolent assimilation of Indians into American society remains a remote possibility. The Indians' plight illustrates a failure of American religion and of American society to achieve full, mutual participation of members of differing races in the common human endeavor.

American religion generated hopes for attainment of personhood and participation by all white men, all white women, and all white children. With regard to their sense of belonging to the human enterprise, the members of the white churches knew no captivity and therefore needed no deliverance; having achieved, they needed no longer aspire, and it was not easy for the churches' members to apply universally this part of the churches' message. Conversely, the failure of American Christianity to bind the Negro into human communities has left to the Negro churches the opportunity and capacity to create and represent a powerful subcommunity of Negroes that is able to demand, on Christian principles in many cases, the full human rights of all men regardless of race. Thus the whites' quest for their own identity had the effect of conquest for the blacks.

The success in the campaign for identity and sociality of all manner of whites has left its peculiar mark on the main denominations. By emphasizing the rights of women and children to exercise their personhood, white religion in America lapsed into a certain effeminacy and infantilism. While stimulating the family to broaden itself beyond the straits of natural-law conceptions and the rigidities of civil-law conceptions into a social unit respecting the particularity of all its members, American religion developed a fixation on familiality from which, in its now predominant suburban form, it has found no release. American religion in all its prominent varieties is domestic in its message, its program, and its character. It bears most heavily upon the home just at that juncture of history when the American home has been most insulated from the decision-making process of a managerial economy serving a technological society. But the critics of churches held captive by suburban mores have a foreshortened view of history unless they recognize that the strong emphasis on the family, on local and laic expressions, on personhood of women and children, is one of the great areas of effectiveness in the religious formation of America. What many reckon as American religion's failure today was the great measure of its success only yesterday.

When the white denominations finally approved the Negroes' bid for full participation in American society, it soon became commonplace to ascribe the exaggerated and agitated finality of their approval to pent-up guilt for their long complicity in keeping the Negro isolated from the mainstream of American affairs. Yet behind these elements of guilt may lurk shame and envy. For the denominational leaders and local ministers, worried by white Christianity's domestication that betokens both neglect of its gospel and irrelevance to the critical affairs of the country, have come near to coveting the Negro churches' facility for clinging to certain essential points of Christian teaching—love, brotherhood, personhood, justice, equality—while maintaining poignant relevance to the basic concern of their members and of the nation.

CHAPTER FOUR

A LITTLE LEARNING

Religion and education followed parallel and often inter-dependent courses throughout American history. All the denomi-nations, even those that played on the anti-intellectual impulse of the frontier, at one time or another sponsored education at every level. Protestants pioneered the endeavors out of which grew the public systems of compulsory instruction, and they established the institutions on which were modeled public col-leges and universities. Finding tax-supported schools deeply colored by Protestant teachings and teachers, Catholics erected the country's only complete system of sectarian education, for which public subventions were repeatedly sought—and gained just when it became clear that the system failed to produce deep sectarian loyalties. Crusading against those same subven-tions as breaches in the wall separating church and state, Protes-tants drove public education to ever loftier neutrality toward religion, and very nearly expunged their own influence from the public school system, which many Protestants then denounced as godless. Americans have reached a broad consensus on dividing education as a worldly enterprise appropriate to public or private sponsorship from catechesis or "religious education" as a sacred enterprise appropriate to denominational sponsorship.

Having stated the consensus, one rushes to qualify the assertion by noticing the many church agencies and groups which claim that instruction reaches its highest quality by combining education and catechesis under denominational control. The Catholic parochial school system, augmented by colleges and universities, endures and is paralleled in certain other denominations, notably The Lutheran Church-Missouri Synod and, at the primary level, the Episcopal Church. The Methodist Church maintains close connection with regional universities from Boston to southern California, and Presbyterians pace the many denominations which maintain colleges.

Amity between religious and profane educational programs is of recent vintage. Behind it lies a long history of education's religious stimulus and worldly response. Throughout most of that history, it has been generally assumed by religionists that learning would automatically yield piety and morality—an assumption which perdured Jefferson's theoretical and practical attacks and which controlled religious leaders' imaginations until well after the Civil War. The assumption is not only illogical, for it also represents misguided obversion of a principle operative through most of the history of Christianity. Since its earliest encounter with Greco-Roman civilization, Christianity found twin enemies in illiteracy and ignorance; it was a religion serving an intelligent deity in an intelligible world on the basis of an intellectual revelation. As an institution bringing civilization to rude European peoples, the church early saw its need for a literate constituency and for learned leaders. To memorize the Decalogue, Paternoster, and "Apostles'" Creed was required by Charlemagne of all his subjects and was the primary means of "Christianizing" Europe. In confronting Islam and later in the Renaissance, European Christendom perceived the latent disjunction between knowledge and piety, but the parts of Europe from which Anglo-America was settled in the seventeenth century had succeeded in holding the disjunction in latency.

Largely isolated from the blatantly secularizing influences of the Enlightenment and recoiling from this disjunction's specific manifestation in the French Revolution, Americans of the main-line religious persuasions clung until the late nineteenth century to the notion that literacy and learning would abet piety and morality. They made a closely related mistake in thinking that education and religion would equally thrive in schools and colleges equipped with devout teachers and ordained presidents.

However wrong these assumptions may have proved in the last hundred years, they reigned long enough to make religion the parent and putative guardian of American education at all levels. When education became the unifier of society and the primary function of the body politic, opinion in religious circles either turned against the growing child or else unsuccessfully sued for his custody.

I. RELIGION AND EDUCATION IN PARTNERSHIP

America's early settlers made their first order of business the establishment of schools to impart piety, morality, and knowledge. Theirs was not by modern criteria a utilitarian motive. Education was designed not to assist the young to get ahead but to help them keep up with their well-schooled, pious parents. Even before the Virginia Company's settlement at Jamestown proved permanent, a large sum of money was collected for schools; ten thousand acres of land were dedicated for a university and another thousand for an Indian college. The dreadful Henrico Massacre of 1622 shelved the plans for college and university until near the end of the century, but schools flourished. A well-known statement tells of the explicitly religious motivation for founding Harvard College in 1636: "After God had carried us safe to *New-England*, and wee had builded our houses, provided necessaries for our liveli-hood, rear'd convenient places for Gods worship, and setled the Civill Government: One of the next things we longed for, and looked after was to advance *Learning* and perpetuate it to Posterity; dreading to leave an illiterate Ministery to the Churches, when our present Ministers shall lie in the Dust." Historian Louis B. Wright thought "the Puritans' most important and most enduring contribution to American society has been a persistent zeal for learning and their equation of religion with education."[1] "Equation" might more accurately read "intimate relation," but otherwise the point applies to the entire Puritan influence on America.

No less notable guardians of the Puritan tradition than Increase Mather (1639–1723), his son, Cotton, and Benjamin Colman in 1718 exhorted their fellow Bostonians to "the honourable support of Learning among us, to which is owing that Reputation which we have among the Provinces, & whereon ye Religion & vertue of this People doy [for 'do'] under God so manifestly depend." To that end these worthies proposed increasing salaries of teachers so that "they can be able to subsist comfortably," and they recommended that the Reverend Mr. Williams receive not only additional money but "some additional Conveniences to his House; without which he neither thinks he has room eno' for his Family, nor that his Servants can be safe in case of sickness."[2] These august gentlemen encouraged higher pay and also spoke the conviction of American Christians of every sort for a century and a half to come, that the basic ground of religion and virtue, after God, was education. Religious men and institutions should support education because education naturally produced religious men and institutions. As long as religion and morality remained the substance of teachers' teachings, the formula worked. But education would become utilitarian and profane when geared to trade, profession, or getting ahead. Religion's inspiration of education warranted no permanent alliance between the two, although inherent enmities lay dormant until universal, free, public education became a main feature of the American dream.

Formal education in America aimed first to transmit information and to inculcate attitudes that society sanctioned. In the colonial period even the better colleges in their hey-days hewed the line of imparting approved, classical lore by rote recitation. Instances of probing unexplored areas of thought or of suggesting new types of action were rare and alarming. "Liberal" pedagogues like John Witherspoon of Princeton and William Smith of the College of Philadelphia were exceptions; the heavy-handed conformist, President Thomas Clap of Yale, represents the rule. The middle colonies developed a society less sure of its traditions, religious or otherwise, than did New England and the south, and proportionately they tolerated inquiry and experimentation. In the national period our colleges—and more lately our universities—multiplied at first under denominational, then public and private, auspices. Before the Civil War institutions which bore the name of college or academy or seminary served primarily as traditioning instruments and therefore commanded common admiration except among studiedly anti-intellectual preachers like Peter Cartwright. Only after the war did universities and some private preparatory schools begin to lead their students forth into untried modes of living and uncharted realms of thought, and only when the corps of teachers had drunk the wine of liberal inquiry did intellectual freedom begin to filter into elementary and intermediate schools.

If the distinction between higher and lower education is taken as broadly reflecting the difference between inquiry and indoctrination, then the lion's share of America's pedagogic energies, even in colleges and universities, has gone into lower education. There is cogency in the stern critique of Morris R. Cohen that even our allegiance to free inquiry of the mind "is in practice a freedom to find new justifications for the accepted and orthodox." In his dictum, "First principles are to be acquired by authority or habit, never by the outcome of critical intelligence," the phrase "never" might well yield to "more often than." Yet it is hard to challenge his conviction that "students must be dosed and instructed, rather than puzzled by logical doubts; they must be 'sold' ideas, rather than probed as to the basis of the ones they have."[3]

American Christianity befriended the main endeavor of education while dosing and instructing prevailed, and with only occasional exceptions it lamented and fought the puzzling of students and the probing of their ideas. Religion promoted education as long as education respected religion. A nameless Virginia Presbyterian about 1800 held in obvious derision the attitude of Sir William Berkeley, governor of Virginia colony from 1642 to 1676, who was represented as having reported to the English commissioners of foreign plantations in these words: "I thank God there are no *free schools*, nor *printing*, & I hope we shall not have [them] these hundred years; for *learning* has brought disobedience & heresy & sects into the world & printing has divulged them & libels against the best governments. God keep us from both!"[4] Yet, as time would tell, Berkeley's words prophetically summarize the inherent enmity between religion and the universal, free, public education that would develop in the United States.

The societies of the colonial and early national periods designed formal instruction to replicate the older generations' learning and manners in the younger, just as Christian catechesis was designed to transmit the faith and morals once delivered to the saints and never to be altered by the pious. In New England and the southern colonies, ecclesiastical and magisterial interests nearly coincided, and religion preserved its traditional influence on learning. In the middle colonies Americans first experienced heterogeneity of class, language, ethnicity, and denomination. While scarcely less devout than their neighbors to north and south, the settlers of New York, New Jersey, and Pennsylvania kept religion distinct from politics and pioneered education under public and secular agencies. They were setting the pattern of things to come. Come they did in the Northwest Ordinance, in local school districts operating under state standards, and eventually in land grant universities which, by purging themselves of denominational rivalries and controls, offered advanced studies that were fully secular. These last were, as the University of Virginia had long been, damned by the denominations, but the burgeoning nation approved their being drawn into the new endeavor of free inquiry.

If it is exaggeration to say that the churches *controlled* old colonial colleges, it is also understatement to say that these institutions made religion the *raison d'être* of learning. Because the roots of education fed in the soil of religion, education served the well-being of man and society. Early in the federal period arose the prophet of a new theory of education, grounded in the pursuit of happiness. That prophet was, of course, Thomas Jefferson. The pursuit of happiness meant that learning and teaching were self-evident values, values that were demeaned and checked, not elevated and revealed, by appeal to religion. Jefferson identified the persistent enemies of his planned University of Virginia as "the priests of the different religious sects, to whose spells on the human mind its improvement is ominous"; the most clamorous of these were the Presbyterians who "pant to re-establish, *by law*, that holy inquisition, which they can now only infuse into *public opinion*."[5] The outburst of 1820 merely specified what Jefferson had long contended.

Jefferson suffered the prophet's dishonor in his own country until, in old age, he built at Charlottesville the prototype of the American university. Only three years after the Declaration of Independence he had advanced a plan, far ahead of its time, to reform William and Mary College, of which he was already the most distinguished alumnus. He projected a general reform of Virginia education by providing "Elementary schools, for all children generally, rich and poor," then "Colleges . . . for all who were in easy circumstances," and a university "for teaching the sciences generally, and in their highest degree."[6] The plan failed in the Old Dominion but began to bear fruit across the mountains with the Northwest Ordinance (1787). The core of Jefferson's revision of Virginia law passed in 1785 and established religious freedom in a manner that set religion's permeation of education on the road to extinction. Although specifically realized only at the University of Virginia in the 1820's, Jefferson's vision, often politically compromised but never personally forfeited, was "that a free society flourished with the freely flowing intelligence of its citzens,"[7] and he knew earlier than most that religion impeded the free flow of intelligence. Education, to be sure, needed a guardian of its freedom; Jefferson tried to mature the child by removing it from its religious parent and by placing it under public protection.

The prophet perhaps faltered when he came, late in life, to organize the very reform he had long preached. But his principle carried the day. After his time, broadly speaking, schools and colleges, whether religiously, publicly, or privately sponsored, took upon themselves the burden of proof that their maintenance was worthwhile in view of the general good. In the cultivation of the American west, whose boundary President Jefferson pushed from the Mississippi River to the Rocky Mountains, the denominations founded and managed a multitude of schools and colleges—far more, in fact, than the general welfare called for, and a majority died after brief, fitful careers. They died not from lack of denominational interest nor from halfheartedness on the part of the representatives of religion. They died because they failed—as the survivors lived because they succeeded —to serve the general welfare. Before 1900 American education was justifying itself according to Jefferson's principle—by the pursuit of happiness under public protection rather than by the inculcation of godliness under sectarian influence. Nor has the renaissance of parochial schools and denominational colleges in the twentieth century fundamentally changed the pattern.

Not that Jefferson was antireligious. He often sounded anti-clerical, as for example in retaliating to the clergy who heaped calumny on him during the presidential campaign of 1800, or when the Presbyterians claimed parts of his university. In the university he actually made room for religion—insofar as it served the general welfare—by allowing that each denomination might establish nearby its school for training ministers. The theologues, he thought, could benefit from university courses of instruction. The denominations saw no such benefits. Virginia Episcopalians were typical; they busied themselves first with an ill-fated theological professorship at William and Mary in 1821 and then in 1823 with founding a seminary which moved to a wilderness campus near Alexandria in 1827.[8] Even in the 1800 campaign Jefferson noted and valued a profound alliance between true Christianity as he understood it and the cultivation of knowledge under the principle of the freedom of the mind. His famous personal oath of "eternal hostility against every form of tyranny over the mind of man" was profoundly religious in its intensity and was "sworn upon the altar of God." Jefferson earnestly believed "that the Christian religion, when divested of the rags" thrown around it by "the clergy, who had got a smell of union between Church and State," and when "brought to the original purity and simplicity of its benevolent institutor, is a religion of all others most friendly to liberty, science, and the freest expansion of the human mind."[9] Just so: perverted Christianity tended to mold the mind; Jefferson measured Christianity's truth and worth by the rod of intellectual freedom.

His plan for Virginia education gave character to educational systems in the old west. "Liberal Kentucky," as Niels H. Sonne's book aptly called it, protested sectarian influences in education, thereby as early as 1787 setting a course that increasingly delivered elementary and intermediate schools from regnant denominational influence. That left advanced training to the churches, and Presbyterians led the way in Kentucky higher education with Transylvania University and later Centre College. Other denominations established rival collegiate institutions in Kentucky during the first third of the nineteenth century. Not every state was as protective of elementary education as early Kentucky, but generally speaking the Protestant churches had made their best contributions to primary and secondary schooling long before the Civil War, and from 1820 to 1860 conceded public control over these areas while clinging to the ideal of denominational or other private sponsorship of higher education.[10]

The great symbols of public claim over education are the Northwest Ordinance and the "Morrill" or Land-Grant Act of 1862 (augmented 1890 and amended 1907). The former set out the bold proviso that "religion, morality, and knowledge being necessary to good government and the happiness of mankind,

schools and the means of education shall forever be encouraged."
The great territory west of Pennsylvania, north of the Ohio
River, and east of the Mississippi was carved into neat blocks
each of which reserved land for schools. The encouragement
of morality came through systems of courts binding the territory
to United States law. Religion, here as in the popular imagination linked to morality and education, was left to voluntary
endeavors, for the federal guarantees separating church and
state and protecting religious liberty applied strictly to the territories. Not only the great northern heartland followed the Ordinance, for its provisions were models of territorial administration
and standards of admission to statehood. Although it associated
religion with education in its preamble, the Ordinance had the
effect of placing lower education firmly in the public sector
under regulation by local districts and later by state agencies.
Henceforth, in effect, religion was instrumental to knowledge,
and denominational schools were expected to meet the criteria
which upgraded public schools.

Not every territory or state developed an identical program
of universal public instruction, and in many localities the denominations were left to impart the A B C's and the three R's as best
they could. Sabbath Schools often did the job. As late as 1858
Horace Muzzy in San Francisco regularly recruited children from
the streets to the church on Sunday afternoons to improve
their religion, morality, and knowledge. He was discouraged
when his efforts produced only two children one vernal Sabbath,
whereas a week earlier he had collared seven.[11] "There were
no free schools in Utah" in 1873, wrote a judge, "& the skeleton
of a school system found on the statute books, made no provision for free schools—all were under the control of the Mormons
& had Mormon teachers & so the Methodists had to establish
a school of their own [in Beaver]. It became a success."[12] But
that was after the Methodists came to regard education as a
good thing. Before 1840 the denomination's leadership prided
itself on religion of the heart that bypassed the head. Then
both Methodist and Baptist anti-intellectualism rapidly waned

and Methodist leaders began to judge education not as to merit but as to sponsorship. In 1844 the Reverend George S. Phillips of northern Ohio thought the minister "that instructs the people should not be an ignoramus. No. He should be . . . [a man] of much learning and deep piety[.] A man of much deep thought and much patience[.]"[13]

As the far west lured pioneers from the east, little anti-intellectualism remained in American religion, even among Methodists. When Seattle was a village of thirty houses, only four of them as much as a year old, the Reverend David E. Blaine (1824–1900) and his wife Catherine arrived from New York as Methodist missionaries. Eternal salvation was the first concern and sound learning a close second. On the Sunday after their arrival late in 1853 Blaine organized a church of four members, counting Catherine whom he hired out as a school teacher at sixty-five dollars a month; classes would begin with the new year. He optioned a lot on which to build a parsonage, and received from one David S. Maynard "for a seminary just outside the village survey" a donation of thirty acres on which to erect the settlement's first literary institution. Not all Blaine's plans matured on schedule. Competing landowners squabbled about the location of the church house, and he never got clear title to the seminary land. But the school began and the congregation prospered, both serving people without regard to denomination. A church and a school—by the middle of the nineteenth century, these were twin hopes of every missionary and twin accomplishments of most new settlements.[14]

II. SOCIAL UTILITY

The great changes in the sponsorship of American higher education have paralleled major shifts in the society's needs. Colonial settlements needed to extend culture and to raise learned leaders. Frontier societies needed stabilizing. Settled communities behind the frontier needed means of replicating themselves down the generations. Growing towns needed a broader base of consensus to absorb new and welcome elements. Urban centers needed mechanisms to break old ways and to accommodate diverse novelties. It is barely too pat to say that these five phases of American social experience have been matched successively by the old school or college, the sectarian institute, the denominational college, the "religiously oriented" or "denominationally affiliated" college, and the secular university. The progression persistently broke close religious control over education. Thus the apparent paradox, that the selfsame Christian churches which founded and fostered higher education in colonial and early national America became jealous foes of the eventually dominant university. Broadly speaking, religious groups nurtured and managed our academies and colleges down to the Civil War; afterward, they restrained and often opposed the development of our leading universities.

Education in the major Anglo-American colonies met specific social needs, as has been noted. Frontier communities frequently rallied behind almost any sectarian effort to provide, beyond the rudiments, such education as would establish a common set of values around which stable community life could be built. There it mattered less *what* the institution taught than *that* the institution taught. Quick to seize any opportunity for service to the society and even quicker when that service allowed for sectarian recruiting, the American denominations hardly without exception set up advanced schools wherever their missionaries met the early settlers. Religious indoctrination became at worst the price and at best the bonus of improved education. Most circuit riders or missionaries brought with them the modicum of culture that most settlers liked; they were at least literate with few exceptions. Perhaps more important, preachers knew persons in older communities who generously would help pay for schools' construction and instruction. As long as sectarianism did not offend the populace, its tendency to restrict inquiry mattered little because education meant inculcation rather than investigation. Under these circumstances, sectarian sponsorship of advanced schools seemed wholly appropriate.

In 1844 Professor Truman Marcellus Post (1810–1886), a Congregationalist minister teaching ancient history at Illinois College in Jacksonville, argued that collegiate education alone could unify the terrifying diversity of the society which was then arising in the west. In urging eastern benevolence for western education, he argued that "only by a system of permanent and efficient Protestant colleges" might Catholic efforts to gain the field be foiled. But Post's profoundest concern was the chaos threatened by a burgeoning population "representative of almost every clime, opinion, sect, language, and social institute" of Europe as well as of America. "Never," he wrote, "was a more intense power of intellectual and moral fusion requisite to prevent the utter disorganization of society." Not religion but education, in Post's judgment, would provide those "principles of stability," those "deep, strong and constant influences, that shall take from the changefulness and excitability of the western mind, by giving it the tranquillity of depth, and shall protect it from delusive and fitful impulses, by enduing it with a calm, profound and pure reason."[15]

Although the vast majority of institutes and seminaries founded on that basis faltered after a short time, mainly because they were carelessly financed, many of them became denominational colleges nurtured by civic pride in communities where the denomination was strong. Nobody surpassed the Presbyterians in founding colleges in the great west, but all American denominations entered the educational race as frontier settlements became stable communities. Where the social need for unity, stability, and self-replication arose, the denominational college became a valued and effective community agency. From colonial Connecticut to contemporary Utah higher education conserved religious consensus and raised sons in the beliefs and manners of fathers. Indoctrination in Christian belief and in denominational idiosyncracies remained compatible with instruction in arts and crafts as long as the arts were traditional and the crafts useful. The denominational colleges which flourished were usually the ones which learned to merge strictly sectarian

tenets into the broadly Protestant consensus that arose in communities sponsoring some religious heterogeneity.

Only when the American communities became complexes of
diverse populations, religions, and ways of living did the denominational colleges thwart an education that now was asked not
to duplicate a settled society but to help create social novelty.
The denominations succeeded in making higher education secure
precisely when higher education was being asked to challenge
accepted patterns of life in America. Religious sponsorship of
higher education reluctantly receded with the rise of scientific
investigations and attitudes which protested dogmatic restraints
on free inquiry. Thus the very religious permeation that made
education thrive also delayed the development of colleges into
universities. For both in its sectarian and in its more broadly
consensual versions, education under religious sponsorship fundamentally extended old values and systems to new generations
by surrounding the accepted with the aura of the sacred. Religion
by its very nature sought to familiarize and domesticate, even
when society demanded broadening the mind beyond the scope
of received knowledge and values. Christianity in America inherited a long experience in teaching, but that teaching was
catechetical.

Catechesis as a style of teaching opposes critical inquiry as the
premise of education, for education under Christian auspices
sought positively to keep the echo of tradition resounding again
and again, and negatively to quiet any new note that might
blur or mingle with the echo or set up independent overtones.
When American life during colonial and early national epochs
prized echoes more than choices, church colleges and sectarian
institutes served the American dream. The late Professor Harbison of Princeton has characterized this kind of instruction as
"inevitably dogmatic, domineering, and divisive. . . . It pounds
in, it does not draw out; it demands conformity, not free response;
it is instruction, but not education."[16]

Opposition between American religion and education arose
because, in the apt phrase of Walter P. Metzger, religion "drew

the doubtful conclusion that age best imparts its wisdom when youth surrenders its style."[17] When that opposition showed itself, two things happened. Many denominational interests turned away from academies and colleges to the simpler tasks of imbuing primary schooling with piety and morality. Simultaneously, denominations invested major efforts in colleges which were at once covertly sectarian and opposed to the free inquiry which inspired universities. Each thrust deserves comment.

Piety and morality were made to permeate American education during the nineteenth century by preachers, parents, and teachers counted in the hundreds of thousands. But the minister who solemnized the marriage of practical religion with elementary education was William Holmes McGuffey (1800–1873). Born in Washington County, Pennsylvania, McGuffey became a Presbyterian preacher, and successively professor at Miami University in Oxford, Ohio (1826), then president of Cincinnati College (1835) and of Ohio University at Athens (1839), then professor of moral philosophy at the University of Virginia (1845). He assuaged westerners' dissastisfaction with the grim doctrine purveyed by New England textbooks when, while still at Miami University, he began preparing what became the famous *Eclectic Readers*—a series which sold 122,000,000 copies in original and revised editions and patterned the *Eclectic Spelling Books* which his brother, Alexander, prepared. From the 1830's until the early 1900's these books were the bread and butter of American primary education. They were masterpieces of religious, moral, patriotic, and literary eclecticism. Perhaps as much as revivalism and the swelling rosters of church membership, they blended a humane and somewhat vague Protestantism with the aspirations of the average American into an archetypal national piety and ethos. To the virtues of kindness, frugality, and sobriety McGuffey brought the sanctions not only of the Bible but also of Shakespeare and Scott, George Washington and Patrick Henry, the founding fathers and the faithful frontiersmen.[18]

The suffusing of primary education with Protestant piety explicitly employed what the McGuffeys' books clearly implied.

Daily readings from the King James Version of the Bible and devotional recitation of the Lord's Prayer (Protestant version) expressed a religious consensus in public schools that distressed sensitive Roman Catholics.

In the 1840's Bishop John J. Hughes (1797–1864) protested the Protestant monopoly on public educational funds, demanding that proportionate amounts be designated for Catholic parochial schools. Higher education was still an open field for each denomination, but quite generally elementary schools received tax money. The Protestant captivity of these schools offended Catholic consciences both by excluding the latter from an assumed American consensus and by doubly taxing Catholic parents who bore the additional cost of parochial-school training for their children. Provincial councils of Catholic bishops in 1829 and 1833 urged parochial schooling for all Catholic children, and the First Plenary Council of Baltimore in 1852 enjoined Catholics to sacrificial efforts for the enterprise. The burden was heavy, and through the rest of the century officials repeated the injunction frequently. Only in the mid-twentieth century did Catholics and other dissenters from the then eroded Protestant consensus find relief in court orders proscribing devotional exercises in public schools and in the provision of public funds benefiting students of parochial schools without endowing sectarian teaching. The point here is not to trace the history of Catholic education in America but to illustrate Protestantism's hold over elementary schools.

Even while stamping their piety on public instruction at the primary level, many denominations defended and expanded their collegiate activities. From about 1850 onward denominational colleges softened overt sectarianism, clung to the older catechetical method, and for the most part viewed the rising university movement with alarm. As a young Methodist preacher in Newberry, Pennsylvania, Charles Maclay (1822–1890) raised money to build dormitories at Dickinson Seminary. In several appeals issued during spring 1849 Maclay pleaded for support on grounds that shifted from enthusiasm for incipient industrialism to the virtues of an educated populace and to Methodist pride in finishing what they undertook. In the style of the day he sang the glories of steam and of the telegraph and made Americans examples to the eyes of the world. The signs of the times indicated to him that "every district [of the denomination must have] its own school . . . to support and we can not expect much foreign aid." Turning to local pride, "Nothing speaks better for a town than an institution of learning flourishing in its midst." And playing on denominational loyalty, "failure" is a word "not found in our vocabulary."[19]

The Methodists had overcome the anti-intellectualism symbolized by Peter Cartwright, who had no use for preachers with book learning yet thought every Methodist minister was entitled to the honorific "Doctor." It came to be that, as Louis Wright wrote, "The circuit rider as book agent, as a carrier of letters and learning, even on the modest level that his own background and the capacity of his saddlebags could provide, is a theme worthy of our respect—and our study." Wright is correct that "a faith in popular education" during the nineteenth century was becoming a substitute in the minds of many "for their former preoccupation with revealed religion. Public education, indeed, became a religion, and Americans looked to it as the way to social salvation. The most intense periods of westward expansion coincided with the growth of faith in education, a fact which helps to explain the multiplication of schools and colleges in the West."[20] The substitution had not quite taken place for Catherine P. Blaine (1829–1908), schoolmarm wife of a Methodist missionary in early Seattle. She wrote her parents in 1854, "Next to religion there is nothing so desirable as a good education. With both of these one can scarcely be placed in circumstances where they will not be happy, and they almost invariably secure their possessor confidence, esteem and honor."[21]

Growing preoccupation with education was an unintended work of the denominations, even of the popular Methodists and Baptists who had earlier cherished in their leadership inspiration certified by ignorance. As they established schools and then colleges to gain and to upgrade members, ministers put themselves in need of sufficient education to hold the respect of members climbing the social ladder of "confidence, esteem and honor." What the Methodists and Baptists experienced in this regard in the 1830's and 1840's is what the new light Presbyterian had learned a century earlier and what the Church of the Nazarene would discover a century later. Education for lay members seemed to produce piety and nourish true religion. In fact it transferred faith from revelation to education and forced learning on preachers who would protect the claims of revelation.

The Reverend George Henry Atkinson, who labored in Oregon most of the latter half of the nineteenth century as a Congregational minister under the American Home Missions Society, recorded in extant letters a lifetime effort to reconcile education and religion. After studying at Dartmouth College and Andover Seminary, Atkinson received his "call" to missionary work in 1846. Early next year he took his Nancy to wife and shifted the object of his evangelistic attention from Africa to Oregon. Sailing around the Horn to Honolulu and thence to the Columbia River, Atkinson was undetained by the Whitman massacre when he began work in Oregon City on July 1, 1848. Immediately he founded a congregation of Presbyterians and Congregationalists and chose trustees for an academy.

Religion was his work; it justified itself by retarding gambling and drunkenness and by inculcating respectable morals and manners. But his ruling passion was always education. He founded the Female Seminary in Oregon City and Tualatin Academy and Pacific University in Washington County. Twice he returned east to raise money for educational projects. The seminary competed with a Roman Catholic school for girls and was sold to the Methodists by 1858.

In Atkinson's view the church provided religious solace, mostly in the face of death, to adults, but its primary duty to the future was educating the young and thus molding a good and moral society while incidentally extending its own influence. After his first trip back to Newbury, Vermont, and environs to raise money and recruit teachers for his schools, he returned to Oregon on February 16, 1853; in early summer he made this poignant report, each sentence of which was its own paragraph: "I have resumed my usual duties here. Our town is increasing slowly though we think surely. Religion makes no apparent progress, except it be in separating its true friends from opposers. Temperance lags, yet has friends. Education prospers, as much as we could expect in a heterogeneous population."[22]

But by 1855 sectarian stifling of liberal education plagued Atkinson, Tualatin Academy, and Pacific University. "Your suggestions, uncle," he replied, "with regard to an unsectarian spirit, and a liberal & ennobling character in our Institutions, accord entirely with a growing conviction in my own mind." He deplored the desire of some constituents to have teachers and trustees subscribe to the Westminster Catechism. Instead, "Our whole spirit now is free thought; free inquiry, in all directions; the discovery and development of all possible knowledge, under the guardian of faith in the Bible, as God's changeless Word, & under the influence of prayer, the Sabbath, & the preaching of the gospel."[23]

Free thought guarded by Bible, prayer, sabbatarianism, and gospel preaching—the plan's sincerity is unassailable, its operability, dubious. The date of the resolution is significant, for down to the Civil War, nine of every ten American college and university presidents were theologians, and the proportion had held steady. By 1940 "no clergyman adorned the presidential chair of any of the leading institutions of learning."[24]

As the modern university movement, harking back to Jefferson, turned sharply away from Bible, prayer, and gospel, and enlarged the conviction that free inquiry needed lay, nonreligious protection, a few churchmen sincerely promoted freedom of thought. Most prominent among these rare birds was the noted theologian, Horace Bushnell. Failing in health and contemplating retirement from his long pastorate in Hartford, Connecticut, Bushnell spent nearly a year (1856–1857) in California to recuperate. He met thoughtful men striving to found an institution of higher learning as cornerstone of a good society. Bushnell acted as president of the institution, without salary, and spent most of his visit appealing for its support, situating the school, and charting its policy as a real university.

In 1853 Presbyterians and Congregationalists had united in founding Contra Costa Academy in Oakland under the Reverend Henry Durant's headship; in 1855 the enterprise was chartered as a university, the College of California. Trustees representing the major Protestant denominations asked Bushnell's help in conceiving and bringing to birth a university worth the name. He envisioned a school of Catholic interest, unstintingly dedicated to the improvement of society, and free from any sectarian control or identity. The great idea took eloquent form in a *Statement* drafted by Bushnell in the Trustees' name and an *Appeal* in his own, which were published together in 1857 as a twenty-three-page pamphlet.

The document is a model of perception as to the role of a university in American society and as to the relation of religion to university education: "The university is the womb in which society is shaped," wrote Bushnell, "and all the determining causes of its operative and observable life are prepared by the silent nurture and secretion of the matrix whence it came. Here is the contact of universalities, whether in matter or mind. Here principles are intellectualized, and thought embraces law. . . . And there is no one interest of society, religion, medicine, law, agriculture, mining and metallurgy, mechanical art and invention, that is not most interiorly related to the university life." Bushnell wanted a university which, "United on the Catholic basis," would "not fulfil its idea till it becomes, on the western shore, what Harvard and Yale are on the other, and finally a complete organization of learning, such as even they are not, except in a rudimental and initial way."[25] Strong words indeed for a dutiful son of Eli!

It is well known that at the opening of The Johns Hopkins University in 1876 Daniel C. Gilman contended that neither state nor church was the appropriate sponsor of genuinely free higher learning. It is not so well known that similar convictions had been voiced in 1860 by Julian Sturtevant of Illinois College, long and then still a bastion of Presbyterian collegiate education. Between Sturtevant's and Gilman's declarations there intervened the Civil War and Reconstruction. The national government became a powerful central impetus in American life, and through the Morrill Act this force was felt on state colleges and universities receiving land grants from Washington. For the most part these land grant colleges declared strict religious neutrality in their charters, and thus tended to follow the lead of private universities such as The Johns Hopkins rather than that of denominational colleges.[26]

But during the war something also happened to drive the denominations toward more single-minded concentration on religion. Their social reform schemes, most notably abolition, had split them more permanently than the nation was rent. The war, like most crises in public life, minified denominational differences and increased the sense of a common American religion, even easing Protestant fears of Catholicism. With resources drained, institutions in disrepair, and interdenominational rivalry abated, fervor for church management of higher education dropped sharply just as the rapidly industrialized society was needing the kind of higher education which could hardly flourish under guardianship of Bible, prayer, and gospel.

Religion had given to all formal education in America initial and enduring impetus. After the Civil War the religious influence on elementary education remained strong but not unchallenged as to the prerogatives of Protestants. Higher education presented a very different picture, for while denominational colleges continued their work the university movement captured leadership and modeled the future. The reasons for this difference are complex, but they hinge on changes in denominational hopes and efforts. That Bushnell and Sturtevant, among some other religionists, saw the wave of the future and promoted free inquiry as the university's goal is plainly attributable to their having sensed the need of American society to explore and to diversify.

They understood that education must serve the society, and that the denominations were ill equipped to foster learning appropriate to the new social needs.

III. RELIGIOUS EDUCATION AS SUCH

By the end of the Civil War religious influence on elementary schools via the Protestant consensus came under direct attack from Roman Catholics just as growing governmental regulation prompted many Protestants to wonder how well and how long they could rejoice univocally in the accomplishments of public education. At the same time, the university idea checked denominational dominance of advanced schooling. The training of ministers was already relegated to divinity schools or theological seminaries. Yet the tortured logic persisted that to make men literate would lead them to learn the Bible whose precepts would guide morals and quicken piety. With the aspiration for formal educational systems well on the way to profane fulfillment, church leaders and devout followers turned attention to three informal means of evincing religious commitment in a populace brought hard against reality by the war, swelled by immigration, and strained by new freedmen.

Each of these informal means was already a well-organized movement of reform and amelioration before being employed to spread piety. Sunday Schools abounded as the result of work by the American Sunday School Union, founded in 1824, but after 1865 they were put to new evangelistic uses because they ran no danger of falling into worldly hands. Bible and religious tract campaigns had spread the religious message, especially in the great valley, through the American Bible Society (1816), the American Tract Society (1825), and denominational publishing enterprises too numerous to catalogue. Colporteurs who canvassed Union or Confederate troops found a new application for the old device, and after the war immigrants and freedmen presented a vast market for Bibles and tracts as well as likely candidates for lessons in literacy. For more sophisticated folk, itinerant lecturers adapted the means of the Lyceum, founded locally in 1826 by Josiah Holbrook, to religious purposes, following Theodore Parker's dictum: "The business of lecturing is an original American contrivance . . . . The world has nothing like it. In it are combined the best things of the Church, and of the College, with some of the fun of the theatre."[27]

The Sunday School movement was spurred by a new theoretical framework emphasizing gradual formation of Christian spirituality, a theory first propounded in Bushnell's *Chritian Nurture* (1847). Dwight Lyman Moody added his inimitable impetus after the war, and in the 1870's John H. Vincent developed his Uniform Lesson Plan and teacher training institutes. Frankly evangelistic, the Sunday Schools were free to enlist, exhort, and catechize in the name of education and without fear of impertinent investigation.[28] Adults were appealed to as (and like) children in an enterprise that was at once intellectually unassailable because of denominational or interdenominational control and also intellectually indefensible because of simplistic adherence to Biblical texts which were being challenged by literary and historical criticism.

To the Sunday Schools may be reckoned much of the educational infantilism of American Protestant churches—a charge hardly evaded by American Catholicism's simplistic inculcation of authoritative dogmas and practices through catechetical instruction in parochial schools. Both enterprises isolated denominational teachings from the mainstream of American intellectual developments.

The isolation sharpened religious attacks on "godless" education in the universities, near whose campuses the Young Men's Christian Association and soon the denominations established centers where pious students were invited for encouragement in their religious beliefs. Understandably, most American universities down to World War II distrusted religon as a dimension of human existence open to fruitful humanistic study. If the university represents the achievement of a religious aspiration for intellectual cultivation as integral to the American dream, the

modern Sunday School and its imitators represent religious disenchantment with that very achievement.

Distributions of tracts, Bibles, and religious periodicals occupied enormous efforts before the Civil War. The American Tract
Society and similar organizations wanted every family to own
a Bible and to include at least one person capable of reading it.
Near success was the effort's reward when the war's dislocations—
especially that of emancipation—loosed a disenchanted generation of whites and a floundering mass of freedmen. The successful work of colporteurs among the troops furnished the pattern
of postwar campaigns for literacy, Bible-reading, and distribution
of religious writings.

The Tract Society's appeal for money followed familiar reason-
ing: if literate, then educable; if educated, then moral; if upright,
then Christian. Reporting on several of the society's schools near
Salisbury, North Carolina, in 1867, Adam H. Erwin turned this
sophistry into rhetorical claim on purses of friends in Maine
where he had recently visited. "Their politeness, intelligence,
and hospitality," he wrote of prospective donors who befriended
him, "proclaimed aloud that God had abundantly bestowed on
them the inestimable blessing of a Christian education." Flattery
was proportionate to the pity Erwin begged for the poor wretches
who were his charges; similar education presumably would make
them polite, intelligent, and hospitable. "To those dear Christian
friends . . . I would say, that if I were able to place before their
eyes, the destitute orphans, whose fathers & mothers were slaves,
whose chains of bondage were broken before they were conscious
of their condition, but who are now conscious of their helpless
condition, their ignorance, and need of teaching in all things,
would I not move the heart of every beholder to tears[?] How
eloquent the silent pleadings to the finer feeling of all who
love dear Jesus!" A contribution to the cause "would be the
means of raising thousands from the degradation of beasts, to
become an honor to our great republic, as olive plants & polished
stones in the palace of our grand Commonwealth." As soon as
"a few primers, tracts & parts of scripture" were provided the

freedmen's schools, he promised, "There will be an unprecedented call for bibles and testaments among the colored people
who are now being taught by hundreds, and are so delighted
with the present of a bible that they cannot find words to express
their heart felt gratitude."[29]

The Reverend R. N. Shedd reported early in 1869 from
Lynchburg, Virginia, to the Richmond agent for the American
Tract Society that his mission day school enrolled "about thirty
of the destitute children of the city," and that he expected "at
least as many more. . . . We hope by bringing them under
the influence of Christian training to prepare them for usefulness
in this life & happiness in the life to come. Another item is—
we require every one who goes to our day school to attend our
Sunday School & Church."[30] Usefulness, indeed, even to the
church!

Across the country eight years later the Presbyterian Board
of Publication commissioned the Reverend William C. Mosher
(1820–1908) "to labor in the Presbyteries of Los Angeles & San
Jose . . . . My duties were to supply vacant Churches, to organize
Sabbath Schools, & put into circulation Christian literature. Also
to supply Sunday Schools with libraries and lesson helps."[31]
Mosher covered the entire southern region of the state and
coastal counties northward to San Francisco Bay.

Certainly the newly taught literates would read Bible and
tracts as long as they owned no other books. But the Negro,
along with the instructed immigrant and the relocated native,
could read inducements to riotous living as well as the Ten Commandments. The logic of Christian motives to increase literacy is
obvious, but to have expected that literacy itself would induce
Christian motives was sentimental. Christians from Virginia
to Maine to California contributed money to Tract Society
schools for freedmen and foreigners, but persons thereby led to
become Christians rarely found welcome at the doors of the
donors' churches. Literacy served better than religion in the
eventual fight for civil liberties.

The Tract Society wanted every white family to own a Bible

as much as it wanted freedmen to be able to read. From Flat Rock, North Carolina, Robert T. Jones reported in 1867 to headquarters in Richmond: "My labors for the past month has showed to me that my mountain country was more destitute then had been expected in the way of Religeous books & Bibles. The troubles of the last few years seems to have distroyed not only the books but the morals of the country." Then euphemism gave way to sentiment: "Many families gave the last Bible or religeous book to a Father or a Son or friend on leaving home for the army to guide the mind in time of trouble & temptation which now leaves many a poor widow & large family of orphant children without that Book of Book's." Jones had "visited many families & ast to sell some good book's & the answer was have you any Bibles[?] . . . the great object of their hart is to read the Bible. Could some cheap Bibles be procured for the destitute it would be the means of placing that Blessed Book in the hands of many a poor family that are scarcely able to supply themselves with food which would be read with prayerfull harts." In another month he hoped "to give some chearing accounts . . . ."[32]

Not all were taken in by the rambling reasonings and maudlin petitions of an Erwin or a Jones. Some thought that denominational or religious-society publishing glutted the market with inferior books at great cost to the churches and little benefit to the readers. In 1875 the Reverend William Ellison Boggs of Memphis, representing the consensus of his presbytery, attacked the very idea of a denominational publishing committee in a letter to William Brown of Richmond, potentate in southern Presbyterian headquarters and editor of *The Central Presbyterian*. "Let our books be able to fight their own way into the world. 'The survival of the fittest' is the only doctrine for them." Sponsored books lacked persuasiveness; "no man ought to write unless a fire burns in his bones."[33] American religion had played a major role in developing and enlarging the publication of books and pamphlets in the century of national independence. Those of Boggs's persuasion would rest on the achievement and leave that business with the people who had peculiar interest in it and special ability to prosecute it. Even the aspiration to flood America with morally uplifting literature became, in this view, a profane achievement from which organized religion should detach itself. Within a generation there arose loud cries that religious interests should sift out from the reading matter offered to Americans everything which failed to be morally uplifting.

As systems of formal education became increasingly profane, American religion resorted to modes of instruction under its own control, to religious education as such. Parochial schools, traveling lecturers, Sunday Schools, and Bible and tract campaigns were means of catechizing by the denominations for their own benefit. When features of these devices fell into the public arena and their religious usefulness became less than apparent, denominational interests either waned in relinquishment or waxed in repossession. Since the Civil War several Protestant denominations have emulated the Catholic strategy of parochial schooling, while more generally the Sunday School movement and denominational publishing activity have known flurries of revival. Increasingly religious education as such has been valued for its direct benefit to the churches, not for its contribution to the general welfare.

IV. THE PARTING OF PARTNERS

Not immediately but not very long after the Civil War came a parting of the ways between religion and formal education. There had been nothing unusual about the fact that the Reverend William C. Mosher, while serving as Presbyterian missionary at Mokelumne Hill, California, was chosen Superintendent of Common Schools for Calaveras County in autumn 1863. From his office in the county courthouse, he conducted institutes for teachers, annually visited every school in his district, and lectured to parents and teachers alike on the benefits of education.[34] Time as well as place were different when the Reverend William Henry Ruffner (1824–1908), Presbyterian minister of Lexington, Virginia, in 1869 received appointment as Superintendent of Public Instruction for the Commonwealth. In asking a friend to support his application for appointment, Ruffner ruefully noted that "Gen. Smith who thinks me well qualified says that *my being a preacher* will militate against me."[35]

Ruffner got the job. Although neither his church nor his state thought his ministerial office precluded the appointment, by 1875 Ruffner himself was regarding his vocation as that of an educator. Apparently having come to agree with General Smith, he requested demission from the ministry and restoration as a lay member of the denomination. The Lexington Presbytery granted the request, but its action elicited a proposal at the 1875 meeting of the Virginia Synod that the presbytery should be censured. The case became a *cause célèbre* of Virginia Presbyterianism. Taking a modern view of the matter, the Reverend Peter Tinsley Penick argued that if God could call blacksmiths to be ministers He could call men from the ministry to pedagogy. "Is not *everybody*," he asked rhetorically, "convinced that there is stronger evidence that God has called Ruf[f]ner to be superintendent of public schools than to be a Minister. If so, what are we contending about?"[36] They were contending precisely whether religion and education were separate enterprises within American society. Penick so readily granted the affirmative that he hardly knew there was a question. His view prevailed in the synod.

From the same Lexington Presbyterians comes a fine example of the trend of American colleges away from church management during the 1870's and afterward. The denomination's local bastion was Washington College, over which presided Episcopalian General Robert E. Lee from shortly after Appomattox until his death in 1870, and to which he bequeathed his share of the school's new name, Washington and Lee University. Originally the college was founded in 1769 under new-school Presbyterian auspices to train ministers for the Great Awakening. The southern reunion of old-school and new-school wings of the denomination continued the proud tradition of the institution but injected dispute over its ecclesiastical servitude.

Soon after Lee's death the issue of continued denominational control was joined. Benjamin Mosby Smith (1811–1893), professor in the church's seminary at Hampden Sidney, Virginia, complained bitterly that Lee's presidency had resulted "in the scheme of (so called) liberalising the College." Even worse was the pursuit of Lee's liberal plans for a small university by the General's successor. "Indeed had all the Presbyterians seen, as I did, the *true purpose* of that *precipatate* [Smith underscored the word twice] election—not three weeks after Gen[.] Lee's death —we might have postponed any election, till, by conference, we could have pitched on some proper Presbyterian minister—likely [Moses Drury] Hoge," Smith wrote. "The election of Pratt" he saw as "a *mere blind* to the evident purpose of the maneuverers to eviscerate Presbyterianism from the College, by degrees," and he accused the Trustees of wishing "*to destroy every trace of a distinctive christian influence in the College, little by little.*" Smith planned soon to ask the Trustees to reassert church control and to censure the administration for losing the denomination's confidence. As to the faculty, "Let the Faculty find, that they are likely to lose the Presbyterian patronage & they will wake from their dream of 'Liberalism.' " Smith was proud of having opposed continuing the law school which made the college into a university, for he had predicted that a professional school and university status would lead "to the charge of sectarianism." Behind all the maneuverings he saw "a deep scheme" which "must be exposed, if it blows up the U[niversity] & calls for a new organization. All this is into my hand for an advocacy of Church control."[37]

Smith was not shadow boxing. The enemy was real and powerful. The university movement was born. Universities cherished independent—to Smith, liberal—pursuit of truth that trod on denominational divinity. A generation earlier, this inherent conflict between liberal science and sectarian theology had been perceived by the skeptical Dr. Rush Nutt (1781–1837), who had moved his family from the northern neck of Virginia to Longwood Plantation near Natchez, Mississippi. "The aim & chief end of an education," Nutt wrote with typical certainty, "is to cultivate the moral & intellectual powers of the mind, & as valuable citizens always have morality, & not being indebted to religion for our virtues & useful attainments, we execrate the principle which couples religion with education; & although religion is found in almost every country, we consider it a standing disgrace to all, where science is cultivated, for it is only appealed to in adversity, & never in prosperity."[38]

The open society preferred by most regions of America after the Civil War was hardly as brash as Dr. Nutt, but it effectively divided religion from higher education by placing a new burden on education, the burden of freeing the new generation from the values, systems, and even the manners of the old. Antiquarian and monumental uses of history, to employ Nietzsche's apt terms, must be exchanged in such circumstances for critical history.[39] But by its very nature, religion prefers antiquarian history and rises to its most daring use of the past when it employs history monumentally. What the open society required was the enemy of both, a critical use of history that carefully revalued all things old by the criteria of their advantage to the new. In the sectarian phases of the American experience, antiquarian history was better than good enough—it was really good. When regions supported a broad Christian consensus but deplored the sectarian spirit as bigotry, religious men still supervised education; monumental uses of history sufficed to spread and perpetuate this consensus. But when society needed primarily a critical use of history to alienate young minds from old confinements, religious sponsorship of education became passé.

The general career of American society through sectarian, consensual, and pluralistic phases has been recapitulated by specific ethnic and religious groups in every region of the country. Therefore the parochial school and the sectarian college—the "sectarian" university is a contradiction in terms, despite familiar appellations to the contrary—continued to catechize certain segments of the population even as they were infiltrated by university-trained teachers who would not catechize if they could. And long after the "secular" university—quotation marks may suggest that the adjective is redundant—dominated American higher education, still religiously oriented and even denominationally affiliated colleges continued to serve a plural society effectively. But since the Civil War the dilemma has posed itself so repeatedly as to seem unavoidable: as educational quality rises in accordance with current criteria, the direct implications of religious sponsorship wane. "Lost to the church" as the lament of the denominations seems often to translate as "won to pluralistic, free, liberal, excellent education."

The trouble that arose for religious sponsorship of education was not that education could brook no religion but that religion preferred induction to education. Denominational management of sectarian colleges, not always visible but increasingly vitiating between 1800 and 1860, used presidential and faculty chairs more than explicit policies to advance the faith and to exclude faithless inquiry. The first great educational explosion had occurred between the American Revolution and the Civil War. Nine permanent colleges and universities existed before 1780; by 1861 more than 180 endured, while three perished for every one that lasted. The colonial nine set the pattern of ministerial presidents and faculties, and by practice if not by policy were denominational: Harvard (1636) and Yale (1701) stood under Congregational establishment as William and Mary (1693) stood under Anglican. Princeton (1746) was revivalist Presbyterian as Brown (1764) was revivalist Baptist, Queen's (1766; later Rutgers) was revivalist Dutch Reformed, and Dartmouth (1769) was revivalist Congregationalist. King's (1754; later Columbia) had strong Anglican connections and rival Presbyterian interests; the same churches vied for influence in the college of Philadelphia (1755; later University of Pennsylvania).[40] The surviving state universities founded before the Civil War number twenty-one; during the period only Jefferson's University of Virginia achieved a consistent academic freedom from denominational incursions, claims, and influences. The vast majority of the others that were organized and chartered in the ante-bellum period bore the marks of denominational foundation and maintenance.

Even where charters and policies invited universal support and open enrollment, promises and practices squared with sectarian interests. Donors of sectarian persuasion received assurances that godlessness, infidelity, and the idolatries of other sects had no entry. Scholars who brought these enemies in their hearts through the gates as they enrolled subjected them to assault by doctrinally pure teachings of sectarian professors and by compulsory, daily religious exercises. Collegiate ethos, ethics, and education remained stanchly denominational even where the college's prospectus lauded its nonsectarian spirit.

The Protestant divisiveness that proliferated colleges and universities also exhibited the multiplicity that helped to improve them. By the time of the Civil War the field was planted full. The large proportion of casualties indicates that it was better planted than fertilized. While many narrowly sectarian institutions survived and more were yet to be founded after the war, the less strict ones became strong and the stronger ones endured. Yet they survived as denominational colleges bent on preserving an old and, by the end of the Civil War, rapidly passing society.

The new society needed universities. Charles W. Eliot accurately "proclaimed that 'a university cannot be built upon a sect' and made this the guiding principle of the post-Civil War era" in American education. In a word, "the needs of the nation started to replace the needs of the church."[41]

But the whole truth is hardly in the final phrase, for throughout the colonial and early national periods education under religious sponsorship was serving the needs of the society and nation as they then existed. Already very early in the nineteenth century the specific needs of the churches for an adequate supply of pious, learned men to serve as ministers brought into being theological seminaries separate from the colleges which had been founded, in most cases, to produce ministers and religious teachers. As early as 1784 the Dutch Reformed Church established an independent professorship to train ministers, and that action led to the founding of New Brunswick (N.J.) Theological Seminary in 1810. Old guard Congregationalists made an independent Andover Seminary in 1807 to counteract Harvard's Unitarianism, and together with Princeton Theological Seminary (1812) it dominated the field for a generation. That generation saw proliferation of seminaries which matched that of colleges after 1830, and there came to be far more seminaries than the churches could well maintain—something like twice as many in the 1870's as in the 1960's. The churches early perceived that their ministerial needs demanded schools distinct from the colleges, and in founding colleges across the land they were intending to serve the nation's needs as then existing. The nation's needs changed after the Civil War so drastically that the denominational colleges could no longer serve both the nation and remain truly loyal to the denominations. The nation called for an educational system based on free inquiry into the very assumptions of humane, sociological, and scientific knowledge for the sake of introducing open discussion and unfettered experimentation in natural and human matters. Religious sponsorship of education knew how to catechize; that worked while the nation needed catechesis. Free inquiry, discussion, and experimentation desanctify the knowledge whose very sanctity was the denominations' stock in trade.

The university that could not be built on a sect also could not but profane a nation. It built itself at Harvard, Princeton, Yale, Columbia, and by those models also at Cornell, The Johns Hopkins, Stanford, and the great state universities as well, often on foundations that had been laid by denominations. From them the universities received legacies both financial and intellectual. But to become true universities the financial legacies needed expansion and the intellectual, transformation. American higher education suckled at the breast of the religious mother who gave it birth, and under her protection grew strong. After the Civil War it became a man and put away childish things, including its mother.

V. "TO CRIPPLE OR DESTROY"

"The worst thing that can be said of the sponsors and promoters of the old [denominational] colleges," according to our best historians of academic freedom, "is not that they failed to foster sufficiently free teaching and research in their own colleges, but that when others attempted to found freer and more advanced institutions [particularly the universities] the denominational forces tried to cripple or destroy their work."[42] By the close of the nineteenth century, Catholicism had officially withdrawn from the public educational system at every level only to learn in the middle of the twentieth century that its educational ghettos were no more productive of ecclesiastical allegiance than the rough-and-tumble worldliness of public education. Perhaps the most representative and certainly the most widely distributed writing of the 1880's and 1890's proposed that the newly populated western regions provided a last chance for religiously controlled education. Josiah Strong's *Our Country* (1885) was an explicit paean of the west and an implicit jeremiad over the east. For eastern education in straying from religion pursued, in Strong's view, a wrong Americanness. He envisioned the exploding western population as the new heart through which America's lifeblood would be circulated and purified. That could happen only if Protestants built and ran western schools and colleges, avoiding the errors of eastern education. Strong voiced the common conviction of official Protestantism that education toward personal freedom and social pluralism was education away from godliness. His later books more realistically recognized urbanity and diversity as the enduring marks of a new age with which Christianity must come to terms, but the profundity of these books is in inverse proportion to their popularity.

To twentieth-century American society, profane education became the unifying force without which social cohesion and its latter-day accomplice, economic growth, are unattainable. Upon recognition of this fact, public education stood ever more firmly on the platform which its leaders called that of religious neutrality and many religionists called that of militant secularism or atheism. The revival of interest in religion among educators after World War II represented no return to religious indoctrination or enlistment but rather a desire to learn critically about religion as an aspect of cultural heritage in a society made to cohere by profane education. The partnership with religion launched education's independent career so successfully that it can afford now to subsidize investigations into the history of the outgrown partnership.

CHAPTER FIVE

"LET MEN BE GOOD"

Although religiously sponsored education aimed in large part at improving American morals and manners, educational enterprises have never fully embraced the religious interest in private and public ethics. All varieties of American religion sought to shape the personal ethics of their constituents and mounted many campaigns to conform social structures with changing conceptions of the kingdom of God on earth. Between the search for personal integrity and the pursuit of social integration, however, notable tensions have long been generated. An astute student of the American novel in the middle period noted these tensions: "A common theme of the American imagination has been the problem of reconciling individual freedom with a mode of social life to which the individual can give his allegiance without danger of impairing his moral, spiritual, or psychological integrity."[1] The religious element of this American imagination has devised many proposals for reconciling personal and social ethics, proposals ranging from the covenant theology to the social gospel. The proposals came as responses to a series of dislocations of American life ranging from that of planting the original settlements to that of the accelerating change which is made possible and inevitable by modern technology. Yet underneath the variety of religious engagements with morality and its tensions between

139

personal and social polarities there lies a fundamental unity of style, a unity which sets American religious morality off from the traditions of European Christendom.

Conventional Christian moralizing proceeded from universal principles to particular cases via fixed procedures. The American style has appealed to flexible norms for guidance in changing circumstances via prudential interests. In a sense this pragmatic, utilitarian ethic of the American religious tradition arose from Renaissance reappropriations of classical, particularly Stoic, insights into problems of good and evil, personhood and society. The Ciceronian doctrine that the good is the advantageous informed patristic theology, most notably of the Greek tradition, but it gave way to authoritarian morality as the Western churches ordered and unified the diverse European peoples from the sixth to the sixteenth centuries. When Renaissance thinkers recovered the old Roman and New Testament correlation of goodness and advantage, European church interests were too far invested in moral theologies of principle and application to share the find.

The explosive chemistry of English Puritanism on its errand to the new world opened a new era in Christian concern for discovering, in changing conditions of personal and public life, pragmatic equations of *bonum* with benefit—of God's will with man's weal. Through severe dislocations down to the end of Reconstruction, American religion invented new ways of stating the old equation and thus remained relevant to the common life. Through most of the period, religious morality in America increasingly set personal above social ethics—never, of course, entirely losing sight of the latter. Since the Civil War, American Christianity has clung to conventionalized personal manners that issued from its earlier moral inventiveness. Thus arose religious moralism with respect to individual ethics. But also since the Civil War, the same religion waged the most important campaign of its history for conforming society to an idea of the kingdom of God. When the social gospel campaign was won, the spoils of victory fell to the citizenry, not to the churches, and disappointment over that fact evoked qualified but distinct repudiation of the social gospel.

The changing moral functions of American religion fit a chronological frame marked off by the great crises of dislocation which Americans have experienced. To proceed within this frame may clarify the distinct character of America's religious morality, may note variations on the common style which new conditions elicited, may see the increasing emphasis on personal ethics and their eventual degeneration into respectable manners, and may embrace in this discussion the social gospelers' concern for religious regeneration of the society's institutions and structures.

It is convenient, however, to group some dozen dislocations of American life into broad periods. Before the Revolution several crises occurred in planting the colonies, in dealing with native generations who had no taste of Europe against which to value America, and in consolidating the seaboard colonies as distinct societies. The middle period saw dislocations affecting morality in the Revolution itself, in the occupation of the middle frontier, in the opening of the far west, and in the flood of new immigrants; the era was closed by the Civil War, the most violent upheaval in American history. Since that war American life has been urbanized, industrialized, internationalized, and technologized. Each of these crises increased the tension between personal, individual freedom and an ordered social life. Thus to state the matter is to be true to the main American experience, in which personal freedom became ever more the base upon which to work out plans of social organization.

I. PRUDENCE IN THE NEW WORLD

Each of the major centers of English colonizing activity in the seventeenth century—New England with its Puritan practicality, the south with its Anglican penchant for order, and the middle settlements with their toleration and diversity—was the scene of a particular effort to base prudential ethics on flexible norms under divine sanctions; such ethical endeavors adjusted to changing conditions while identifying the good with human advantage. Each area developed a moral mind of its own in the seventeenth century, and each handed over its unique experience to the American moral mind which emerged during the eighteenth century. Every region cast religion in the role of improving men and their societies.

Puritan theologians in New England drew heavily on the theoretical endeavors of Cambridge scholars like William Perkins, John Preston, and William Ames, who built a new type of covenant theology out of overriding concerns for human depravity, divine sovereignty, and scriptural authority. According to this conception man on his own could neither know nor do what would please God. By His own justice, the Almighty would condemn all men, but by His mercy He chose some to be His saints on earth. The nexus between these otherwise disparate themes was the Bible. What God kept to Himself (including the identity of His saints) man could never know, but the Scriptures told man all he needed to know about what God would have him do or eschew. Moreover, obedience would lead to a human welfare which in turn hinted a person's inclusion in the list of saints. In England this theological melange opened controversies about God's will for the order and organization of the church. In America the early Puritans had little reason for such disputes. As members of a colony they were like-minded, and in their rude circumstances only a congregational arrangement of the churches made sense. All this is to say that the American Puritans were practical men—practical almost to a fault, for blindness to theory is the beginning of conformity.

The federal theology was undisputed truth for early New England religion. Yet the Bible was not held to be, as it had been for most European Christians (including English Puritans), a book about religion, doctrine, church, and general principles of conduct. The Bible was consulted more as a historical almanac than as the rule book of life. It chartered every feature of human life, private and public, not as precept or code but as a rich and flexible set of normative precedents. And the early New Englanders did not doubt that Providence prospered faithful men and communities who followed these precepts. Thereby they struck an equation between the good and the advantageous.

No Christians since the Greek Fathers (best exemplified by John Chrysostom) had so thoroughly made Christ's teachings compatible with Cicero's. "And the holy Scriptures are now also soe perfect," decreed the Massachusetts Bay divines in their famous Cambridge Platform of 1648, "as they are able to make the man of God perfect & thorough-ly furnished vnto euery good work; and therefore doubtless to the well ordering of the house of God."[2] Even though this Platform on the whole defends the congregational arrangement of the churches, the passage quoted is crucial and makes its final phrase an addendum.

The ruling intention of New England's early saints was to enact the good life as God would have it lived. To that end, well-ordered churches were the means, and of it, the proof. The human community walking in the New England Way was exemplified by the congregation of saints, but it was actualized by the daily life of persons, families, towns, and colonies. That their laws were meant to cohere with old England's laws has been amply argued by Daniel Boorstin. The great innovation lies first in the validation of law by appeal to the Bible, and second in the flexibility by which Biblical precedent and British legislation were adapted to new-world circumstances. In the midst of his argument, Boorstin quoted a long passage from John Winthrop's *Journal* for November 1639, a passage most notable for the telling insistence that "such laws would be fittest for us, which should arise pro re nata upon occasions, etc."; indeed Winthrop saw the fundamental laws of England and other states as having arisen in the same way—as "customs, consuetudines."[3]

Long after pristine Puritanism had spent its energies for homogeneity, preachers all along the seaboard still interpreted calamities as signals of disobedience to the divine will. On such occasions everybody standing in the Puritan tradition expected that the men who knew Scripture best would discover what breach of precedent had stirred God's wrath and what line of action would regain divine favor.

As the dramatic record of God's revealed will, the Bible was a sufficient charter for all human activity, neither unreasonable nor un-English, not the enunciation of fixed moral principles but a collection of flexible norms to be consulted for guidance in meeting conditions "pro re nata." Precisely because manners and modes of living changed, Puritan morality was regulatory but not precisianist, authoritative and rigorous yet prudential and innovative. *The Book of General Lawes and Libertyes* (1648) of Massachusetts proclaimed that ". . . surely there is no humane law that tendeth to common good . . . but the same is mediately a law of God, and that in way of an Ordinance which all are to submit unto and that for conscience sake."[4] For Puritanism, fresh or stale, the proposition might be obverted: there is no expression of the will of God but the same tendeth to common good for saints on earth.

Prudence and flexibility are immediately apparent in the adjustment of rules for church membership by the Half-way Covenant and in the bold instrumentalism of Solomon Stoddard's ecclesiology, which were adequately discussed above. Both features stand out again in Cotton Mather's concern for doing good, a concern most eloquently stated in his *Bonifacius*. In his better-known *Magnalia Christi Americana*, Mather made examples out of saints and sinners, positively and negatively: obedience to God issued in prosperous beneficence, and disobedience in shame and malevolence. Jonathan Edwards' ethics were prudent and flexible applications of the early Puritan tradition to the settled town life of mid-eighteenth-century Massachusetts; true religion produced public harmony. His heir, Samuel Hopkins, explicated the master's thought in the *System of Doctrines* (1793) by making holiness produce "disinterested benevolence" which primarily yielded the common good.[5] Hopkins brought to full utility what American Puritan morality had been all about since Bradford's and Winthrop's time: rooted in God's will as revealed in holy

writ, benevolence both divine and human is beneficial to man
and his society.

New Englanders found in the new world a place to erect their
new Zion, their city upon a hill. If at first they hoped that
Englishmen would receive moral light from that hill, by the
Interregnum their beacon was already shining westward. By
contrast the early Virginians found in the new world less the
place for a holy experiment than the new space for extending
and improving the best old English values.

No opportunity should be passed to emphasize that the
Virginians had much in common with their nonseparatist New
England cousins. Both groups prized a reformation of the English
Church. Both suspected Stuart kings of distorting true religion.
Virginians calmly accepted the de facto congregationalism which
New Englanders strove to justify theologically. Both built communities on the foundation of religious conformity under magisterial constraint and public support. Only by leaping over most
of the seventeenth-century experience can one affirm a strong
contrast between wishing to "escape from English vices" in
the northern settlements and wishing to "fulfill English virtues"
in Virginia.[6] The differences are there in more subtle ways. In
early Virginia the ethical theory for equating God's will with
man's welfare appealed to the divine reasonableness for the
sake of public order. New Englanders looked to the Bible as
charter for holy community. Middle-colony Quakers went to their
inner light for sanctions of personal righteousness. Each group
in its own way found religious reasons to identify the good with
the advantageous.

It is a commonplace that Virginia's earliest ministers belonged
to the purifying wing of the Church of England. The religious
uniformity inaugurated by seventeenth-century planters remained
the letter of the law until revolutionary times. During the formative century legislation concerning Virginians' religion reveals
even keener interest in morality than do New England laws.
Swearing, sabbath breaking, blasphemy, irreverence, drunkenness,
adultery, and fornication were punishable by fines, beatings, and,

on third offense, death. Lay vestries supervised personal morality for the sake of peace and order, which according to Anglican tradition were religion's chief interests and products. The Anglo-American experience altered the hierarchical form of England's official church by this lay supervision of local congregations and their ministers, thereby making religion the conservator of parochial decency. Conformity was to the Book of Common Prayer rather than to the mother church's doctrine and discipline, a conformity which came to allow informal toleration of any religion that maintained peace and patrolled morality.

Without philosophical or theological effort the southern Anglicans tested varieties of Christianity by their capacity to uphold genteel manners as the basis of harmony and prosperity on remote plantations. The planter himself became a religious and moral governor over his family, tenants, indentured servants, and slaves. The church strengthened his hand by sanctioning the stratified communities in which parsons themselves were lesser gentry holding tenure at the behest of churchwardens and vestrymen who were planters. Once the spatially diffused settlements were secure and amply supplied with labor, the clergyman found himself conducting rituals of baptism, marriage, and burial in the great houses, and on Sundays preaching moralistic applications of Christian teachings to flocks gathered in homelike church buildings set in old fields no longer productive of tobacco, at the rural junctions of several plantations. The leading religious figure of colonial Virginia was the Reverend James Blair (1656–1743), who was appointed in 1689 commissary of the bishop of London to supervise the colony's clergy. The vestry system left him little better than token authority, but he paced the colony's preaching from the pulpit of Bruton Parish Church in Williamsburg. On modern ears his sermons fall like cold ashes of rationalistic moralizing, while to contemporaries they accomplished the important function of heaping religion's and God's approval onto that moderation in public and private life which was the singular benefit of mankind in an agrarian, aristocratic society.

In north and south different means yielded the same end: religion made men good by proving that good men prospered. At the end of the seventeenth century Richard Coote (1636–1701), first Earl of Bellomont and colonial governor, told New York legislators what they knew as well as their northern and southern fellow colonists:

I have observ'd great Marks of Irreligion and Immorality in this place, and I take it to proceed from a long Habit of breaking the Laws, which has introduced Liscentious and Dissolute Living: And nothing can rectifie and reform our Lives and Manners but Religion. *Religion* is of that admirable frame and temper, it inflames us with a true Devotion to our great Maker, which is our most reasonable Service. Then it fits us for all the ends of Civil Society, by uniting our Minds, Affections and Interests; it makes us good Men: And good Men will of course be good Friends, good Neighbours, good Subjects; and good Patriots, that is, Lovers of their Country, and obedient to its Laws.[7]

Nor did middle-colony Quakers, who worked out yet a third way to identify divine purposes with human prosperity, disagree with Governor Coote. If the early Massachusetts Puritans set society above persons as the bearer of goodness on earth, and if the Virginia Anglicans wanted private virtue to serve public order, both of them eventually lost the future of American morals to the early Quaker who was nettlesome precisely for his insistence upon personal integrity through obedience to the individual's inner light.

Just when the social-ethical utility of colonial religion was growing trite on the tongues of magistrates and preachers alike, the Quaker injected a rampantly individualistic ethic which, in its own way, was no less prudential. Puritan moral flexibility poured more stuff into American history than did the Quaker's ossified practices and customs, but the Quaker set the American style by insisting on the priority of persons over institutions in the pursuit of happiness.

William Penn is the great spokesman. His preface to Pennsylvania's Frame of Government (1682) laid down the principle that "governments rather depend upon men, than men upon governments." Specifically regarding morality, "Let men be good and the government cannot be bad; if it be ill, they will cure it. But, if men be bad, let the government be never so good, they will endeavor to warp and spoil it to their turn." Fourteen years later Penn formulated the same maxim theologically: ". . . a main *Fundamental* in Religion is this, *That God, through Christ, hath placed a Principle in every Man, to inform him of his Duty and to enable him to do it; and that those that Live up to this Principle, are the People of God, and those that Live in Disobedience to it, are not God's People, what ever Name they may bear, or Profession they may make of Religion.*"[8]

Penn's priority and his "Principle" were not fixities of moral theory but divinely sanctioned rules of thumb variously fitted to changing conditions. Thus they belong with the foundations of American religious morality. In fact his equation of conscientiousness and Christianity—in its time a bold reduction of religion to moral essence—found ever wider acceptance during the eighteenth century among Anglicans and Arminian Congregationalists. There is little in the writings, for example, of Samuel Johnson or Charles Chauncy that would dispute Penn's "main Fundamental," although of course they differed with him and with one another over institutional manifestations of the true people of God. Already in Penn's dictum is the typically American connection between believing and doing, between knowledge of duty and enablement to perform what one knows to be right. In Quaker parlance this connection meant that listening to the still, small voice was worthless without following its dictates.

New Englanders on both sides of the controversy between Arminian reserve and Awakening enthusiasm prized sincerity as the highest virtue, the virtue which conquered deception by thrusting conviction into action. Indeed the very success of the Puritan theology and theocracy was its tendency to profane itself into a code of citizenship. Sydney E. Ahlstrom pointed out this irreversible thrust of the covenant theology. "Puritanism," he wrote, "thus can almost be said to have offered itself as a sacrifice to responsible citizenship. It was enormously influential almost *because* it was secularized."[9] Here is the point of merger between the Puritan theme of prudential morality for a holy society and the Quaker theme of doing what the individual conscience dictated. By thinking of God as covenanting legislator, Puritans saw life in terms of law—not of cult or creed but of conduct. The saint's vocation in the world made the profane arena the proving ground of his sacred concern. Piety in action produced prosperity; there is a "steady line of progression from the Puritan doctrine of vocation to the Yankee gospel of work, and from that, in due course, to the Gilded Age's gospel of wealth." Bishop William Lawrence's reverence for the prosperity of an Andrew Carnegie sprang from distant but not remote fountains in Thomas Hooker's worship of Almighty God.[10]

The pragmatic, prudential ethic of early Anglo-Americans bridged the traditional Christian separation of God's commandments from man's accomplishments by various devices—federal theology, appeal to order, and the inner light. The variety of means is of little importance alongside the identity of ends. Before the Revolution a common Christian ethic (disregarding such peculiarities as Quaker pacifism) had become an advantageous morality for all Anglo-Americans. On the personal level and stripped of theological niceties, it found clearest and cleverest expression in Franklin's maxims. "Honesty is the best policy" is a profane rule already in danger of making advantage the test of goodness. But Franklin only counseled what Puritans had proved without displaying the apparatus of their proof. Getting ahead by being good was what God intended for His children, intended so avidly that He wrote it into the laws of nature as well as upon the hearts of men. If this personal ethic be profane, that is so only because it so vaguely recollects its origin in the temple. Transferred to the social scene, as it perhaps was most memorably by President John Witherspoon (1723–1794) of Princeton, the same prudential ethic of flexible norms would reduce the necessity of numerous legal restraints and make a better, freer society. The mentor of Madison and other founding fathers, known as the only clergyman to sign the Declaration of Independence, wrote in his "Lectures on Moral Philosophy" that religion was instrumental to public morality. "If, as we have seen above, virtue and piety are inseparably connected, then to promote true religion is the best and most effectual way of making a virtuous and regular people. Love to God, and love to man, is the substance of religion; when these prevail, civil laws will have little to do."[11]

The way by which people were taught this common colonial ethic was transcendently the sermon, in one or another form the central ritual of all colonial religion. Indeed American religion devised a homiletical genre for the purpose, the jeremiad. On July 28, 1756, the Reverend John Moncure of Stafford County, Virginia, preached "For a Fast appointed by Public Authority" on the story of Ahab and Naboth's vineyard, by way of pointing out that the colonies' troubles at the hands of Indians were righteous judgments of God against the sins of the settlers. "Are not Atheism & Profaneness, Fraud & Violence openly professed & practised? Are not Religion & its professors reviled & contemned?—Our Corruptions & Iniquities multiplied, & does not a general depravity of Manners prevail amongst us?" he asked. He reasoned that "a National Guilt necessarily requires a Nation[a]l Punishment"; whereas "Some great & notorious Sinners, may by the Permission of God be sufferd to escape Punishment in this World, because it is certain they will meet with it in Weight and Measure in the next,—but it is not so with Countries & Kingdoms;—Their Sins when grown ripe for Vengeance, if not prevented by a general Repentance, will not fail sooner or later to meet with a Punishment proportion'd to their Guilt,—as well to serve for Examples to the rest of the World, as to manifest the Power & Justice of God." The remedy was "Repentance & Reformation"; that meant for each person "to promote true Religion & Virtue,—to discountenance all Irreligion & Vice." Moncure repeated the sermon to another congregation on a public fast in September 1757, and yet again from the original pulpit on a public fast in 1758.[12] Good persons prosper. Societies avoid calamity by widespread righteousness. To do evil is to suffer—corporately here, individually here or hereafter. Such was the *quid pro quo* clarity of prudence in the religious campaign for morality in colonial America.

In the early national years before the second awakening, many minds detached prudential morality from religious sanctions. An anonymous preacher, probably from the south, proclaimed about 1795: "Universal experience justifies the Maxim . . . that Righteousness exalteth a nation & that vice is not only a reproach, but will be the ruin of any people." Such was the order of things; almost as an afterthought and certainly as an addendum, he noted, "But, my brethren that our virtue, may be uniform[,] extensive & permanent, we must call in to her aid the sanctions of religion."[13]

Making religion ancillary to the constancy of virtue is only a short stride from reducing religion to mere moral agency. When Thomas Jefferson took that step he incited preachers to denounce him as a deist at best and a French infidel at worst. Beneath this famous Protestant polemic against Jefferson's presidential candidacy ran a strong undertow of resentment against the profane success of religion's campaign for prudential morality in America. Linked with cries of mobocracy against the Democratic-Republican candidate were calumnies upon outspoken anticlericalism which in Jefferson's view struck toward restoring pure, undiluted religion—religion, that is to say, stripped of ceremony and dogma and hieratic authority, which meant religion subservient to personal and public ethics. Except when replying to calumny, Jefferson's moderation ruled his views on preachers and heightened his appreciation of the moral sublimity of which essential religion seemed the enabling agent.[14] Within a decade after Jefferson's death the new revivals reached their height. Religion in America swung away from rationality toward feeling, and a cynic like Rush Nutt, who thought himself in the Jeffersonian tradition, portrayed religion and morality as antipodal. As an eloquent testimony for morality unfettered by faith, Nutt's long paragraph merits quotation:

If then it is found that religion & morality are distinct properties or tendencies of our nature, as daily experience most evidently prove[s], & we look upon religion as a mental alienation, & morality as a power approximating towards the perfection of mental gualities; we should labor to keep them separated, knowing the danger of the one, & the value of the other. The religionist relies upon God to work a miracle in his nature & render him honest, while the moralist, relying upon the exercise of his own faculties, judges between right & wrong, & persues a course which he considers most beneficial to the best interests of mankind. The moralist should no longer be relied upon, if he becomes religious, in the common acceptation of the term, for in such case we always find him to rely more & more on God to direct his course; & ceasing to reason & rather to be hunting after some ideal operation of a supernatural nature, he becomes more selfish & conceited in his views; nay fanatical, & he is ready to shed the blood of his neighbor for a difference in feeling & sentiment. Of all the curses that ever afflicted the human family, & of all the obstacles ever thrown into the way of human improv[e]ment, & the successful cultivation of the sciences, religious insanity, & the rapacity & roguery of the priests, have been the most fatal.[15]

Nutt's point was not lost on American history, for a century later John Dewey would declare, "The opposition between religious values as I conceive them and religions is not to be bridged. Just because the release of these values is so important, their identification with the creeds and cults of religion must be dissolved."[16]

II. REVIVALIST AND PIONEER ETHICS

Although Dewey of course spoke to the modern American mind, Nutt's excoriation of religion as detrimental to morality reflected the attitude of late colonial and early national sophisticates. Religionists replied in kind by denouncing the humanistic, self-validating pursuit of happiness by young America as a dangerous flirtation with the French revolutionary spirit; the American pulpit depicted French liberty and libertinism as interchangeable. The Great Awakening is marked from the middle-period revivals by the self-consciousness of the latter's effort to stir religious excitation; on the seaboard where the revivals began, their self-consciousness arose directly out of a sense of danger that French atheism might sweep America. The eastern revivals opened with the century at Yale where President Timothy Dwight inveighed against infidelity and lax morals as causally connected, always rising to rhetorical heights over illustrations drawn from Europe, particularly France. Three published addresses by Dwight bear titles that sufficiently expose his dislike for the independent spirit of his time and his desire to rejoin morality to religion as effect to cause. He became famous for such printed addresses as *The Nature and Danger of Infidel Philosophy* (1797), *The Duty of Americans at the Present Crisis* (1798), and *A Discourse, on Some Events of the Last Century* (1801). William Meade (1789–1862), later bishop of the Episcopal Church in Virginia, studied at Princeton during the century's first decade. Meade later recalled that deism and infidelity rampaged there, destroying decency and good morals.

In one of its dimensions the protest of men like Dwight and Meade attacked the heady success of colonial religion's effort to equate the good with the advantageous. If "honesty is the best policy" without explicit reference to God's will, then the work of religion was done and "infidels" could pursue happiness by their natural lights. In another dimension the protest became a proposal that new times called for a new equation of godliness and goodness in which both entities were apparent. The great revivals, almost continuous between 1800 and 1835 and resuscitated locally down to the Civil War, repeatedly struck that new equation.

The Reverend Charles P. McIlvaine (1799–1873), chaplain at West Point and then Episcopal Bishop of Ohio, has been quoted by Perry Miller as designating in 1832 the overriding objective of a revival to be *"the quickening of the people of God to a spirit and walk becoming the gospel."*[17] Their general success is indicated by Louis B. Wright's remark that "the revivalists who swarmed into the backcountry put an end to complacence about iniquity."[18] In the second decade of the century eastern church groups poured money and men into spreading religion over the middle frontier. Their appeal and their campaign focused on turning iniquity into uprightness for the sake of human improvement. In summer 1812 Schermerhorn and Mills began touring "the west"; for a year they did stopgap evangelistic work and surveyed missionary needs and opportunities. Their report described "the state of churches, religion, and morals" on a wide frontier: transmontane Pennsylvania, "New Virginia" (west of the Blue Ridge), Ohio, Kentucky, Tennessee, the Territories of Mississippi, Indiana, Illinois, and Missouri, and the State of Louisiana. Everywhere they found the same vices—gambling, drunkenness, "visiting," "parties of pleasure," theatrical amusements, "dining parties," dancing, swearing, disregard of the sabbath. They noted occasional infidelity of the active kind together with widespread illiteracy and lack of educational facilities. In Catholic areas they lamented ignorance of the Bible. Everywhere they found Baptists and Methodists who seemed unlettered, enthusiastic, and at best temporarily effective. In concluding the report, Schermerhorn described the range and work of Presbyterians, Baptists, Methodists, New Lights, and "Halcyons" (a sect devoted to uniting Christian denominations). Naturally they proposed vigorous missionary measures, especially distributing tracts and Bibles. These men set the tone of a flood of writings down through the 1850's calling a Christian crusade to save the Great Valley from barbarism—and, after mid-century, California. Moral laxity degraded America and Americans, this literature agreed; Christianization would upgrade morality, rescue men and women from evil living, and civilize America.[19]

The task of frontier preachers was to cure special maladies by religious remedies proceeding from God's decree and issuing in man's happiness. The crusading literature soon reached a consensus on the major ills, a consensus that lasted through the Civil War. Liquor, gambling, and sexual license were the devil's trinity. At mid-century a thoughtful moral diagnostician of America in general and California in particular declared that each such evil had "some part of our nature to attack and destroy, as neither of the others could. Intemperance levels its forces against our physical natures; gambling bewilders, assails, and ruins our intellectual natures; and licentiousness stupefies, deadens, and destroys our moral natures."[20] Joseph A. Benton (1818–1892) was cataloguing the cardinal sins against which American religionists preached during the middle period and he made their avoidance prudent. But since he thought in terms of burgeoning town life, his analysis is transparently more artificial than the concrete advantage that accrued to the frontiersman who kept himself in physical sobriety, economic frugality, and matrimonial fidelity. Preachers elevated these particular virtues by ingenious insight into pioneer living.

Biblical backing for the first two is less than fully convincing but effective. By emphasizing certain admonitions to sobriety and by interpreting other passages so as to supress Biblical praise of wine, it was borne in upon the frontiersman's or villager's conscience (or at least upon his wife's) that moderation in alcoholic drink was good and abstinence much better. At its simplest, drinking wasted money needed for wholesome things. Worse than that, inebriation forfeited the alertness that was the pioneer's necessary weapon against the ravages of fire or flood or animal which constantly threatened to wrest from him his possessions and his meager gains over the ominous wilderness. Worst of all, intemperance drove its slaves to the madhouse, prison, pauperism, or early death, in any case leaving destitute wives and children in misery of mind and body. By the 1830's when major Protestant denominations launched a massive temperance campaign, thousands of sermons and tracts echoed the same theme. For palpable evils brought by much drink the only remedy was abstinence from all liquors—vinous, maltous, and spiritous. To be effective, moreover, the remedy must be universal. "Let the multitude continue to drink a little," intoned Bishop McIlvaine in one of the American Tract Society's most widely circulated temperance pamphlets, "and still our hundreds of thousands will annually drink to death." In his peroration he declared, "The deliverance of this land from its present degradation, and from the increasing woes attendant upon this vice, depends altogether upon the extent to which the principle of total abstinence shall be adopted by our citizens."[21] The purely prudential concern for temperance was thinly disguised by appeal to a few overworked scriptural verses wrested out of context to condemn drinking and by allegorically applying apocalyptic passages to the scourge, pestilence, plague, bondage, corruption, etc., of liquor.

Similarly prudent if less publicized sanctions were invoked against gambling. Pioneer life wrenched people from home, kin, and accustomed work—each an aspect of the time's economic security and personal stability. Its drudgery invited the conviviality of card playing and horse racing whose excitement doubled with wagers. Its isolation made men easy prey to sharpers. Personal advantage drew on religious resources to avoid the small wagers—not grand risks like the Gold Rush—of petty betting because cash was needed for commodities unavailable by tillage or hunting or husbandry.

Even men playing the great games of chance turned piety to advantage. One G. A. Cassil wrote in 1850 from California home to Ohio: "When I left Marysville a little more than a year ago I left it a different being. Circumstances came to me a day or two before I left which awoke my moral nature from a trance in which it had slumbered for a few years previous. From that day a profane word has not been utered, no drop of liquor drank, nor a card been played, by your wayward brother. I have forsaken them for better companions." With Cassil had gone John Thompson Kinkade, who after nine years of mining in Placer County deplored gambling and attendant vices: "Quallifycations of Citizenship, in a man: Drink Rum Gamble Sharply. Stand his hand in a knock down, and dabble in Politics. Of a married Lady, to dress beyond her means flirt with every man. An[d] run away from her Husband once a year. Of a Boy Snoke [for 'smoke'] and chew, drink Rum. And swear fluently in English, French and Spanish. &c I would have you know, however that my family are exceptions to this Rule."[22] Other letters from Kinkade show concern for manners and morals producing and protecting familial well-being but deeply founded in piety. The preachers' admonitions against gambling took root.

Frontier prudence dictated sexual behavior easily adapted to traditional Christian sanctions of premarital continence and monogamous fidelity. As long as the family remained economically primary as a producing and consuming unit, maturing sons and daughters were assets. Cooperative labor among man, wife, and children was necessary to livelihood. Under these circumstances, premarital pregnancy and extramarital promiscuity seriously disrupted a familial society whose harmony with nature's seasons was the condition of food and shelter. In regions where slave labor prevailed a serious alteration took place, and plantation life transferred westward continued its traditional merriment, dancing, and greater sexual permissiveness. From 1835 to the Civil War preachers in slave areas (with notable exceptions) adduced Biblical sanctions for slavery as prudentially as their rural, free-state brethren preached against drinking, gambling, and dancing. American religion thus kept in touch with the prevailing style of life and adapted its moral norms to changing circumstances by making new identities between God's will and man's well-being.

Sabbath observance better than any other single issue illustrates this equation of goodness with advantage in American religious morality on the personal side. From the colonies' foundation down through the Civil War, keeping Sundays as days of rest preoccupied religious people. In the seventeenth century hardly any distinction can be drawn between New England and Virginia laws regarding the Sabbath. In both regions as well as in the middle colonies universal attendance at divine worship served equally as obedience to God's will and as ritual renewal

of community life. These fragile societies reenacted their solidarity and learned from their holy men how they should respond
to current events. Carried over into the prospering town life of
the next century, sabbatarianism became more routine and custo-
mary, but still served the useful purpose of binding new members
into social traditions. Moreover, it punctuated the drudgery of
labor. When men pitted themselves against the natural wilderness
lying westward, new advantages arose from Sunday rest.

Prudential considerations largely determined the sabbatarianism
of the pious (and promiscuous) Anglican aristocrat of Westover
plantation on the James River, William Byrd II (1674–1744).
On his treks westward, he called halt each Sunday. If lacking the
company of clergy, he himself led devotions for members of his
parties. Byrd's twice-recorded journeys (1728) tracing the boundary line between Virginia and North Carolina are notable for
the fact that the Virginia commissioners attached to their company the Reverend Peter Fontaine as chaplain, whom Byrd lam-
pooned as "Doctor Humdrum" and the "bishop of Beardom" in
the *Secret History*. On only one Sunday (November 3) of the
long trip Byrd allowed travel because all his men were anxious to
hasten from the wilds toward their homes, but the dispensation
came after Fontaine "put on his casuistical face and offered to
take the sin upon himself." In the *History of the Dividing Line*
Byrd justified his action as reasonableness and flexibility before
necessity, contrasting himself with certain Jewish and New England precisianists. His true feelings about the incident surface in
the *Secret History*. He wanted to lay over that Sunday "on account of resting the horses, which they greatly needed, as well as
because of the duty of the day . . . ." Gleefully Byrd vindicated
himself when time gained by Sunday travel was lost waiting for
a swollen river to subside before fording. "But, as I think our
present march could not strictly be justified by any of these
rules ["of necessity, charity, and self-preservation"], it was but
just we should suffer a little for it."[23]

On the middle frontier Byrd's principle of rest on Sundays applied to unnecessary labor, but in remote places worship awaited

the circuit rider's periodic arrival. Recovery from arduous toil rather than praising God served human needs. John Schermerhorn noted in 1812 that in the district of southern Ohio "the Sabbath is greatly polluted, by visiting, hunting, fishing, and neglecting public worship even where they [the settlers] can enjoy it."[24] Regular labor is conspicuously absent from the list of pollutants. Yet one task of missionaries was to establish Sunday Schools designed, as Robert J. Breckinridge (1800–1871) and his fellow elders in Lexington, Kentucky, nicely put it in 1831, to exert "a most happy influence upon the rising generation."[25] Educational employment of free time on Sundays catechized young people into the values and ways of their elders. Thus a social function was performed which differed primarily from the early Puritans' owning of the covenant in that the coming generation simply conformed to an unchallenged tradition without voluntarily taking it upon themselves. In both cases the Sabbath was made for man.

On overland routes to the Pacific at mid-century, wagon trains which lay over every Sunday were thought by experienced travelers to reach California much sooner than trains traveling seven days each week. While religious observance of Sundays was a constant undercurrent of concern to pious pilgrims, the real intent of Sabbath rest was to refresh the animals. "Sunday 6ʰ [May 1849] We made it a rule to lay by Sundays," wrote Stanislaus Laselle, "but as the ground we had campᵈ on was bad on the account of grass we went some three miles, and pitched our tents for the rest of the day." Six weeks later at the forty-third camp of the New Jersey Overland Company, Charles R. Gray, cook and factotum, wrote, "The condition of our cattle was such as to make us lay by for to day . . . besides every body else seemᵈ to respect the day & why not we? . . . At about 10 o'clock a clerical looking young chap invited us to church in a grove about a mile distant and *one* of our men did actually attend—in the afternoon he preachᵈ in a grove quite near us & I believe no one condescended to pay their respects to him." The editor of a famous overland journal has quoted diaries of several travelers to the effect that Sabbath rest saved time; one was ready to "guarantee that if you lay by on the Sabbath, and rest yourselves and teams, that you will get to California 20 days sooner than those who travel seven days in the week."[26]

Sabbath observance was deeply ingrained in many Forty-Niners who sought gold in California. Professional religionists among them damned their failure or refusal to attend church and to refrain from sports, but the miners themselves employed Sundays as occasions of rest and refreshment, physical and spiritual. William Heath Davis (1822–1909), who knew California intimately from his first touch with it in 1831 at age nine until his death, noted "The Habits of the Miners on Sundays" in a sketch that never found its way into his *Sixty Years in California* (1889) or *Seventy-Five Years in California* (1929). Conceding that "Sunday in a typical Mining camp" lacked "anything that would remind one of the presence of the Lord among men," Davis noted that almost universally it was "a day of peculiar interest." Miners could "rest and wash their shirts and socks and patch up their overalls," go to town for provisions and supplies, stop leisurely to observe a cockfight or a brawl between riled or drunken miners, fetch letters and newspapers from back home, eat a more sumptuous meal than usual although still one of bread and bacon and beans, converse and tell tales of home, think nostalgic thoughts and sing familiar songs, and relax from gaining gold by spending it. All that comprised Sabbath observance of a kind. Religious men replaced the more raucous activities with attending worship if possible or prayer meeting or hymn sing if not. Rough men refused to become Sunday soft, but they were mellower than they were from Monday through Saturday.[27]

Once in California "the forty-niners delivered themselves with abandon into the hands of saloonkeepers and gamblers. Drinking was universal except during working hours; 'liquoring' usually began early Sunday morning with a few 'flashes of lightning,' and continued all day." Ray Allen Billington's vivid picture accurately portrays many miners, but there were prominent exceptions in such men as Peter Y. Cool who during seven months in the Mother Lode country normally attended church twice or thrice each Sunday, rarely missed midweek prayer meeting, associated only with intensely pious fellows, and refused to trade with merchants who sold liquor.[28] And then there was Horace Muzzy of Maine, who on a typical 1857 Sunday in wicked San Francisco arose at six for morning exercise, breakfasted at nine, went to Methodist class meeting at nine-thirty, strolled through the city and chanced upon a Baptist service at the Episcopal church which he attended. In the afternoon he went to the Methodist chapel for service and sermon and baptizing, then administration of Communion to the congregation. In the evening he heard a lecture on the life of Samson attended by eight hundred people at the Presbyterian church, and then carefully wrote his wife Fidelia all about it.[29] This ecumenical harbinger was no doubt lonely and homesick—conditions as common to the great dislocations of American living as carousing.

The tendency of American religion to demand morality and to settle for good manners is most prominent in its impact upon rural and western life where prudence equated ethics with etiquette. Precisely that equation collapsed American religious morality into petty moralism, especially when the etiquette came to be of dubious advantage. Professional religionists on the frontier generally represented a higher degree of culture than their constituents exhibited, and most men agreed that religion was a civilizing force. Strict Sabbath observance as interpreted by American Protestants of the middle period required a modicum of literacy and sufficient economic security to sustain a little leisure. On the frontier literacy and leisure signaled culture and were promised as the fruits of religion. To that end preachers elevated such misdemeanors as indelicate dress, immodest acts, profane language, strong drink, gambling at cards or horses, dancing and frivolity, and particularly Sabbath breaking into the specters of Antichrist. Whether the virtues of modesty, propriety, sobriety, and staidness improved Americans is, on the face of it, a debatable question. Nevertheless, they did much, in the name of heaven, to make America what it is.

During the Civil War soldiers on both sides experienced well-known revivals of religious fervor which issued in moral improvements such as observing the Sabbath, praying, Bible reading, eschewing profanity and strong drink and loose women, and keeping company with fellow Christians. After the Civil War precisely the same religiously sanctioned personal morality lost touch with human advantage on the American scene. When that happened, ethics indeed became etiquette and prudent morals indeed became petty moralism. Recalling the prior era of earlier ethical virility, Charles Maclay, retired Methodist missionary and successful California politician, addressed the State Assembly in 1862 advocating a stricter Sunday law. "Communities, states & governments," he argued, "prosper just [in proportion] as they observe this day." Harking back to the horror of the French Revolution, he connected "anarchy, Bloodshed & dessolation" with "the period when they blotted out the Sabbath, & closed up the churches. . . . A nation without, I should say a State without a Sabbath, will be a state without harmony & peace[.]"[30]

III. TOWARD SOCIAL REGENERATION

Seven years later and in the same state, the Reverend Laurentine Hamilton (1826–1882) preached "that religion sh'd avoid as far as possible making *religious* sins; that is, turning those actions & enjoyments & amusements innocent in themselves into a snare to the conscience by putting a religious ban upon them, making them a distinction between the Ch[urch] & the world. The tendency of this is to make religion seem a matter occupied about trifles," he continued, "& religious people a set of carping triflers or petty critics on manners . . . neglecting the weightier matters of the law, judgment, mercy & faith . . . . I will only add now that the true spirit of religion is to be indulgent on things indifferent that it may be rigid on things essential."[31]

Maclay and Hamilton, although contemporaries by the calendar, spoke for the different generations to which they respectively belonged. In central Pennsylvania as a Methodist circuit rider in the 1840's Maclay raised money to build Dickinson College at Williamsport, gaining experience in finance and land speculation. In 1851 he took his new bride to San Jose and Santa Clara, California, where he built churches and learned real estate development, imported and sold goods from the Atlantic country as a merchant, organized a steam mill, farmed, bought and sold land, and profited from a boarding house he ran for employees and carpenters and masons attending his enterprises. He was elected to the California Assembly and later the Senate, and received typical political favors such as the concession to construct a turnpike at public expense. He aided the railroad builder, Leland Stanford, by buying lands which railroads would occupy and by splitting profits from developments along rights of way. In one such enterprise he bought San Fernando Mission and developed the town of San Fernando. After assuring his family's comfort, his fortune endowed Maclay College of Theology at the Methodist University of Southern California; as a trustee he installed his brother as dean of the college. Maclay did well by being upright.

On the other hand, Hamilton busily envisioned the new society which was emerging in America after the Civil War, and by his sermons helped it take shape in California. As a young man he graduated from Hamilton College (1850) and Auburn Theological Seminary (1853) in New York, set out for California where he was pastor of Presbyterian churches in Columbia, San Jose, and Oakland, was deposed as a universalist heretic in 1869, and founded Oakland's Independent Presbyterian Church where he preached until 1882. His liberal bent turned religion into the instrument of humanity and freedom, attacking local prejudice, isolation, provincialism, and bigotry. "But mark this fact," he typically proposed in 1870, "of religion—its aim, its ruling passion is moral perfection. Its peculiarity is that it proposes for its object *To become the best we know* [doubly underscored]. It cultivates humanity for the sake of humanity, goodness for the sake of goodness, man for the glorious being he was made to become; not for what he may have, eat or drink."[32]

The measure of the distance between these average men's minds is that Maclay hailed the values of pioneer, rural, individualistic America; Hamilton, those of cosmopolitan, urban, pluralistic society. Even more important, Hamilton perceived the folly of "making religious sins" out of mere bad manners, and thus accurately diagnosed the dominant influence of American religion on personal morals. He placed in the social sphere the old equation between God's will and human welfare, stating summarily that "the essential principle of true Manhood is a supreme interest in man . . . ."[33]

Actually, Hamilton derived the insight from Horace Bushnell, who in 1856 published an important sermon adapting the social-reform implications of Puritan covenant theology to the urban-industrial America that prophetic men then saw arising. Bushnell subtitled his "Society and Religion" as "a Sermon for California," and preached it at the First Congregational Church in San Francisco shortly after Independence Day (the occasion was the installation of a new pastor). Bushnell laid down the principle *"that true religion, including the pulpit and the church, is the only sufficient spring of civil order and social happiness."* The principle, as old as Israel's prophets, meant "that religion is the arbiter of state and nations; rooting out, pulling down, destroying, what is opposite to God; planting and building and so erecting into social beauty and establishing in virtue and happiness with God . . ." the social structures of justice and righteousness. While he thought that separation of church and state allowed religious influence on society to be more profound—because more subtle, indirect, and personal—than did ecclesiocratic arrangements, Bushnell flatly denied the notion of natural progress as "only a glimmer of literary moonshine, just now taken by its credulous admirers for the day." Nevertheless, societies and nations influenced by Christianity "are in a law of progress, just so far as they are in the power of Christ," because that power was supernatural. Moreover, American society represented a peculiar penetration of "the great principles of the gospel . . . into the order of states"; Americans, "as a nation, are witnesses to all mankind of the power there is in the gospel to establish at once, equality and order, liberty and justice, and so to organize a free commonwealth." For the American system, to the extent that it derived from Puritan ideas, began in prayer and continued by the practical pattern of congregational life to set "all men on a footing of spiritual equality and fraternity"; it cultivated domestic virtue and peace, and its consecration of a Sabbath furnished "a kind of public sacrament" that sanctified all time. Religion in America further made men responsible for, not excused by, society, because religion "fosters intelligence, endows institutions of learning, and values the good of the mind over all external gifts of fortune."[34]

As much as any single utterance, Bushnell's sermon originated the social gospel movement in American religion. Just when the center of gravity in American life shifted from the individual to the social, Bushnell and the refiners of his idea transferred the identity between divine benevolence and human benefits from personal to politico-economic spheres, thus applying the variable norms of Christian goodness to the new conditions of advantage for Americans. To be sure, Bushnell was not the first to complain about Protestantism's lack of a social gospel; that belongs, A. N. Kaul pointed out, to the elder Henry James.[35] Bushnell drew, indeed, on an older tradition of infusing society with religious values, a tradition which in principle had been reconciled with voluntaryism and congregationalism by the political philosopher, John Witherspoon, and by the theologian, Samuel Hopkins; both linked Christian benevolence directly with social order. But Bushnell first applied the prophetic function of religion to the structure of a society perceptibly dominated by mass politics and economics. In his own mind, as the following chapter will show, Bushnell's idea fruited more richly in an original concept of American nationality than in programs for social salvation. But others took up the latter implications and made religion into a prominent force for social change between the end of the Civil War and the beginnings of World War I.

The problem which the social gospel leaders faced self-consciously had subconsciously tortured every age of American history: how preserve an individual's freedom to pursue his personal advantage while perpetuating social structures which at once protect and restrict just that freedom? The old American ways of meeting this dilemma were the idea of the covenanted communities of colonial religion and the principle of government by consent which animated early national life. The former lost force as Americans occupied a mammoth continental expanse, and the latter, by any strict interpretation, surrendered its viability for all the people to the war's angry animosities.

The dilemma between personal advantage and public order stands unsolved, but has produced constructive rather than disruptive tension whenever the American imagination was deeply stirred by visions of a nobler society. Kaul stated the dilemma as the impossibility of reconciling moral principles with social expediency, and properly looked to poets and philosophers for ways of rendering that impossibility possible. "An ideal society," in his words, "could be created as soon as the individuals concerned subscribed to the ideal principle which was to inform it. Since Americans were no longer the victims of old institutions but the prospective creators of new ones, the decisive factor was the moral regeneration of the individual."[36] Quite true, as long as the sense of novelty prevailed, but, as we saw, the Civil War revealed a certain staleness in institutions which indeed victimized an increasing proportion of Americans.

As a specific religious aspiration, the social gospel proposed that American institutions themselves stood in need of moral and spiritual, economic and political regeneration, a pervasive regeneration proffered by social Christianity under the name of the kingdom of God upon earth. The awakening and revivals had begun with "moral regeneration of the individual" and erected thereon certain institutions fit for a good society: the stable family, the protective and identifying home town, the common law as identical with the law of God (*vox populi est vox Dei*), and the congregation—even, for most southern Americans between 1835 and 1860, chattel slavery. None endured the Civil

War fully intact. All eroded in the storms of industrial revolution which swept cities spawned by industry.

Americans had long concentrated upon social organization, not from idealism but from knowing that whatever institutions were built here must be of their own building. Americans were thus realistically utopian and idealistically mundane—for only by surprising if not paradoxical juxtapositions can we speak accurately of the American dream. After the Civil War came the realization that some institutions, notably those controlled by the capitalist hegemony installed by President Grant's Reconstruction (and progressively dismantled since President Theodore Roosevelt's "Square Deal"), served badly. Thinking institutionally rather than individually, social gospelers expected the highest reaches of human imagination to fructify in possible justice among men. Therefore, following Bushnell's lead, they attacked the *laissez-faire* idea of a natural law of progress and set in its place the conviction that "true religion . . . is the only sufficient spring of civil order and social happiness."

Precisely the era of the capitalist hegemony, 1869–1901, elicited from American religion—Catholic as well as Protestant—its most active and enduring interest in social ethics. The major social gospel leaders, after Bushnell, were Josiah Strong, Washington Gladden, Lyman Abbott, Richard T. Ely (1854–1943), and Walter Rauschenbusch, and a score of names might help fill out the ranks. All were influenced by the Marxian doctrine of *homo economicus,* but the movement successfully avoided ideological dogmas which a priori would arrange human society and a posteriori justify the arrangement. If any social plan drew support from diverse streams of the movement it was Henry George's single tax scheme. Negative criticisms of *laissez-faire,* such as George N. Boardman's 1866 essay on "Political Economy and the Christian Ministry,"[37] gave way to positive proposals for shared wealth and equal protection for poor and rich.

The favorite technique for spreading and enacting the movement's message had been the usual instrument of American religion throughout the preceding generation—the voluntary so-

ciety; among the notable ones was the Society of Christian So-
cialists, organized in 1889 by Boston clergymen. Indeed concern
for social reform in American religion arose from the late revivals
of the two decades preceding the Civil War, and what distin-
guishes the social gospel movement from this earlier impulse
is the belief that a spiritually regenerated social order would redeem individuals more effectively than regenerated persons could
redeem society. That belief permeated the religious movement
after the Civil War, and found its full theological expression as
well as official endorsement by major church bodies only in the
early decades of the twentieth century. The social gospel was
cast in doctrinal form best by Rauschenbusch in *Christianity and
the Social Crisis* (1907), *Christianizing the Social Order* (1912),
and *A Theology for the Social Gospel* (1917). Reform programs
were adopted by the Protestant Federal Council of Churches
in 1912, and in 1919 the American Catholic "Bishops' Program
of Social Reconstruction," drafted by Monsignor John A. Ryan,
was issued in the name of the National Catholic War Council
(called the National Catholic Welfare Conference 1921–1966).

All the social beliefs, principles, and programs we have so
far mentioned were formulated by religious leaders, mostly by
clergymen. As such they indiciate the direction in which many
religious people were willing to be led, which is indirect evidence
of the nexus between religious and social concerns in the thought
and action of believers. For most sectors of the populace, such
indirect evidence is all that has been studied. Recent historians
of American religion have blushed their way through the Gilded
Age, acknowledging collusion between such preachers of the
gospel of wealth as Bishop William Lawrence of Massachusetts
and such harvesters of that gospel as Andrew Carnegie. It has
been less widely acknowledged that the Reverend William Rainsford of St. George's Church in New York City remained a constant moral burr under the conscientious saddle of John Pierpont
Morgan, or that many "Robber Barons" sought religious guidance
for the philanthropic use of their often ill-acquired fortunes.

If the gospel of wealth conformed itself to large-scale avarice, it was avarice writ small to which the social gospel conformed itself by supporting organized labor and the federal government's regulation of mammoth business. Justice, relatively speaking, was on the side of the latter when the two conflicted, but they did not always clash. A major function of Gilded Age Protestantism was to sanction both the accumulation and the philanthropic use of wealth whose very enormity made it seem immoral. That function was different but not less social-ethical in its interest than the proposals to ban such great wealth. A detailed study of the social gospel of justice by Robert R. Roberts concluded that "before the issue was dramatized by the . . . activities of 'Teddy' Roosevelt," a devastating "critique of monopoly capitalism" had been mounted between 1875 and 1900 by R. Heber Newton, T. Edwin Brown, George D. Herron, and George C. Lorrimer, as well as by the more famous Strong, Gladden, and Abbott.[38] In both these instances religion was employed to bless socially beneficial approaches to new economic programs created by industrialization.

Hans Kohn's generalization that religion in America as in England "has been on the whole liberal, broad, and practical, not an 'opium' of people, but a strong active force behind most of the reform and humanitarian movements," has been shown to be peculiarly applicable to the period 1850–1900 by Herbert G. Gutman's study of primary sources for the labor history of these decades.[39] Americans saw economic distress as the result of sin more commonly than they attributed affluence to personal righteousness. The congregational arrangement endemic to American religion produced socio-economic homogeneity when residential areas became highly stratified in the major industrial and commercial cities of the period. This condition naturally led to the equation of Christian justice with interest of laborers and of owners. The latter equation could hardly avoid widespread recognition, but the abrupt change wrought by industrialism drove workers as well as owners to find in the past both sacred and profane sanctions for their behavior, circumstances, and aspirations.

Gutman has shown that "the discontented nineteenth-century American worker" found "a transcendent and sanctioning 'notion of right'" not only in the country's "republican political tradition" but also in "traditional American Protestantism." From the latter tradition, premillennial pessimism took a place subordinate to that of "a postmillennial Christian justification of trade-unionism and even more radical social reform." As one would expect, "The intensity of religious commitment varied among individuals: it depended upon particular life experiences, and its sources drew from the many strands that made up the web of Protestant tradition." Many "labor evangels" (a species of social gospelers) preached that the regnant order in American industry violated God's will, and Jesus Christ became the figure of a prototypical laborer or labor leader. "The most important early UMW [United Mine Worker] Negro leader, Richard L. Davis, . . . in 1896 and 1897 . . . found in the union a secular church that promised redemption from an evil social order." Christian "truths" were employed to undercut major "myths" of the Gilded Age.

While Gutman cautiously guarded against concluding more than his early studies justified, he found "tentative connections between the religious mode of expression of many Gilded Age trade-unionists and labor radicals and the behavior of larger numbers of disaffected Gilded Age Protestant workers." It is especially interesting that these connections broke sooner (about 1900) among citified unionists than among those of more isolated regions. Although the main-line social gospelers developed their protest out of a religious intellectualism little shared by the early trade-union movement, Gutman concluded "that the social gospel early found expression among those who professed to speak for the discontented lower classes and that the behavior of these critics of industrial capitalism cannot be understood without first exploring the religious (and secular) dimensions of their thought."

The downtrodden workers, then, along with middle-class, pious intellectuals who are the social gospel's canonized heroes, and even with the economic giants who could not sleep easily until they justified their accumulation of wealth by its philanthropic use—all found in the traditions of American Protestantism some "notion of right" by which to make their way into the jungle of industrial society. Each notion so used, moreover, placed in the social sphere the same religio-ethical prudence and flexibility which had served well for changing personal mores. The fact that Catholicism and Judaism espoused the workers' cause is more accurately referred to these religions' large immigrant constituencies, concentrated in urban-industrial areas, than to doctrinal or cultic or political idiosyncracies.

Simply stated, the religious aspirations after the Civil War to conform American institutions with the kingdom of God on earth were multiple crusades which while being waged as well as in retrospect often worked at cross-purposes. The main-line social gospelers are convenient candidates to represent the epoch's religion because in effect they occupied a middle ground between workers' and owners' interests and therefore appear to escape the conflict. The cross-purposes, however, are embraceable within a single functional interpretation of religion so long as we remember that the Gilded Age also generated America's unabashedly pluralistic society.

IV. "THEOLOGICAL HUSKS" RESTORED

Nevertheless, it remains convenient to focus attention on the middle-class social gospel when asking how the religious aspirations for a society given to public welfare became profane accomplishments. For it is too neat—but not untrue—to show that labor eventually coveted capital's security and capital copied labor's love for a broad base, both of course under governmental regulations which protected even as they restrained. Middle-class aspirations could hardly accommodate to a nonexistent opposite. Instead, the social gospel's hopes for the kingdom of God on earth became profane achievements in the reform programs legislated under the administrations of the Roosevelts, Wilson,

Truman, and L. B. Johnson. As these sacred dreams became worldly realities, theological heirs of Rauschenbusch repudiated the achievements as illusions of progress and delusions of utopia.

"The American core of Puritanism," wrote Nelson R. Burr, "without its theological husks, is an intense moral zeal for individual and community salvation."[40] Religious opposition to the social gospel's success in federal social legislation restored Puritanism's theological husks, particularly around the concept of man.

What became the dominant reaction found its first homegrown manifesto in Reinhold Niebuhr's *Moral Man in Immoral Society* (1932). The book was hailed almost overnight as having collapsed the entire edifice of liberal Protestantism that had been erected on foundations laid by Bushnell. While European forerunners of neo-orthodoxy were already translated into English, Niebuhr's revival of traditional Christian pessimism about man derived less from Barth and Tillich than from his own acknowledged frustration in face of unyielding socio-economic realities in Detroit where he was a pastor from 1915 to 1928. Niebuhr's fundamental concern throughout a long career as social critic, lecturer, and seminary teacher has been to establish conceptually the accurate limits of human achievement in the struggle to master history. His appeal to Biblical themes has sought to validate these limits theoretically as his discussions of American politics have sought to legitimate them pragmatically. Always given to paradoxical statements and disclaiming the title of "theologian," Niebuhr devised fascinating variations on the single theme that man's personal yearning for innocence invariably turns to guilt when social institutions come into play. All hope for the human enterprise he placed in divine, not human, powers; thus his strong emphasis upon original sin fell quite short of quietism—although activism was more his recommendation than his own métier. He saw isolation as the impossible precondition of innocence; thus man, primordially moral, always became polluted by the immoral societies in which he inevitably lived. While this statement by no means exhausts the subtlety and variety of Niebuhr's thought, his preaching and teaching effec-

tively destroyed the social gospel's belief in the religious regener-
ability of human institutions as such. His ingenuity appears in
the capacity to bend this wholly negative principle into a social
ethic concerned less with doing good than with avoiding the
greater of alternative evils.

Of course, not all who were concerned with American religion
from 1930 to the 1960's followed Reinhold Niebuhr, although his
influence has been virtually inescapable. Fundamentalists and
"positive thinkers" in all denominations found his teachings incompatible with their primary tenets, but neither has set much
store on social welfare as a proper religious aspiration. A young
generation of activists seemed in the 1960's to expect more from
social reform than Niebuhr's teachings would allow, but it is
by no means certain that religion is their starting point. Thus as
nearly as it may be said of any one person, Niebuhr's pessimism
about the redeemability of social institutions effectively disenchanted the main reforming elements among American Protestants, Catholics, and Jews with social gospel "utopianism."

That disenchantment is crucial to a functional interpretation
of religiously inspired social reform because it condemned the
social gospel less for the optimism of its visions than for lending
religious sanctity to worldly successes. Sidney E. Mead, who
ranks high for soberly critical appraisals of American Protestant
history, found since 1930 in the churches "a common spirit"
characterized by such unrelieved virtues as "a heightened theological consciousness, a willingness to re-examine the traditional
content of the Christian faith of Protestants, a critical attitude
toward the liberalism and modernism of the immediate past, and
positive attempts to revitalize the life of the denominations on
the basis of theological formulations of the nature of the church
and its relation to the general culture."[41] However accurate, all
these characteristics have in common a distinctly theological
nature. If we add to them the issuing of denominational decrees on matters of public policy, we only underscore the same
concern, for these decrees generally invoked theologico-ethical
principles as solving such public problems as segregation, war,

and poverty. *Mutatis mutandis,* the same theological revival entranced articulate American Catholics. Since about 1930 the main work of American Christianity has been to replace the theological husks whose disappearance had activated the social gospel.

The grand tradition of American religious morality, both private and public, developed a historically conditioned ethic which was fluidly normative, dynamically flexible, and prudentially teleological. But since the Civil War in the private sector and since the great depression in the public, American religion has reverted from this tradition to private manners of respectability and to public concern for theological integrity. The old pragmatic norms hardened into prescriptive principles before new conditions or else crumbled under the weight of newly imposed doctrinal burdens. The spiritual regeneration of the American people in their personhood as well as in their common life is no longer the primary religious goal, not because past campaigns consistently failed but rather because their successes were profane.

CHAPTER SIX

"THIS NATION, UNDER GOD"

America entire staggers the imagination, whether it is considered as place, people, society, or civilization. Even when telegraph, telephone, television, jet airplanes, and interstate highways bring the expanse and the multiformity within conceptual reach, the nation as a whole is not easily comprehended, so many-faced and many-voiced are its people and so varied their ways of life. Their common space remains vast despite the recent artifact of common time, and the allegedly common tongue in any of its dialects has always been for many an ill-learned second language. Prior to the New Deal, only during the Civil War and World War I did common government touch the masses more formatively than by post office and national elections. Historically, the sense of one American nation is the creation neither of kings nor presidents, congresses nor courts, but of an aspiration to and an ideal of liberties inherent and guaranteed. For the American people united themselves by introducing themselves to one another through voluntary enlistment in societies of mutual benefit —in towns, counties, and congregations.

The mark of mother England is unforgettable only because her language and literature, law and lore were both adoptable by and repeatedly adapted to a new scene that spurred new hopes and wrought new havoc in human lives. Unabashed pride in the mother awaited the daughter's marrying her own country, managing her own affairs, and eventually guarding the maternal homestead. American national self-respect demanded standardizing a dialect without imposing it, listening to native poets without believing them, shaping unique laws and customs without universally enforcing them, building a peculiar government not on royalty or rank but responsiveness to popular opinion, and attaining full—even brash—status in the Atlantic community of nations.

Thus American nationality was neither fathered by the state nor mothered by old-world history but rather generated by the will of man answering what he took to be the call of Providence. If to understand well the nationhood of America we must look to vocation and repose in their religious dimension, all the more to understand American religion we must heed its function in generating the sense of common nationality. The matter began with felt need for human company in the hard wilderness, a need classically stated in the familiar 1642 passage from John Winthrop's *Journal*: "For such as come together into a wilderness, where are nothing but wild beasts and beastlike men, and there confederate together in civil and church estate, whereby they do, implicity at least, bind themselves to support each other, and all of them that society, whether civil or sacred, whereof they are members, how they can break from this without free consent, is hard to find, so as may satisfy a tender or good conscience in time of trial . . . ; for if one may go, another may, and so the greater part, and so church and commonwealth may be left destitute in a wilderness, exposed to misery and reproach. . . ."[1] And it proceeded through the organizing of congregations—which, unlike towns and counties, embodied universal ideals—to colonial and national heroes in the form of wandering evangelists of God and America.

The most arresting religious aspiration to nationhood appeared when the Civil War was interpreted to be baptism into genuine national identity. That identity took ever more profane form. Since Reconstruction, religion in America has equivocated between denominational regionalism and supranational cosmopolitanism, but also has reserved the right to be supernationalistic in time of major wars. To trace the effect of religion on the national aspiration and the disenchantment of religion with the national achievement is to examine the churches, heroes, and theories of the colonial and early national epochs, then to pay close attention to religio-national interpretations of the Civil War, and then to note the regionalism and cosmopolitanism of post-Reconstruction American religion.

I. CHURCHES, HEROES, AND THEORIES

It detracts neither from the primacy of the Jamestown settlers nor from the bravery before privations of the Pilgrim fathers to find in those Puritans who first built their settlements at Boston and Watertown and Charlestown and the Connecticut Valley a peculiar purposefulness. Their "Errand into the Wilderness" was that of "A society despatched upon an errand that is its own reward [which] would want no other rewards: it could go forth to possess a land without ever becoming possessed by it," the late Perry Miller wrote in 1952.[2] These men with their women and children took up a new home on a new continent in a new spirit to inaugurate a new age. In the third generation their sense of novelty about the experiment begat an embryonic sense of nationality, a preoccupation with the peculiar Americanness of the Puritan enterprise. The preachers of the jeremiads lamenting visitations of the Lord's wrath after 1670 began to wonder (as Miller noted in the same essay) why Winthrop's experiment had not worked out as he planned but had instead become a society which, still taking the errand as its own reward, nevertheless accumulated the extra rewards of expanding communities in an expansive land.

The first generation anticipated that only the spiritually elite should receive from God the signs of their standing within the covenant of grace—signs which included good health, long life, and prosperity. With the Half-way Covenant of 1662, the novelty

of the experiment officially went native—the first step toward
nationhood—when even the grandchildren of saints could ride
into church membership on their grandparents' coattails. The
city set on a hill, beaming light of pure reform toward England,
became a new Zion in the wilderness facing westward. The
ministers who raised Massachusetts' lamentations in the 1670's
and 1680's were still wondering whether compromise had not
trespassed the divine prerogative; they were realizing that no
longer could they expect England to pattern itself after their
model society, built as a temporary exemplar.

Their business with history must instead be settled in and
for New England itself as part of the new world. Cotton
Mather gave explicit articulation to the permanence of the new
society in the new world at the opening of the new century in
his *Magnalia Christi Americana* (1702). The book lamented the
failure of New Englanders to achieve what Winthrop had envisioned, but, more than a lament, it also invoked theological sanctions for the New England experiment as setting standards for
the future in America.

Only two years before Mather's *magnum opus* was published
the "pope of the Connecticut Valley," Stoddard of Northhampton, reaper of "harvests of souls," made religion instrumental to
the well-being of man in society; every ordinance given to the
church was a means of regeneration. Stoddard no doubt expected
that purified church polity and purged body politic would sail
forever together in the same historical boat. The church had a
duty to use every ordinance for the comfort of all persons save
those visibly condemned by God, and Stoddard expected the
latter to comprise a distinct minority. He replaced the founding
fathers' vision of a spiritual elite demonstrating their rectitude
in grace as in governance and thus showing England the way
on which it would best be led by recalling them to lead it; now
the great responsibility of spiritual watchmen was to utilize God's
word and sacraments for the strength and perseverance of a
society set permanently in New England and already moving
westward.

Stoddard's stubborn adherence to a conception of religion as upbuilding American society removed him a giant's step from perplexities of the jeremiads a generation earlier. That conception neatly complemented Cotton Mather's awareness of the permanence of America as a scene of Christ's great works, although Mather remained wistful for Winthrop's brief experiment. And men of New England's first century had thought of a long future in the new world. When Charles II complained against the presumptuous independence of Massachusetts and proposed to recover that generous slip by which Charles I had allowed charter and company to be domiciled three thousand miles from Whitehall, church elders answered certain questions propounded to them by the General Court assembled in Boston, as follows: "It is our undoubted duty to abide by what rights & Priviledges the Lord our God in his mercifull providence hath bestowed upon us," they wrote in appreciation for the past; more important was their confidence in the American future, "and what ever the event may be the Lord forbid that wee should be any way active in parting w[i]th them."[3]

The troubles of the 1670's brought Puritans to terms with history and with America. Old Puritans were on an errand for somebody else no matter how significant they may have thought it; new Puritans were on their own errand learning that the errand took place in their own wilderness. Belatedly, adjustments of church polity in Massachusetts in 1705 and three years later in Connecticut reflected the change. The Cambridge Platform (1648) had steered a middle course between separatism and presbyterialism, for old Puritanism anathematized religious toleration on the left as well as any complete church system on the right. This middle course shrewdly eschewed the theories of polity that were debated at the Westminster Assembly and clung to New England's aspiration to exemplary uniqueness. By the eighteenth century, however, church polity in Massachusetts and Connecticut was meant as a model for America rather than for England. The adjusted Puritan polity developed a national sense in America, for it presaged the formation of those religious denominations which were intercolonial long before specific political bonds linked the colonies as American entities.

As the eighteenth century opened, a large number of settlers thought themselves not only members of a local community and church, but also Congregationalists or Anglicans or Presbyterians or Catholics. Even in Massachusetts, where congregational independence had been an article of faith, there developed consociations and associations that anticipated denominational organization. An impressive group of ministers met in Boston on September 13, 1705, as delegates of the associations to ask, "What further steps are to be taken, that Councils may have their due constitution and Efficacy, in supporting, preserving, and well-ordering, the Interests of the Chh[s] in the Countrey?" Cotton Mather, Moderator Samuel Willard, and Ebenezer Pemberton of Boston, Samuel Torry and John Danforth of Waymouth, Samuel Cheever and Joseph Gerrish of Salem, Grindal Rawson of Sherborne, and Samuel Danforth for the Bristol association gave New England congregationalism a mildly presbyterial polity, but more important than the political theory, which they believed to be Biblically sanctioned, is the fact that American religion was enlisted to serve "the Interests of the Chh[s] in the Countrey."[4]

What the Puritans did to transform a temporary experiment into a permanent enterprise was repeated by members of other churches elsewhere. By no means all the colonists adhered to religious groups, but those who did so discovered an important instrument of solidarity with fellow Americans beyond their own families, villages, and colonies. All experienced colonial governments that were variously related to European sovereignties in the seventeenth century; the trend toward royal colonies during the eighteenth gave the crown representation by royal governors. Churchmen, whether Puritan, Baptist, Quaker, Anglican, or Catholic, shared another identity wider than the colony and more powerfully present than the crown. This identity engendered a sense of involvement in a new-world movement, in an American enterprise.

For all their resistance to externalism, colonial Friends were loyal to London Yearly Meetings until the 1680's, when Yearly Meetings in Burlington and Philadelphia united Quakers in the middle colonies. New England congregationalists federated into consociations that heightened their sense of common religion and region independent of English ecclesiastical judicatories. While Anglican church life developed differently in the individual colonies throughout the seventeenth century, during the eighteenth century the Society for the Propagation of the Gospel provided a symbol of common American experience for the clergy it commissioned and for the congregations it aided. As did New England Puritans, Anglicans gained a sense of America as a single, continuing enterprise. The reality of this continuity led Thomas Bray, the bishop of London's agent supervising the Church of England in Maryland, to form the S.P.G. and its sister Society for Promoting Christian Knowledge. The S.P.C.K. from 1698 furnished libraries for colonials and clergymen. The S.P.G. was chartered in 1701 for the "better support and Maintenance of an Orthodox Clergy in Forreigne Parts." Although quite denominational in their interests both societies achieved and inculcated a synoptic understanding of Anglo-America.

The S.P.G. commissioned the Reverend George Keith (1639?–1716), Anglican priest and Quaker apostate, to survey the condition and opportunities of the Church of England in all the colonies. He toured seaboard communities from New Hampshire to Currituck, North Carolina, kept a careful journal of his travels, and in November 1702 he and six other clergymen issued "An Account of the State of the Church in North America."[5] Various proposals, aimed at "reducing the main body of Dissenters of all sorts to ye Church of England," showed Keith's almost fanatical animus against his former faith. In New England he entered pamphlet warfare with Increase Mather and Samuel Willard, whom he regarded as "Independents." Throughout his tour Keith visited and preached to churchmen, disputed against Quakers, and above all strove to impart a sense of the Church of England as commanding a religious loyalty that bound its adherents to one another in a common endeavor.

Keith spent from June 1702 to August 1704 traveling the coast. For associate and companion he chose the Reverend John Talbot, later an S.P.G. missionary in Burlington, New Jersey. As an itinerant preacher, lecturer, and author, Keith became one of the few widely known colonial men of the early eighteenth century, to head a long line of peripatetic religionists who gave many Americans a common acquaintance with prominent men. His journals record more than one public appearance each week during his travels—as preacher, disputer with Quakers, or conductor of public arguments on religious topics. Everywhere he went he distributed the pamphlets he wrote during the tour, four sermons and six polemical leaflets against dissenters and Quakers. He held long conversations with churchmen to establish their commitment and with Quakers to undermine theirs. He preached on one hundred and twenty-two occasions in Massachusetts, Rhode Island, Connecticut, New York, New Jersey, Pennsylvania, Delaware, Maryland, Virginia, and North Carolina, and he held open disputes with Quakers and others in Massachusetts, Rhode Island, New York, New Jersey, Pennsylvania, and Maryland. Talbot preached as often. Both baptized adults and children at every opportunity.

Earlier experience as a Quaker missionary in America taught Keith to adopt the tactics of his irrepressible adversaries. He represented the official Church of England and the S.P.G., and he meant to return to England after his tour, but he always assumed that the colonists were in America to stay. He encountered them less as a visitor from England than as one experienced in American ways common to all the colonies. Like many mobile preachers after him in the American experience, he brought plain news with the Good News, taught his ways with the Way, sowed his writings alongside God's Word, won disciples to himself among disciples of the Lord, and portrayed his enemies—especially the Quakers—as enemies of God.

Keith was America's first "nationally known" revivalist, notwithstanding his distaste for "enthusiasm." He was neither the last nor the greatest. In the 1740's a far less sectarian parson succeeded to the title when George Whitefield began his colonial tours. From Savannah to Boston and to Jonathan Edwards' district in the Connecticut Valley Whitefield marched, a combination of John the Baptist chastening with his message and William Jennings Bryan charming with his voice the men and women who left plows in fields and pots on stoves to throng towns and villages where he preached. Franklin, who admired his eloquence and used his influence to foster the charity school in Philadelphia, estimated that twenty thousand persons at once heard Whitefield exhort repentance and love. Whitefield raised money for his own pet projects in Georgia—schools, orphanages, and other benevolences. Yet he clearly implied that the settled ministers, who were unhappy over his mulcting their parishioners, were uncommitted to God and gospel. Like Keith, Whitefield called attention to himself as he called souls to redemption, and he became an intercolonial hero. His name was perhaps more widely known to American colonials than any other eighteenth-century name save those of George III, Franklin, and Washington.

What Whitefield was to the colonies in the mid-eighteenth century, Francis Asbury became to the states in the three decades centering on 1800. Charles Grandison Finney, Henry Ward Beecher, and Dwight Lyman Moody carry the lineage to 1899. As American politics furnished leaders for the nascent nation, religion furnished inspirers. For the sense of solidarity which had spread through the colonies from Charlestown to Charleston was enlarging to bind what Jefferson feared would be two trans-Appalachian republics into a single nation. Religion was one of several factors engendering American aspirations for independence from England, for confederation, and for covenanting the states into a union, and it cannot be overlooked if we are to understand incipient American nationalism. The Great Awakening's leaders saw and commended their revivals as a movement by which God opened a new chapter in the history of human redemption on a new continent held in virginal purity for the special purpose of binding diverse folk into a single people. The same task was taken up under new circumstances after the Revolution.

It has been reckoned that when Asbury died in 1816 he had been seen and heard by more Americans than ever had any other person.[6] Asbury's accomplishment was so far greater than Whitefield's as the United States of 1785–1815 was greater than the seaboard from Saint Simon's to Nantucket Islands. Asbury was almost accidentally an American colonist; having been appointed a missionary by and under John Wesley, he refused to return when Wesley recalled him at the opening of the Revolution. He was also instinctively American, and in 1784 refused to accept joint headship with Thomas Coke over the Methodist Episcopal Church merely at Wesley's behest, preferring ministerial election by the founding Christmas Conference in Baltimore. This double defiance of the autocratic Wesley measures Asbury's own arbitrariness. He ruled the Methodist movement while it burgeoned from a small sect centered in Maryland and Virginia into the major popular denomination with work in every state and territory.

Asbury symbolizes the uniting work. He left theorizing to others. His career neatly spans the era of federation, for he came to America in 1771 while schemes of independence were taking shape; when, after criss-crossing the whole land, he died in 1816, Britain had come to terms with the loss of her mainland colonies south of the St. Lawrence. To stir common aspirations for an independent nation, Asbury pleaded that common evangelical Christianity was a stronger bond between Americans of every region than any political bond could be. At his death he was the commander-in-chief of circuit riders whose adherents numbered perhaps one in every twenty-five American men, women, and children. Asbury's organization regularly touched the lives of as many United States citizens as did the administration of President Madison. The bishop was indeed a parent of his country.

In theory the religious basis of American nationality was an extension of covenant theology from congregation to nation.

Under God proved saints were received into a covenant of grace which impelled them to covenant with one another to work for the common weal. Before the Revolution Jonathan Edwards had tried to return covenant theology to the strict congregational application which its framers intended. Ironically, it was Edwards' disciple who changed the master's theology to empower the theory of a nation. Samuel Hopkins accomplished the delicate adjustment by expanding the notion of "disinterested benevolence" (a theme common to New England theologians since Cotton Mather): "holiness consists in disinterested benevolence" and he who possesses such benevolence "will have a greater regard for the inhabitants of the nation to which he belongs, and be more concerned for their interest, than for those of other nations."[7]

An anonymous sermon on Psalm 147:12–14, preached about 1795, specifically applied to the American nation this Hopkinsian extension of the covenant. Finding in "Our Union" what he took to be "the only solid foundation, under God, of our present happy situation & future prospects as a people," the preacher exhorted "such a friendly & Affectionate disposition towards our fellow-citizens throughout the Union as will conduce to the removing of all local prejudices, distinctions, & policies, & substitute in their place those Mutual concessions & sacrifices which are on particular occasions so *essential* in every community to the general prosperity." What could bring about this happy circumstance?

The Religion which we profess is acknowledged by all, even by those who doubt or deny its Authority, to be of all others the most friendly to the interests of civil society & the best calculated to promote the happiness of Mankind. It inculcates all the social & relative duties, the private and public virtues, by the most awful sanctions. It excites our hopes, rouses our fears, & strikes all the powers of the human soul. Whilst it unites us to the Supreme Father of all it connects us, by the strongest ties, to our fellow-creatures. It represents us as composing one grand family, under one common head, as Brethren, nay, as members one of Another.

That man who has most largely imbibed its spirit or who is a ['real' struck out] Christian indeed becomes thereby a useful citizen, for it is impossible for him to be united to This Creator by religious adoration without having at the same time with his fellow citizens all those other relations of charity & justice which constitute the character of a man of integrity and real worth.[8]

Little wonder that Francis Grund (1805–1863) thought "The Americans look upon religion as a promoter of civil and political liberty; and have, therefore, transferred to it a large portion of the affection which they cherish for the institutions of their country." Grund saw here America's uniqueness; its religion, unlike "the instrument of oppression" it had been in other countries, served freedom and nationality so powerfully that "its promotion is essential to the constitution."[9] To quote Perry Miller, if "the Revolutionary divines combined the law of nature with the tuition of the Old Testament in order to encourage resistance to the house of Hanover," then the Second Awakening sought to protect the newly independent nation from incursions of French infidelity as an external threat. But revivalism in the early nineteenth century "progressively endeavored to conceive of itself as exclusively internal," and indeed "the steady burning of the Revival, sometimes smoldering, now blazing into flame, never quite extinguished (even in Boston) until the Civil War had been fought, was a central mode of this culture's search for national identity." And when the Revival found its special form in the many-boothed camp meeting, people "congregated . . . from everywhere and nowhere," not knowing "to what church they belonged, or which they would join, and accepted Baptist, Methodist, Presbyterian alike. They were not preaching nationalism, they were enacting it."[10]

Not only did religion theoretically explain how men of good intention voluntarily compacted themselves into a unity yielding resources of benevolence to maintain healthy relations between those thus united. Religion also gave Americans, especially during the revivals, a heightened sense of corporate purpose and an exalted consciousness of their own voluntary creation of social wholeness. But voluntaryism applied to an entire society was corollary to Arminianism applied to the covenant theology. In theory and, as events would prove, in practice, unless the covenant of grace made saints wholly dependent on a sovereign God, their covenanting together was not only voluntary but temporary; as Winthrop knew, one might opt out as well as opt in. Transferred to the politics of nationality, unless the allegiance of citizenship engendered loyalty to a sovereign nation—which does not necessarily mean "state" or "government"—the voluntary principle was wonderfully inclusive but not binding. This unsettled point became crucial in America's mid-passage.

The revivalistic production of national aspirations faced less crucial perplexities than that essential one. Within decades it spawned not only benevolent societies but the foreign missionary movement. Where the former vindicated evangelical religion by fructifying the national welfare, the latter suggested that the revivals aimed at a cosmopolitan rather than a national goal. Was it God's design to use the religion of the heart to pump lifeblood through American arteries, or was the Christianizing of Americans meant to produce transfusions of redemptive plasma for the rest of the world?

That issue posed itself in the decades before and after the Civil War. It was poignant because either goal lay within reach of Christian soldiers marching as to war, but they must march to one war or the other! The issue was not really new, for it resembled early seventeenth-century New England's question whether to be a temporary exemplar for England or a permanent new Zion in the wilderness. In each instance there were those who would have it both ways. Interregnum and Restoration turned the Massachusetts Puritans' demonstration into a permanent society. In the case of the revivals and missions Americans tried to choose both wars. "America has the divinely appointed task in history to become itself completely regenerated so that it may then legitimately convert the heathen world."[11] But the prior task was both obvious and Gargantuan, what with immigrant popery to be put down as well as Protestant piety to be upbuilt.

II. GOD, WAR, AND NATIONALITY

But men do not choose their wars; wars come to men. And the war came. Revivals did not cease, but the question came to be whether American nationality was something lost to be recovered or something yet to be discovered. The quandary about foreign missions was automatically settled for a time, and after the Civil War American Christians carried the cross abroad in a parade led by the Red, White, and Blue. Secession and Sumter's cannon dinned away most intellectual questions, unless "How establish the Confederacy?" and "How restore the Union?" count as questions of the mind. Underneath the inimical preoccupations of the majestic tragedy, however, writhed the question that would not lie still: where has American nationality gone? Moderate southerners sought it in constructions of the Constitution that set protection of property above guarantees of liberty, and thought the true nationhood—which northern industrial materialism had forfeited—might be salvaged by eleven agrarian states loosely conjoined. Northerners commonly saw the true nation as frayed but not parted so long as the rebellious south could be brought to sanity and submission—some added emancipation. Few in the south could seriously contend that they were about really new business with their Confederate States of America, whose Constitution and law were simply those of the old Union with topics touching slavery and secession elided. But in the north were differing religionists who, on the one hand, contended that American nationality, however severely strained, was written into the constitution of the universe by its creator, and who, on the other hand, argued that at best a spurious pretense to nationhood had sprung from the contract theory and spread through the voluntary religion of the revivalists, while the true American nationality was emerging in the war. For instruction in the first theory, we may place ourselves under the tutelage of a little known preacher, George S. Phillips of Ohio. For the latter, we best seek instruction from Horace Bushnell of Connecticut.

Phillips invoked divine sanctions direct and complete for the American nation as established by Declaration and Constitution and preserved by the Union Government. He lectured on the subject in winter 1863. Next year, having enlarged the arguments with evidences of divine blessing in Union victories, Phillips published *The American Republic and Human Liberty Foreshadowed in Scripture* (Cincinnati: Poe and Hitchcock, for the author, 1864). The obscure book imaginatively uncovers neat Biblical indications of God's plan to crown His work with a republic which in every detail corresponded to the United States of America, and it typifies a kind of religious nationalism kindled by Christians during and after the Civil War.

Phillips began laboring for the Lord as a circuit rider of the Northern Ohio Methodist Conference in the early 1840's, served the decade before the war under the California Missionary Conference, returned to Ohio and became chaplain to the Forty-ninth Infantry of Ohio Volunteer Regiment, saw battle in Tennessee and Georgia. While back home in Tiffin in the hard winter of 1863–1864 before returning to his chaplain's post, he delivered his lectures at St. Paul's Methodist Church. The book was printed, after several delays, largely on the author's borrowed money. After resigning his chaplaincy, Phillips worked briefly in Denver as an educator, and died in Ohio just before the war ended. More interesting than his career is Phillips' sure conviction that God promised in the Old Testament to found a nation fully complying with His will, and fulfilled that promise by establishing the United States. Onto a theological stock resembling Joseph Smith's revelations of America as the true Holy Land he grafted a supernationalistic stem much like that of Senator Charles Sumner's.

The prototype of the American republic was the "United States of Israel" under the written constitution of the Ten Commandments and the presidency of Moses. Therefore civil liberty derived from the God of Christianity and its forerunner, not from the classical world. (Like many early church fathers, Phillips thought Plato's *Republic* plagiarized the Pentateuch.) The Hebrews defaulted their vocation by submitting to monarchy, but their prophetic and apocalyptic books, particularly Isaiah and Daniel, kept open God's plan for mankind and foretold the day and hour of the Declaration of Independence. Phillips identified the United States as the final empire which Daniel envisioned; Isaiah 33:21 predicted in detail the Boston Tea Party, and Isaiah 49:12 foretold the coming of Chinese immigrants to California. Even the national apostasy of slavery and the Civil War as the purge of that apostasy were foretold in Old Testament passages. Although Washington's U.S.A. was the first nation since Moses' U.S.I. to repudiate monarchy by a written constitution guaranteeing religious and civil freedom, through the intervening centuries God raised up a series of men to keep alive among mankind the hope and vision of the great nation He planned. Abraham, Moses, Daniel, Paul, Luther, Calvin, Cromwell, and Wesley all stood in the same lineage of liberty. American colonial leaders were God's nearer precursors of the anointed, "the immortal Washington," who, surrounded by Christian "coadjutors . . . of rare qualities" erected a Christian nation, without king and with written constitution. "These facts of history . . . clearly show that the Government of the United States was set up by the God of heaven."[12]

That the Almighty might have intended a nation other than the United States was a thought lying entirely beyond Phillips' imagination, for on his reading of the evidence there could be no doubt. "God seems to have kept the New World, with its vast forests and grand prairies, as the place of his Christian Israel. Here for ages the wilderness remained unbroken; kings and kingdoms rose and fell in other portions of the world, while Jehovah, in his mysterious providence, was preparing the way for the coming nation, which was not to grow up upon the ruins of another, but was to receive its birth outside of all other nations, to grow up where monarchy had never cast its dark shadow as an occu-

pant of the country." God's design for man to be above Government, to have it serve him and not him it, aimed at liberating
man ultimately to serve God alone. This liberty was based on
"equal dignity and worth of the common humanity . . ."[13] But
from the early national period the popular conception of social
contract went abroad, infecting the national body with the pois-
onous idea of secession. This disease sprang from misunderstanding and, he thought, could be cured by the historical realization
of all Americans' mutual responsibilities and interdependence.

But the abomination of desolation, the national apostasy, was
slavery, an institution in absolute violation of the nation's "covenant of life." This evil permeated the entire country when the
Fugitive Slave Law passed, and even the churches—especially the
Methodist Episcopal Church, South—followed the apostasy. The
Civil War, whose prototype was Michael's war with the dragon,
at first wrongly turned on preserving the union. Only on the first
day of 1863 with the Emancipation Proclamation did it become
for the north a righteous war. God approved war for emancipation by granting victories at Gettysburg, at Vicksburg, in the capture of Morgan in Ohio, at Port Hudson, at Murfreesboro, and
at Chattanooga.

Since in 1864 many seceded states were reconstructed as free
states, Phillips could declare: "We have come back to our solemn
Life Covenant, and to-day the nation stands up in its own
majesty . . . ." Thereafter, the genius and mission of the American
republic would be to destroy, by example, all monarchies of the
world, and to free mankind for government under written constitutions. The "United States is to fill the earth"; its destiny
was "so to occupy the place of government in the world, as to
leave room for no other government." Such was the will of God
and the universal law of mind, to make the world Christian.
Only two forces—Christianity and republican government—fully
accorded with God's will as permanent forces in history, and
therefore they, as initially combined in America, "shall prevail
throughout the world."[14]

The patent unoriginality of Phillips' book signifies its representing a major body of religious and nationalistic sentiment in the north. Neither the threads of argument nor the cloth of conception belonged uniquely to the author. He piled long quotations borrowed from politicians and preachers upon heaps of Biblical allegories.

The revivals, despite their waning since the late 1830's, had been the great common experience of the country; the outburst of lay enthusiasm in the late 1850's gave the appearance of a nation that was religious and a religion that was national. This interchangeable theme—Christian America, American Christianity—gave Phillips' book the modicum of unity it exhibits as a collection of revised lectures laden with homiletical rhetoric—despite the alteration of "dear hearer" to "dear reader." The war came as a sudden thunderstorm routing the picnic of American national and religious optimism. Phillips voiced common sentiment by turning bane into blessing; the rain nourished national pastures and washed away dunghills that putrefied the southern sector and befouled the northern. A cleansed nation now greeted a this-worldly, millennial dawn for which all history had been preparing. What the explanation lacked in profundity it exuded in popularity.

Southern sentiments during the war devised a parallel providential interpretation which specified the national apostasy conversely, not as slavery but as the central government's invasion of the rights of property on the pretense of guarding liberty. Had Vicksburg and Gettysburg and Chattanooga gone to the Grey, the prophecies of Robert Lewis Dabney and James Henley Thornwell could have come true. Then the Confederacy would have borne the national continuity with neither discrepancy nor remainder in the interchangeability of America and Christianity.

Simplistic conversion of tragedy into triumph was not the only religious interpretation of the Civil War bearing importantly on an aspiring nationality. By combining his learning in jurisprudence and in theology, Horace Bushnell adumbrated an alternative at once more accountable to fact and more profound in its seriousness. He had trained as a lawyer and worked as a journalist before entering the Yale Divinity School in 1831, and two years later he began at North Church (Congregational) in Hartford, Connecticut, a pastorate that lasted until failing health led him to retire in 1859. Seventeen more years he spent traveling, writing, and occasionally preaching. As one of the few theological giants arising from American religion, Bushnell was eclectic, practical, and distinctive in the content and in the form of his thought. The reality he apprehended was organic, dynamic, and mysterious. Apprehension of it entailed the entire human faculty. Articulation could at best be evocative; thus many expressions of insights into truth must be comprehended and composed before much truth could be grasped.

Bushnell is famous for his theories of Christian education, is more widely hailed than deeply studied as a creative theologian, and is badly misunderstood when judged by isolated citations depicting him as a radical Republican during Reconstruction. Not in a few topical comments but in the whole body of his thought the concept of "the nation" is a leading motif. He viewed societies as organic human entities working out their destinies in the framework of a history that was subtly enticed, not coerced, toward human fulfillment by a benign Providence.

Bushnell was no utopian, social-contract, voluntaryistic theorist of man and history. Man seemed to him political by nature, and his politicality originated prior to consent or consciousness of it. "Without this political equipment," he wrote in an essay on "The Doctrine of Loyalty," men "should not even be complete men."[15] In the divine economy, he believed, nations are called into being by God's guidance of history. When human response answers divine vocation, there arise the power of law and the spirit of loyalty. Therefore in the human economy, nations begin as fragile entities, perilously sensing and pursuing their callings and only gradually becoming strong through wars, literature, and religion. Nationality, a "given" in principle, must therefore emerge in the actualities of constitutions and governments. Nationality comes to be voiced in law and received in loyalty. But governments are run by men, and it did not surprise Bushnell that legislation could abrogate rather than express the true law of a nation. In America the Fugitive Slave Law palpably reneged the national vocation, and in such a case disobedience to positive law was not only permissible but morally mandatory. For true law was not man's creature; rather, men learned their creatureliness from the fact that they are by nature legal.

Law in itself, then, was a "power of God" which erected the nation as "perpetual, beneficent, the safeguard of the homes and of industry, the condition of a public feeling and a consciously organic life." Bushnell was a "higher law man" with a vengeance and a vindication. He saw in loyalty the human response to law, and therefore a second necessary condition of nationality. But neither law in itself (which might be broken by positive law) nor loyalty in itself (which might be misdirected into mistaken legislation) was a sufficient condition of nationhood. Looking back to the American past, Bushnell found interesting illustrations of his theology of nationality; or, more precisely, being steeped in the theology and politics of the American past, he ingeniously devised his unique conception of nationality. The old covenant theology of the Puritans had recognized the proper relation between law and loyalty: "it is the glory . . . of our founders and first fathers," he wrote, that "in their unconsciousness" they "prepared us to such a state."[16]

That is, the Puritan fathers knew that true nationality arose from a covenant relation between divine law and popular loyalty. A quite different idea, Bushnell reasoned, pervaded the mood of the framers of the independent American government. They assumed that sovereign man made his own law, articulated it neatly in legislation, engendered his own loyalty, and by compact created nations. The fallacy of this view became patent in the claim that government derives its just power only from the consent of the governed; were that true, never before had nation been! On Bushnell's reading, this artificial doctrine had precluded the emergence of American nationality in the founding era. The Constitution merely "kenneled together" independent states. Thus the Civil War was to be understood as the dissolution of an illusion of nationality on the negative side, and, on the positive, the birth of a genuine nationhood.

The war subjected America's self-consciousness to tragic circumstance, thereby renewing the divine calling by means of law and eliciting an enduring loyalty in response to the country's vocation. Bushnell was not sanguine, certainly not militaristic. By his preaching, lecturing, and writing before the war he had sought to instill a true sense of nationality by pointing out that the country chased an illusion. The war came as a tragic but therefore grand event, at once revealing the emptiness of flimsy theories of social contract and bringing a true nation to painful, bloody birth.

Here nationhood was actualized, just as the Revolution had actualized an already existing independence from England. Then the colonies had not seceded because they were already their own center of historic and social gravity. Southern secession per contra was pretentious because the south was not its own center of gravity. Seventy-five years of nationalistic pretension had brought the American people "to the point where only blood, much blood, long years of bleeding, can resanctify what we [north and south] have so loosely held and so badly desecrated."[17] In the war, blame for which fell equally on northerners and southerners, the old pretensions died, and through the vicarious suffering of fighting men there came into being a nation. The government came to its historic completion as, through shedding of blood, there was atonement between two previously conflicting principles, freedom and authority.

Shocking as Bushnell's enthusiasm for the war may be on the face of it, he was by no means unpained by the experience. What is central is that he included tragedy in his sense of history. If, as he thought, reconciliation between God and man entailed vicarious sacrifice, so the dissolution of contention between peoples sharing a historic destiny, a common heritage, and a single land could be achieved only by tragic bloodshed. The unity won in the Civil War was a true nationhood, "a sacredly heroic, Providentially tragic unity, where God's cherubim stand guard over grudges and hates and remembered jealousies, and the sense of nationality becomes even a kind of religion."[18] If the phrase sounds supernationalistic, it must be underscored that Bushnell regarded language as more evocative than descriptive. These words are drawn from his oration at Yale College's commemoration of her alumni who died in the war, an oration delivered just after the end of hostilities.

Bushnell thought that the enigma of America's pretentious career as a protonation had been solved by the Civil War. He also thought that a religiously and theologically true nationality had been achieved. He held, however, to no positive, hypostatized notion of "nation" as such, save as a particular people's collective acceptance of their divine vocation. Thus he spoke evocatively of the tradition to be cherished as exemplifying that response, and of the response's embodiment in law, literature, government, and other organically interrelated institutions. In contrast to Phillips, who sought vindication for northern victory by appeal to divine sanction for all American history except that of the south, Bushnell tried to adumbrate a conception of nationality that would engender religious aspirations for mutual acknowledgment of guilt and mutual sense of achievement with regard to nationhood for united Americans. If one can speak of theologies of Reconstruction, then Bushnell's ideas befit the plans of Lincoln; Phillips endorsed the program of the radicals and Grant.

Nobody rivals Bushnell in advancing a novel theology of American nationality, although similar views appealed to the Swiss-born theologian, Philip Schaff, who adopted the United States for his country in 1844. The Civil War, he believed, fell on Americans as providential punishment for having deserted their calling to unify a polyglot people in a heterogeneous land by guaranteed freedom. The broken union only did explicitly what the antipodal institution of slavery did implicitly. Each defaulted the national vocation. Thus, Schaff thought, both north and south incurred blame for and judgment by the war. Yet out of the very judgment came national and vocational rebirth. Then America "first entered upon the age of manly vigor and independence"; or, in explicitly sacramental terms, "this very baptism of blood entitles us also to hope for a glorious regeneration."[19]

Nor were such interpretations of the war as providentially leading Americans into their true nationhood confined to northern theologians. Stephen Elliott (1806–1866), Episcopal bishop of Georgia, referred the war's desolation to the question of national vocation. He thought that the prewar federal government failed to elicit the country's intended nationality. Although the southern states' regional attempt to embody that ideal fell under adverse judgment by God and history, southerners should be thankful that Providence was using their defeat to fasten on all Americans their calling to be a harmonious, united, just, compact nation. Elliott had thought of the Confederacy as potentially grounding the national ideal in historic institutions. Defeat forced him to concede that Providence intended no remnant America, and he urged southerners to think gladly of themselves as receiving, through their reunion with a transformed national government, the nationality they had separately sought.[20]

If profound interpretations of the Civil War's initiation of American nationality came from south as well as north, there were of course southern preachers who vaunted the Confederacy's righteousness. Perhaps the most unrelieved encomium came from Robert Lewis Dabney (1820–1898), Virginia Presbyterian who was Stonewall Jackson's adjutant and biographer and who in 1883 became a founding professor of the University of Texas in Austin. At the war's beginning "There was no 'nation'; for the United States were then a confederation of sovereign States, and consequently there was no 'national life.'" Therefore "it was . . . impossible that one of these sovereign constituents could commit 'treason' against its own creature, the common agent," Dabney wrote in 1897. He never changed his opinion that "the task which duty and Providence assigned us was, to demonstrate by our own defeat, after intense struggle, the unfitness of the age for that blessing [free government] we would fain have preserved . . . ."[21] As jaundiced as this unreconstructed son of

Dixie was, he found the issue of nationhood central to the meaning of the Civil War.

How far and which of these theologies of nationality reached into people's imaginations would be difficult indeed to assess had one of them not been enunciated in prominent statements by President Lincoln. By his eloquence the spokesman and by his assassination the personification of the war's significance for America, Lincoln became "the representative man of the nation . . ." in person and not only "as the constitutional President of the United States."[22] If Washington is father of the country and Jefferson father of the government, then Lincoln is indeed father of the nation. Slavery and emancipation, he insisted, must subserve the cause of union—not only governmental but national. His "*official* duty" to "save the Union," as he wrote to Horace Greeley, eventually but not necessarily coincided with his "oft-expressed *personal* wish that all men every where could be free."[23] By throwing down a particular challenge to the endurance of the United States government, the war also tested the seriousness of Americans in actualizing the universally significant principle of government of, by, and for the people. The two were linked in the Gettysburg Address. The war was "testing whether that nation, or any nation so conceived and so dedicated, can long endure," and "the great task remaining before us" was "that this nation, under God, shall have a new birth of freedom" so that such government "shall not perish from the earth."[24]

The universal principle is "that all men are created equal." Lincoln thought the war accountable neither to secession nor to slavery as such but rather to the issue of nationality. His last writings after Appomattox indicate that he saw in the war an unclosed chapter in American history, an episode which was at once preserving, testing, regenerating, and transforming American nationality. There was indeed continuity between it and Jefferson's "hard mystery," as Robert Frost called it.[25] It tested both the particular nation and its universal principle. Yet the nation needed "a new birth of freedom." The Gettysburg dead "nobly advanced" an "unfinished work," for there was "the great task remaining before" Americans living and unborn. With remarkable thoroughness, Lincoln's interpretation of the Civil War gathered together the themes and motifs of national death and rebirth, of national baptism and regeneration, of national vocation under God, which preoccupied Christian spokesmen for a new nationality, and Lincoln printed them, so far indelibly, on the American imagination.

Whether in the stridently nationalistic tones of sectional men or in the grand conceptions which Lincoln summarized, religious aspirations for a renewed American nationality rose to a definite peak during and immediately after the Civil War. Moreover, these aspirations were distinctly American as well as palpably religious, for in most cases they appealed to a divine vocation laid upon Americans through their peculiar experiment in human freedom. That calling indeed surpassed European visions of man's liberty, but more important than its human quality is its conception as a divine-human covenant worked out in a historical process which itself respected that liberty. Unlike the principles of organic genius and mission which generated modern European nationalisms, these proposals (most insistently stated by Bushnell) placed human solidarity on the basis of a certain willful acceptance of public duties levied by deity.

Perhaps nobody saw this difference more clearly than the Paulist priest, Father Isaac Thomas Hecker (1819–1888), whose transcendentalist convictions found religious fulfillment in Catholicism to which he was converted in 1844. In *The Church and the Age*, written near the end of his life, Hecker attacked the adequacy of Calvinism, with its pessimism and determinism, to support the American national ideal of liberty, and proposed that Catholicism's emphasis on human freedom to do God's work on earth cohered with democracy. When liberal Catholics in France exaggerated Hecker's accommodation of Catholic teachings to Americanism, Pope Leo XIII in 1899 condemned that particular form of modernism. But if Hecker failed to realize how far the American experience had eroded old Calvinism, he successfully brought Catholic thought and attitudes into affirma-

tive connection with the two main features of religious nationalism—divine calling and man's voluntary response.

III. NATION VERSUS COSMOPOLIS

While religious impulses toward a uniquely American nationality reached a climax during and after the Civil War, there were
arising significant rivalries between national and cosmopolitan
interests. These rivalries had developed into inherent conflicts
by World War I.

Two vantage points allowed the broader vision. In the first
instance, new concern for the liberty and welfare of mankind
arose out of America's new role, accepted soon after Reconstruction, as a muscular member of the family of nations. That role
extended the American experiment's universal significance, which
the founding fathers had emphasized and Lincoln had nurtured
through the Civil War. In the second instance, religious thinkers
caught a fresh glimpse of Christianity's universalism by reflecting
on disparities between increased denominational tensions at home
and heightened missionary activities abroad. If the perspective
was half profane and half religious, the vision was none the less
truly ecumenical, in the general sense of the word.

In its religious expression the cosmopolitan spirit wanted peace
among nations, and the Spanish-American War as well as World
War I were supported as military means to peaceful ends. In
both these cases Protestants were more sanguine than Catholics,
not so much because of theological disagreements as because
America's adversaries belonged for the most part to the Catholic
camp. Yet pacifism remained a major product of American religion between 1865 and World War II, repeatedly checking tendencies toward militant nationalism. The contest between national
and cosmopolitan interests raged in several arenas of religion:
denominationalism, foreign missions and international relations,
ecclesiastical ecumenism, and decisions for war or peace.

The denominations' contribution to a sense of common Americanness during the colonial period was assessed at the beginning

of this chapter. Now it is appropriate to indicate that, just when a theological rationale for nationhood was made possible by the Civil War, denominational divisiveness ironically intensified.

Roman Catholics suffered no organizational breach although they had no immunity against sectional sympathies during and after the war. The Methodists and Baptists, then the two most populous denominations, divided over the slavery issue in 1844 and 1845, respectively; the Methodists reunited only in 1939. New school Presbyterians likewise split in 1857 and old school Presbyterians followed suit in 1861; during the war regional bonds transcended religious issues sufficiently to unite both schools into southern and northern churches which remained separate in the 1960's. Episcopalians and Lutherans healed their formal divisions after Appomattox but the former remained regional in spirit while ethnic differences rent the latter. "Ecclesiastical division not only foreshadowed political disunion," according to H. Shelton Smith, "but actually prepared the moral ground for it."[26]

The ground was so well prepared that it still yielded cultural enmities a century after political reunion was won. Down to World War II religion prominently specified the southernness or northernness (more accurately, "nonsouthernness") of American Christians, thus undercutting the very sense of common nationality the yearning for which was a chief function of antebellum religion. Insofar as the war produced this nationality, the churches provided a refuge from the hard work of actualizing it. One perspective from which to oppose the new national spirit was that of religious regionalism.

Only a nation of sure integrity could have undertaken the international involvements which the United States assumed after Reconstruction. Dollar diplomacy made America a major power in the Pacific and actually the hemispheric watchdog which President Monroe had theoretically proclaimed it to be. The new internationalism reversed the pattern prevailing since the Treaty of Ghent (1814) when interest in foreign affairs was mostly stirred in the churches by foreign missionaries. Now the cross indeed followed the flag to Pacific islands, to Latin American countries, and to Alaska.

The shift is familiarly interpreted as feeding evangelical convictions to American imperialism, and the fox in the henhouse is usually said to be Josiah Strong's famous book, *Our Country*.[27] Careful study of Strong's writings indicates that his Anglo-Saxonism changed with changing social-scientific conceptions of "race," and, moreover, was never an exclusivistic notion. Rather Strong, who in this regard represents a wide range of religious leaders, advanced an inclusive and cosmopolitan plan whereby North Americans would receive into partnership all sorts and conditions of men in the enterprise to spread civilization and enlightenment over the face of the globe. As his thought developed from the undeniably tendentious positions of *Our Country*, Strong joined sagacious concern for metropolitan society with his overriding cosmopolitanism. But the present point is that typical social gospel endorsements of America's revived "Manifest Destiny" outreached nationalism as well as racialism (in the current sense) and countervailed the secular achievement of American nationality by calling religious attention to "the evangelization of the world in this generation."

With that slogan as title of his 1900 book, John Raleigh Mott (1865–1955) summoned a crusade for Protestant Christianity and democracy as two sides of a single coin to be proffered every man without delay. Granting the difference between evangelization and conversion, the campaign is startling less for having taken an enormous goal than for having almost achieved it. Mott had already founded the supranational World's Student Christian Federation (1895) and went on to blend interdenominationalism and internationalism into the Protestant ecumenical movement.

A similar religious internationalism, arising from but transcending American nationality, in part changed the Roman Catholic Church in the United States from a missionary recipient into a missionary sender. In 1908 the Vatican officially recognized this change, sealing in fact both the success of Father Hecker's Catholic nationalism and the church's transformation of it into international and ecumenical concerns. Catholicism's role in the United States became that of a full partner in the history of American religion, and a truly national church played its increasingly responsible part in Christian and religious ecumenism. The Catholic Foreign Missionary Society of America, known as the Maryknoll Fathers, was officially established in 1911 as a distinctly American endeavor whose remarkable foreign missionary activities spread the American ideal of religious liberty into Catholicism in the Far East, Africa, and much of Latin America.[28]

American practicality, pragmatism, and cooperativeness were suffused through the Christian world missionary movement and gave significant impetus to the conferences which eventuated in the World Council of Churches (1948) and in the Second Vatican Council (1962–1965). Renewal within and rapprochement between Protestant, Catholic, and Eastern Orthodox Churches throughout the world sprang undeniably and perhaps most significantly from the recent missionary revival for which American Christianity assumed heavy responsibility. European theological and liturgical renewal not only guided the course of modern ecumenism but also drew American religion toward cosmopolitan concerns that effectively counterbalanced nationalism. Moreover, ecumenical activities produced in most major American denominations a new sense of identification with groups spread over the world who shared their ecclesiastical traditions. For example, decennial Lambeth Conferences of Anglican bishops began in 1867 at the request of American Episcopalians, and since the 1950's have been supplemented by Anglican Congresses; thus American Episcopalians increasingly (and quite anomalously) think of themselves as "members of the Anglican Church." Many American Lutherans similarly "belong" to the Lutheran World Federation, and there are world alliances of Baptists, Methodists, and Presbyterians.

With some exceptions, the important mergers of denominations in America have reunited groups sharing a single confessional heritage. By contrast, transconfessional unions along national lines characterize the ecumenical movement in Asia,

Africa, and also Canada. Trends toward interdenominational cooperation and reunion have so far in America found national expression only in the National Council of the Churches of Christ in the U.S.A. (1950; formerly the Federal Council of Churches, 1908), which speaks to rather than for its constituents, who do not include Catholics, the majority of Baptists, many Lutherans, and a large number of smaller denominations.

The national integrity achieved in the United States through the Civil War was at once undercut by denominational regionalism and transcended by religious cosmopolitanism. While all but the most strictly pacifist denominations endorsed the major wars in which the reunited nation engaged, in times of peace American religious groups categorically condemned war as an instrument of national policy, again paradoxically finessing the nationalism they helped produce. Of churchmen "who had been drawn into the progressive movement," Winthrop S. Hudson noted that "William Jennings Bryan rather than Theodore Roosevelt was their spokesman."[29]

The old pre-Civil War peace movement took new form in the hopes of supranationalistic Christians for a world without wars. The effort of these reformers was to engage religion with grandly universal hopes and hurts of mankind by disengaging its interests from specifically American nationality. Thinking that nations as such willfully helped Satan by resorting to war, energetic elements within the churches cultivated programmatic pacifism not as an individual's conscientious protest against collective evil but as a panacea for human happiness in uncoercive and uncoerced societies. This spirit made World War I a holy war to end war by safeguarding democracy, and for two decades thereafter American religion basked in a pacific calm before the awful storm. Apparent inconsistencies between Christian pacifism and American assistance to the European Allies melted in a fervor for universal peace which justified military means. That war discouraged the great social gospelers, and when it ended Strong and Gladden and Rauschenbusch were dead.

The popular hero who thought to apply principles of the Prince of Peace to disputes between nations was indeed Bryan, to whom Christianity was "not only a solution but the Best solution of international problems."[30] Resigning after a brief term as Wilson's Secretary of State in protest against the second note to Germany concerning the sinking of *Lusitania*, Bryan thought surely the southern and western United States would stand with him against the President. Characteristically, he proceeded from pious belief to political certainty in an easy stride, and he never saw a possibly irreconcilable conflict between religious ideals and international realities. But for that reason he remained until his death the model Christian statesman in the minds of throngs of pious Americans.

Nobody has stated the absoluteness of Christian pacifism better than Rufus M. Jones (1863–1948), Quaker philosopher of Haverford College in Pennsylvania. "Christianity and war are utterly incompatible," he wrote. For "war interferes with all these [liberal] social undertakings; it postpones the realization of all ideals and human hopes." Therefore good men in America and elsewhere must "form in as large groups as possible higher convictions, more idealistic faiths, and greater compulsions, which in the long run—in these matters the run is often very long!—will penetrate and permeate ever wider groups, and so make *new nations*, or at least a *new national spirit*. . . ." International justice, peace, and happiness, on this view, were "the true glory of a nation and . . . the real business of the best patriots."[31]

Whether primarily political or theological, pacifism and cosmopolitan internationalism were inseparable between the two World Wars. Like ecclesiastical ecumenism and foreign missions, the combination vaulted religious Americans across national identities as soon as the American nationality to which religion aspired had been realized. A similarly antinational impulse kept the old popular Protestant churches—Baptist, Methodist, Presbyterian—regionally separated. These contrary impulses seemed to Sidney E. Mead most characteristic of Protestantism after the Civil War. The denominational pattern "was generally accepted in the United States," he wrote, "and was assumed to be the proper organizational form of Christianity under religious freedom and the separation of church and state." But under one form, the substance of religion was twofold: "the religion of the denominations . . . was commonly articulated in the terms of scholastic Protestant orthodoxy and almost universally practiced in terms of the experimental religion of pietistic revivalism," while "the religion of the democratic society and nation . . . was articulated in terms of the democratic way of life for the example and betterment of all mankind."[32]

Viewed functionally in relation to American nationality, these counterthrusts do not contradict one another, for both reject the profane achievement of a nationhood long religiously sought after. The denominations' religion particularized a human identity that fell short of nationality while the "religion of democracy" universalized human ideals on a cosmopolitan scale which overreached nationality. That the nation stood impervious to both impulses was proved repeatedly in America's wars since the Civil War, for in these times of crisis the denominations' restlessness subsided into compliant sanctioning of national goals. Thus the churches which prominently inspired Americans to seek and find a genuine nationality proceeded to oppose it once it was found. Explicit denunciations of the American national ideal are as uncommon among churchmen as politicians, and the reasons are obvious in both cases. Yet national integrity has been held suspect by the religious sector, which quite generally preferred either to deepen the regionalism that threatened the nation a century ago or else to pitch all issues on a grandly cosmopolitan scale of worldwide churches, Christianity, or humanity. Both devices avoid rejoicing in or transforming the profane nationalism that is the *sine qua non* of that social cohesion without which no American church can perdure.

The great solvent of religious suspicion toward the national spirit in America has been active engagement in international war, which the majority of churches have supported at least down to the Vietnam War. Even so, religious ambivalence toward American nationality quickly hardened in peacetime, no matter whether into denominationalism, churchly ecumenism, or pacifism. Thus religion subtly opposed what it engendered.

CHAPTER SEVEN

A "POLYPOLITAN" CULTURE

Since 1710 when Cotton Mather preached about his vision of *Theopolis Americana,* the American experience has been ramifying and plurifying a different reality—the pluralistic culture of "polypolitan" America. Each member city of this culture has justified itself by its contribution to the general welfare, and each has represented itself as a path along which men and women may pursue happiness.

The preceding chapters have shown that religion profoundly affected the laying out and the building of five such cities—those of novelty, egalitarian society, education, personal and public morality, and nationality. It remains by way of recapitulation and conclusion to indicate how the religious enterprise became an internally pluralistic city within a diverse society. But to delineate here all constituent elements of America's cultural pluralism would be quite another task. The introductory chapter more comprehensively enumerated the cities in which Americans are living: religious, economic, political, familial, intellectual, and recreational. Subsequent chapters have dealt, more or less systematically with each.[1] Their argument has undercut the tendentious argument that the religious city by influencing the rest unifies all. Rather American religion cultivated pluralism within and without itself.

A contrary tendency of American thought, religious and secular, has indeed proposed the ordering of pluralism by some unifying loyalty. Josiah Royce taught that five cities demanded loyalty from individuals—domestic, professional, commercial, religious, and political—and that the fundamental problem was finding one loyalty transcendent over and thus capable of uniting the others. Yet even Royce was searching for "the city out of sight."[2] In its own day and own way each of the five cities discussed in these chapters—plus of course the religious city itself—has provided some Americans with such an overarching cause.

More recent American experience indicates that this pluralistic culture's genius lies precisely in being content with a multiplicity that is harmonious and productive without being unified. Such was the observation of Royce's student and successor, William James. In a classic statement, James wrote, "Things are 'with' one another in many ways, but nothing includes everything, or dominates over everything." According to this distinctively American thinker, "The pluralistic world is thus more like a federal republic than like an empire or a kingdom. However much may be collected, . . . something else is self-governed and absent and unreduced to unity."[3]

In America pluralism has been resolved less and less by appeal to order that yields unity and more and more by tolerance that diminishes the ultimacy implicit in any cause's demand for loyalty. Save for nationalism in time of putative military danger, the religious city alone states its claims over modern Americans in ultimate terms of absolute allegiance. But these claims ring hollow; American religion increasingly finds ways to express in doctrine its new-world experience and therefore also its distance from European Christendom. Although lacking explicit testimony to its own relativity as one cause among many, as one tolerant member of this plural culture, religion tacitly concedes by its internally pluralistic form that it is not the overarching cause which collects all other loyalties.

While religious impulses were shaping independent, profane cities in America, the religious city was becoming one entity among many, "unreduced to unity." Concurrently, the religious city expressed itself in a self-accepting pluralism. Cultural pluralism is in part the sponsor and in part the yield of its twin, religious diversity. Therefore to treat the theme of pluralism in the American dream's religious dimension is not to name one more city but is rather to specify the character of and relation between the several cities already described. The American aspiration for plural culture and plural religion has reached achievement, and to trace the religious influences on this interlocking aspiration is also to recapitulate major themes of the foregoing chapters. The double task of this conclusion, then, is to analyze religious pluralism and cultural pluralism in their reciprocal, intimate relations.

I. MANY CITIES OF GOD

Religious pluralism arose from a historical accident whose convenience and beneficence generated legal sanctions in the form of governmental neutrality toward religion. Accidentally the American colonies provided separate places for people of differing faiths, then drew them into tolerant intercourse with one another. Nobody in Western Christendom between the Emperor Constantine and Roger Williams seriously proposed that social cohesion could perdure religious liberty. Reformation radicals and later the Quakers wanted religious toleration without regard for social cohesion. But Williams fathered the distinctly American theory that unrestrained varieties of religious expression heightened the spiritual vigor of a single society. Not that Williams himself worried much about the welfare of worldly society. He pleaded that God's chosen people needed, in the famous phrase, a "hedge or wall of separation between the garden of the church and the wilderness of the world." The garden belonged to God's elect, for in it He transplanted His saints. But if His plan, as Williams saw it, did not include taming the wilderness, the project soon attracted the attention of self-declared saints.

Quite accurately, Mark DeWolfe Howe distinguished Williams'

primarily theological from Jefferson's primarily political use of the "wall" metaphor.[4] But the distinction did not endure when the sacred aspiration for religious liberty became the profane achievement of religious pluralism. The history of colonial religion details how Williams' protest against civil restraints in the name of God melted into Jefferson's objection to civil constraints in the name of man. In the process Jefferson's ideal was embracing and not replacing that of Williams. Quakers invaded every colony where there was an established church. Presbyterians and Baptists claimed quarters in the Anglican south while Anglicans won a foothold in New England. Freedom of religion generated rivalry during the Great Awakening and again during the antebellum revivals. Each denomination, jealousy defending every man's right to join it, perforce extended him the right to join another—or none.

Whether the authors of the "Bill of Rights" intended to check or advance religion by Article I (taken in conjunction with Article VI of the original Constitution), eventually a Jeffersonian construction of the issues prevailed in the disestablishment of New England Congregationalism and again in the Fourteenth Amendment. Down to the time of that amendment, the United States Supreme Court and other courts were usually conceding that the nation was built upon a Christian, Protestant, evangelical consensus. More important than the courts' decrees, this consensus was itself stimulating multiplication of denominations.

That each group must tolerate all the others robbed the consensus of specificity. As far back as the Maryland Colony's original charter, it had been clear that any church would flourish by allowing others to exist alongside it, and the early national experience taught even the Congregationalists in New England what southern Anglicans had learned in late colonial times— that establishment brought mixed and eventually harmful privileges. To endure in America, each church had to thrust westward with the population, and the new territories' nascent cultural pluralism, in part begotten by the multiple sects that invaded them, pronounced an anathema on religious conformity. Of the denominations indigenous to national America only the Mormons dominated a political territory, and Utah awaited admission to the Union until its proposed constitution of 1895 outlawed polygamy and forbade church control of state government.

The incoming American population of course brought fresher recollections, not all unpleasant, of ecclesiastical establishments in Europe. But the region from Long Island Sound to Delaware Bay, increasingly after 1700 the portal of immigrants, had known establishment only very briefly in New Netherland in the seventeenth century, and was then holding high the torch of toleration which Lord Baltimore had lighted. Here (as also in Rhode Island) colonists objected to constrained religion, and their objections gloried in pluralism as liberty's sacramental sign. Particularly where Quaker attitudes prevailed, the formalism of measuring faithfulness by conformity fell under righteous indignation. When the rate of immigration quickened after 1700, seaboard lands had been claimed, and the newer Americans pushed into piedmont and valley regions. Their gateway, the middle colonies, displayed multiple, tolerant churches. Religious uniformity and intolerance were features of the Europe they had departed. Plurality of religion characterized the new home they were occupying. Since the transition left their preferred faiths intact, it did not rankle.

Choice between churches implied the alternative of no church. When the Great Awakening flared in mid-century, incidence of irreligious folk had risen to heights unknown in Western Christendom for perhaps a millennium. Although enthusiastic preaching enlisted many, the American Revolution ended with no more than one in ten citizens of the new states enrolled in a congregation. The doctrine of neutrality, restricting the United States government from establishing religion or infringing its exercise, kept hands off an activity which, in its institutional form, was already well plurified and just as well neglected. As establishment receded and then disappeared in New England, robustly religious voices answered, "Amen," for already the revivals were proving that voluntary, rival denominations could gain members and influence the common life more effectively than could publicly privileged ones.

Religious pluralism was the American way of doing things. It worked. It even received theological sanctions. As Sidney E. Mead noted, "a largely neglected strand in the Protestant tradition" was construing pluralism "as a positive good." From "some of the Independent divines of seventeenth-century England" this strand "might be traced historically through eighteenth-century pietistic and evangelical movements to its flowering in the formation of the Evangelical Alliance in 1846." (Founded in London, that organization had a strong American branch.) "By that time its leaders," continued Mead, "had adumbrated a doctrine of the church (denominationalism as over against sectarianism) consistent with the practice of religious freedom. But . . . their work has become an almost forgotten chapter in American church history."[5] Yet not really forgotten, for in the American religious experience the good and right of religious pluralism (not to gainsay accompanying ecumenical thrusts) is everywhere assumed. In lectures focusing the issues of his large history of freedom on modern religion, Herbert J. Muller noted that all major American demonimations take "for granted the existence of other free churches no less when they claim absolute truth for their own doctrines; however disposed to intolerance, none would dare to call for the supression of their rivals."[6]

Indeed, precisely those groups most concerned for the finality of their own teachings knew best of all that they must grant to others the very toleration which was the condition of their own existence. In the first national decades the pattern of religious pluralism proved itself almost too well by eliciting the broadly Protestant consensus. Against that unofficial "establishment" arose sectarian protests ranging from the indigenous Mormon religion through the imported Anglo-Catholicism espoused by Episcopalian partisans to the transplanted Roman Catholicism of the Irish—and other nationally identified—Catholic immigrants. Each denounced Protestantism as false; with equal vigor each found the others' protests to be spurious. But each demanded the right to exist, and each granted the same right to all other denominations.

A religious pluralism that was good for the denominations gradually became also good for the country, less because it actualized the antiestablishment convictions of Jefferson and more because it inculcated mutual understanding and tolerance among otherwise diverse peoples who joined together in the American enterprise.

In the mid-twentieth century the agreement to disagree agreeably, on which American religion was thriving, reached an apex of prominence as a model of popular diversity within national unity. In reviewing United States Supreme Court decisions regarding church and state controversies since 1947 (the year of the famous decision in *Everson v. Board of Education*), two constitutional lawyers found a distinct trend toward recognizing the legality of public expenditures which promote religious pluralism and the toleration that is its simultaneous premise and promise. Indirect, equitable public assistance to denominational endeavors, far from breaching the wall of separation—whether in Jefferson's or Williams' sense—deepened and broadened religious pluralism as contributing to the common good; Wilber G. Katz and Harold P. Southerland wrote, "The Court is commending to the citizens of a country with many faiths the ideal of an expanding and deepening religious freedom." These writers were ready to "trust that the Court will not consider educational aids to be so hot that they must at all costs be kept off the agendas of Congress and state legislatures. These are issues that can be left to the democratic process because of the healthy vigor of American religious pluralism: a pluralism that is finding its unity in a spreading trust in the common belief in religious freedom."[7]

Thus the American expression of religious pluralism attained a pinnacle of success by producing healthy cultural pluralism. Through tolerant rivalry with one another the denominations not only taught tolerance but competed for the right to shape American common life by commending themselves to the common mind. To convince people in the open market of popular opinion that a denomination served the general welfare became the sure way for a denomination in fact to influence social affairs and public policy. As Leo Pfeffer wrote, "the objective of competition [between denominations] is not to capture the state but to convince the community. The religious groups wish to translate their values into communal values mainly through the operation of law. . . . They seek to achieve it by convincing the masters of the state in a democracy—the people—that the values they urge are the best for the community and should be adopted by the political representatives of the community."[8] The City of God in America does well by itself and good for the society by being several cities.

II. MANY CITIES OF MAN

More than a few denominations participated in successful campaigns for each of the five features of the American dream which previous chapters have detailed. Since the campaigns were numerous, each successive victory increasingly marked off the religious movement from the profane achievements it helped to inspire. Thus American religion, partly by being plural, worked to create a cultural pluralism, simultaneously making itself one of several members in a frankly "polypolitan" society. In both these connections, "pluralism" is used in the positive, constructive sense of describing "a society in which there prevails an attitude toward differences that reinforces and contributes to social cohesiveness."[9]

In America no denomination polarizes the entire religious constellation and no sector of the culture controls related sectors. In this peculiarly fluid arrangement of constituent social factors, each factor establishes its relation to the others by suasion and with a high degree of autonomy. The result is a combination characterized by interdependence instead of dominance. Making possible such a society are the mood of tolerance and the liking for difference. The social consensus is broad enough to be forceful even though it is taken for granted and does not require specific, concrete symbolization. Each element, moreover, manifests its own mixtures of distinct but ultimately concordant parts. A mixed economy of private and public and corporate interests is paralleled by a political blend of local and regional and national parties and administrations. Among all the pluralized members stands the religious mixture as a distinct partner to the rest.

From the beginning of each American community the plural paradigm foretold what the whole American community would itself become. Varied religious institutions took part in the general diversity. "The population of Oregon City is set down," wrote David E. Blaine in 1856, "at five hundred. There are two public houses—temperance—two liquor saloons, and one grocery. There are a Methodist Church, Congregational Church, Baptist Church, Catholic Church; the Episcopalians hold regular services. There is a Masonic Lodge, an Oddfellows Lodge and a Division of the Sons of Temperance in the city."[10] Like the lodges and the saloons, the religious groups were purely voluntary associations. Yet as such they also manifested a unique quality, which allowed them to seek thorough diversity in the community. The special feature of the American denomination among voluntary associations has always been its universalism, its declaration and determination to serve—and by serving to enlist, if possible—everybody, regardless of age, sex, wealth, language, religion, and (to an extent whose limits have been discussed) race.[11] While the many denominations were helping to plurify American society, a distinct arena was being reserved for religion.

Perhaps the chief gift that religion gave to variety in American life was assistance to newly immigrant communities in preserving certain old-world characteristics even while they placed themselves in the new world's melting pot. Most nineteenth-century immigrants from Sweden, for example, were Lutherans and therefore Protestants, anxious at once to guard their "national traits" and to adapt themselves to America. At mid-century a Swedish intellectual, Fredrika Bremer, toured the United States; after having visited a settlement of her fellow countrymen in Wisconsin, she urged, "The Swedes must continue to be Swedes, even in the New World; and their national life and temperament, their dances and games, their star-songs and hymns, must give to the western land a new element of life and beauty." But the advice did not stop there; meanwhile, they were to absorb American traits, especially "that regularity and perseverance, that systematising in life, in which they are yet deficient."[12]

Catholics and Jews of many national traditions had similar hopes of retaining certain geniuses while absorbing new ones, and they looked to their religion for guidance and help in the transition. Thus was borne out the hope that James Madison recorded in the fifty-first Federalist Paper, that the new country should secure civil and religious rights as belonging to the coin of freedom, guaranteeing "the multiplicity of interests" on the one side and "the multiplicity of sects" on the other. Religious pluralism became the sacred and sanctifying corollary to cultural pluralism.

Late in the nineteenth century voices of Protestantism at home and of Catholicism abroad recognized but deplored this complicity of religion with pluralism. Although Josiah Strong revised his ideas when he came to reflect on the urbanization of American society, his earlier notions about the great west issued in calling a missionary crusade to preserve or restore the old Protestant consensus against corrosive dangers of "Mammonism," "materialism," "luxuriousness," "the centralization of wealth," "socialism," "the saloon," "Mormonism," "Romanism," and "the foreign element."[13] Pope Leo XIII condemned "Americanism" in 1899 by weaving a net that caught no fish in the American hierarchy, yet he was justifiably suspicious "that there are some among you who conceive and desire a church in America different from that which is in the rest of the world."[14] Insofar as the difference consisted in becoming one among many faiths in a society where many faiths were together becoming one of many cultural cities, the difference would be resolved by the Second Vatican Council in favor of the American dream. Judaism meanwhile generated an internal diversity between orthodox, conservative, and reform elements, and earned its place as the "third American religion" without protesting the culture's pluralism.

On the other (winning) hand, voices praised the independence of plural religion in a plural culture. Concerted efforts to enthrone an interdenominational deity in the United States Constitution evoked religious opposition in many quarters, on the grounds that religion must maintain distance from government if it would retain its distinctness in society. In the first volume of *Millennial Dawn* (1886), Charles Taze Russell (1852–1916), founder of the Jehovah's Witnesses, struck notes which anticipated those of prominent neo-orthodox Protestants after the 1930's. Russell derided any such nominal Christianization as spurious and hypocritical. A later, more liberal writer pleaded that "God is put in the Constitution and laws of a Christian people not by legislative fiat, but by the moral conscience and Christian practices of that people; he is kept there in the same way."[15] The health of America and the integrity of the denominations again coincided in the prevailing views. Religion must be free from society's other articulations if it would be free to influence them profoundly. Summarily (if cautiously) stated and "Viewed positively," according to William Lee Miller, "the main current of American religious thought, the marrow of American divinity, has been a unique free church spirit and tradition that arises out of the Protestant past and in some ways is reinforced by the pluralistic present."[16] On our argument, "some" should read "most."

The introductory chapter advanced the suggestion that religion's relation to the main features of contemporary American society may today have become polarized and static. While prediction is forbidden fruit in Clio's garden, it must be noted that the great genius of cultural pluralism is that it allows dynamism and change to characterize relations between its members. There seem to be good reasons for wondering whether religious impulses will again generate new aspirations in the American dream as definite as novelty, participation, education, morality, and nationality.

Nevertheless, the options for relating religion to the many cities of modern America are vital and viable. Existing experiments to advance education, guide public policy, increase economic justice, shape social welfare, promote spiritual and mental health, and the like, chart ways in which the religious element may more or less creatively engage a "polypolitan" culture. To assess their respective shares of the future would require perspectives not granted to historical investigation and would carry us far afield. The cultural pluralism of America which pluralistic religion helped bring into being is in principle accomplished. The success can be called thoroughly profane, with the important reservation that one of the many cities in which American life is lived is the religious city. This culture allows no City of God to rule, much less chiefly to inspire, all its many cities of man. Notwithstanding, for religion to remain one of many cities is to be, if not *the* City of God, at least *one* city of man.

NOTES

PREFACE

1. See Hans W. Frei, "Theological Reflections on the Accounts of Jesus' Death and Resurrection," *The Christian Scholar*, 49 (Winter 1966), especially pp. 275–285, for summary analyses of these modes of identity or description, relying in part upon work of Gilbert Ryle and P. F. Strawson.

CHAPTER ONE: THE PARADOX OF SUCCESS AND FAILURE

1. *New York Times* story in *San Francisco Chronicle*, July 25, 1966, p. 2.

2. Fine examples of such essays are found in *Religious Perspectives in American Culture*, ed. James Ward Smith and A. Leland Jamison (Religion in American Life, 2, Princeton: Princeton University Press, 1961).

3. The study was made possible by an opportunity to examine manuscript collections of the Henry E. Huntington Library, San Marino, Calif., under a grant from the Library's Trustees. Subsequently the Librarian has granted my every request to cite these manuscripts.

4. Lawrence W. Levine, *Defender of the Faith* (New York: Oxford University Press, 1965), p. 292; Reinhold Niebuhr, *Leaves from the Notebook of a Tamed Cynic* (New York: Willett, Clark & Colby, 1929; Hamden, Conn.: Shoe String Press, 1956), p. 36.

5. An interesting example is monasticism for women, the demolition of whose traditions was surveyed with unconcealed delight by Michael Novak in "The New Nuns," *The Saturday Evening Post*, July 30, 1966.

6. An eloquent statement of disillusionment with Christian apologetics was made by William H. Poteat, "Christianity and the Intellectual," in *Viewpoints*, ed. John C. Coburn and W. Norman Pittenger (Greenwich, Conn.: Seabury Press, 1959), reprinted under the same title but with telling revisions in *The Church Review*, 24 (April–May 1966), 3–5. Turmoil over the inapplicability of continental neo-orthodoxy to American secularity

underlies and motivates Paul M. van Buren, *The Secular Meaning of the Gospel* (New York: Macmillan, 1963). The voluminous writings which make the point in very brash ways need not concern us here.

7. Henry F. May, "The Recovery of American Religious History," *American Historical Review*, 70 (Oct. 1964), 79, 92. That such a synthesis had been gained by church historians was noted by William A. Clebsch, "A New Historiography of American Religion," *Historical Magazine of the Protestant Episcopal Church*, 32 (Sept. 1963), 224–257.

8. This paragraph is taken from Clebsch, "A New Historiography," p. 232.

9. Martin E. Marty, *The New Shape of American Religion* (New York: Harper & Brothers, 1959), pp. 78, 80.

10. Perry Miller, "The Marrow of Puritan Divinity," *Errand Into the Wilderness* (Cambridge, Mass.: Harvard University Press, 1956), p. 94. See William A. Clebsch, "New Morality and Old Religion," *Stanford Today*, Winter 1967, pp. 11–16.

11. James Truslow Adams, *The Epic of America* (Boston: Little, Brown, 1931), pp. 404–405. I have discovered no serious interpreter of American history prior to Adams who used "the American dream" as a major interpretive tool.

12. Nathaniel W. Taylor, *Concio ad Clerum. A Sermon delivered in the Chapel of Yale College, September 10, 1828* (New Haven: Hezekiah Howe, 1828), p. 22; see H. Shelton Smith, Robert T. Handy, and Lefferts A. Loetscher, *American Christianity; An Historical Interpretation with Representative Documents* (2 vols., New York: Scribner's, 1960, 1963), 2, 35 (hereafter abbreviated as "*Am. Chr.*").

13. Some such combination of ideas is generally agreed upon as comprising the covenant theology; their origin in Tyndale's thought is argued by William A. Clebsch, *England's Earliest Protestants, 1520–1535* (Yale Studies in Religion, 11, New Haven: Yale University Press, 1964).

14. Perry Miller, "From the Covenant to the Revival," in *The Shaping of American Religion*, ed. James Ward Smith and A. Leland Jamison (Religion in American Life, 1, Princeton: Princeton University Press, 1961), p. 360.

CHAPTER TWO: "AHEAD OF HISTORY"

1. All these lines are widely anthologized and may be found in compendia of famous quotations. Such sources usually give the last line of Berkeley's stanza as "Time's noblest offspring is the last," but see Berkeley, "America or the Muse's Refuge, A Prophecy" (1726), *The Works of George Berkeley of Cloyne*, ed. A. A. Luce and T. E. Jessop (7 vols., London: Thomas Nelson, 1955), 7, 370. Sewall's abstract piece is cited from the 2nd ed., p. 31, as quoted by Charles Sumner, *Prophetic Voices Concerning America, A Monograph* (Boston: Lee and Shepard, 1874; New York: Lee, Shepard, and Dillingham, 1874), p. 30.

2. Philip Schaff, *Der Buergerkrieg und das christliche Leben in Nord-Amerika* (3rd ed., Berlin: Wiegandt und Grieben, 1886), p. 6. See also

Schaff, *America*, p. 31 *et passim*, and Schaff, *American Nationality* (Chambersburg, Pa.: no printer, 1856), pp. 8, 12, 21.

3.   Josiah Strong, *Our Country* (New York: Baker & Taylor, 1885), p. 166; John Adams to Benjamin Rush, May 23, 1807, *The Works of John Adams* (10 vols., Boston: Little, Brown, 1854), 9, 599–600.

4.   Winthrop S. Hudson, *Religion in America* (New York: Scribner's, 1965), pp. 21–22.

5.   David W. Noble, *Historians against History; The Frontier Thesis and the National Covenant in American Historical Writing since 1830* (Minneapolis: University of Minnesota Press, 1965), p. 177.

6.   Roland Van Zandt, *The Metaphysical Foundations of American History* ('s-Gravenhage: Mouton, 1959), pp. 26, 236.

7.   Edward Johnson, *Johnson's Wonder-Working Providence 1628–1651*, ed. J. Franklin Jameson (Original Narratives of Early American History, New York: Scribner's, 1910), p. 25.

8.   Alexis de Tocqueville, *Democracy in America*, trans. Henry Reeve, rev. Francis Bowen, ed. Phillips Bradley (2 vols., New York: Vintage, 1954), *1*, 319; *2*, 135.

9.   Jacques Maritain, *Reflections on America* (New York: Scribner's, 1958), p. 27.

10.   Roger Williams, *The Bloudy Tenent of Persecution for Cause of Conscience, The Complete Writings of Roger Williams*, ed. Samuel L. Caldwell (7 vols., New York: Russell & Russell, 1963), *3*, 3.

11.   Solomon Stoddard, *The Doctrine of Instituted Churches Explained and Proved from the Word of God* (London: for Ralph Smith, 1700), fol. F [4]; see *Am. Chr.*, *1*, 223.

12.   Miller, "From the Covenant to the Revival," p. 346.

13.   Jefferson, Monticello, Va., Aug. 1, 1816, to John Adams, *Writings*, ed. Andrew A. Lipscomb and Albert E. Bergh (20 vols., Washington: Thomas Jefferson Memorial Association, 1904), *15*, 59; see Hans Kohn, *American Nationalism; an Interpretative Essay* (New York: Macmillan, 1957), p 156.

14.   Adams, *Epic of America*, pp. 416–417.

15.   Samuel Cooper, sermon on a text from Jeremiah 2:14–17, preached in Boston, August 28, 1755, p. 7 verso, Cooper Papers, no. 150, Huntington Library. By permission.

16.   Ferdinando Galiani, Naples, May 18, 1776, to Madame d'Épinay, *Correspondance . . .*, ed. Lucien Perey and Gaston Maugras (2 vols., Paris: Michel Lévy Frères, 1881), 2, 443: " . . . *religion, lois, arts, sciences . . . . N'achetez donc pas votre maison à la Chausée-d'Antin, vous l'achèterez à Philadelphie. La malheur est pour moi, puisqu'il n'y a point d'abbayes en Amérique.*" Like many such approbations of America, this one was popularized by Sumner, *Prophetic Voices*, p. 106, and was repeated by Kohn, p. 23. The following citations of Richard Price are from Sumner, pp. 111–113.

17.   Samuel Cooper, *A Sermon Preached Before . . . John Hancock . . .* (Boston: T. and J. Fleet, and J. Gill, 1780), pp. 2–3.

18.   For similar views of George S. Phillips at the time of the Civil War, see below, pp. 188–192.

19. Blair, A Thanksgiving Sermon, pp. [5, 6, 13-14], Brock Collection, box 46, Huntington Library. By permission.

20. *The Federalist*, ed. Jacob E. Cooke (Middletown, Conn.: Wesleyan University Press, 1961), pp. 88-89.

21. Miller, *The Life of the Mind in America from the Revolution to the Civil War* (New York: Harcourt, Brace & World, 1965), pp. 3, 4.

22. *Ibid.*, p. 9.

23. Hartford: Peter B. Gleason, 1814. The pamphlet of 52 close pages is packed with detailed information about each region visited.

24. Charles G. Finney, *Memoirs* . . . (New York: A. S. Barnes, 1876), and *Lectures on Revivals of Religion* (1835), ed William G. McLoughlin (John Harvard Library, Cambridge, Mass.: Belknap Press of Harvard University Press, 1960).

25. Blair, A Thanksgiving Sermon, pp. [1-2], Huntington Library. By permission.

26. *Short Sayings on Times, Men, Measures and Religion* (Pittsfield, Mass.: Phineas Allen and Son, 1830?), p. 4; see LeRoy Moore, "Religious Liberty: Roger Williams and the Revolutionary Era," *Church History, 34* (Mar. 1965), 69, 75. Leland's career is outlined and an extract from his *The Rights of Conscience* . . . is printed in *Am. Chr.*, 1, 469-475.

27. Sidney E. Mead, *The Lively Experiment* (New York: Harper & Row, 1963), p. 38; the previously cited phrases are from p. 52.

28. William Ransom Johnson, Petersburg, Va., July 4, 1833, Oration, pp. 9-10, Brock Collection, box 98, Huntington Library. By permission.

29. Emerson, "An Address Delivered Before the Senior Class in Divinity College, Cambridge, Sunday Evening, July 15, 1838," *Nature, Addresses, and Lectures* (new and rev. ed., Boston: Houghton, Mifflin, 1874), p. 142; see *Am. Chr.*, 2, 139.

30. Charles Philip Krauth, "The Lutheran Church in the United States," *The Evangelical Review*, 2 (July 1850), 9, as quoted by *Am. Chr.*, 2, 103.

31. Jefferson Martenet, Harbaugh Camp, Tuolumne Co., Calif., May 13, 1853, to C. M. Richardson, Martenet Correspondence, no. 0476, Huntington Library. By permission.

32. George Sherman, Journal of a voyage . . . to Astoria, Ore., 1849-53, p. 18 verso, Huntington Manuscripts, no. 2178, Huntington Library. By permission.

33. Charles G. Gray, An overland passage, from Independence, Mo., to San Francisco, Cala. in 1849, 2 vols.; the references, in order, are to *1*, 40, 62, 19, Huntington Manuscripts, no. 16520, Huntington Library. By permission.

34. Lorin[g] Hodge, Mackinaw, July 28, 1820, to Benjamin Hodge; same, Jefferson, Ohio, May 21, 1828, to same, Hodge Papers, nos. 202, 209, Huntington Library. By permission.

35. James Edward Glazier, New Bern, N. C., May 27-29, 1862, to Annie G. Monroe, Glazier Collection, no. 57, Huntington Library. By permission.

36. George Henry Atkinson, Portland, Ore., March 28, 1868, to Sarah Little, Atkinson Collection, Huntington Manuscripts, no. 4495, Huntington Library. By permission.

37. George Wythe Munford, *The Two Parsons; Cupid's Sports; The Dream; and The Jewels of Virginia* (Richmond: J. D. K. Sleight, 1884), pp. 462–463, quoting "from a recent article in the *Selma Times . . . .*"

38. George Santayana, *Character & Opinion in the United States* (New York: Scribner's, 1921), p. vii.

CHAPTER THREE: EQUALS—AND SOME MORE EQUAL

1. Maritain, *Reflections on America*, p. 168. In the same book this philosopher proposed that "we may believe that if a new Christian Civilization, a new Christendom is ever to come about in human history, it is on American soil that it will find its starting point." *Ibid.*, p. 188.

2. John Heuss, "Organizing Our Interdependence," *Overseas Mission Review*, 10, 1 (Michaelmas 1964), 18.

3. G. F. T[ittmann], "Bureaucracy," *ibid.*, 10, 3 (Whitsunday 1965), 3.

4. T. Scott Miyakawa, *Protestants and Pioneers, Individualism and Conformity on the American Frontier* (Chicago: University of Chicago Press, 1964), pp. 213–215.

5. Timothy L. Smith, *Revivalism and Social Reform in Mid-Nineteenth-Century America* (New York: Abingdon, 1957).

6. Miller, *Life of the Mind in America*, book I.

7. For a brief discussion of discipline among American Baptists, see William A. Clebsch and Charles R. Jaekle, *Pastoral Care in Historical Perspective* (New York: Harper Torchbooks, 1967), pp. 62–63; for voluminous records of Baptist meetings involving women as well as men, see William Warren Sweet, *Religion on the American Frontier, The Baptists 1783–1830, A Collection of Source Material* (Chicago: University of Chicago Press, 1931).

8. Alice Felt Tyler, *Freedom's Ferment; Phases of American Social History from the Colonial Period to the Civil War* (Minneapolis: University of Minnesota Press, 1944; New York: Harper Torchbooks, 1962), p. 428.

9. George S. Phillips, Journal of G. S. Phillips . . . 1843–4 North Ohio Conference, Phillips Collection, box 2, Huntington Library. By permission.

10. The title was conferred by Lloyd C. M. Hare, *The Greatest American Woman: Lucretia Mott* (New York: American Historical Society, 1937). The connection between her feminism and Quakerism is asserted by her granddaughter, Anna Davis Hallowell, *James and Lucretia Mott: Life and Letters* (Boston: Houghton, Mifflin, 1884), pp. 298 ff.; see also Otelia Cromwell, *Lucretia Mott* (Cambridge, Mass.: Harvard University Press, 1958), ch. 11.

11. Quoted by Tyler, p. 458.

12. Stoddard, *Doctrine of Instituted Churches*, fol. F [4]; see Am. Chr., 1, 223.

13. Edwards, "Personal Narrative," *Representative Selections*, ed. Clarence H. Faust and Thomas H. Johnson (rev. ed., New York: Hill and Wang, 1962), p. 57.

14. "Narrative of Surprising Conversion," *ibid.*, pp. 73–75 and 85 ff.

15. See Frank J. Klingberg, *Anglican Humanitarianism in Colonial New York* (Philadelphia: Church Historical Society, 1940); *An Appraisal of the*

Negro in Colonial South Carolina (Washington: Associated Publishers, 1941); "The S. P. G. Program for Negroes in Colonial New York," *Historical Magazine of the Protestant Episcopal Church*, 8 (Dec. 1939), 306–371; "The African Immigrant in Colonial Pennsylvania and Delaware," *ibid.*, 11 (Mar. 1942), 126–153; and Samuel Clyde McCulloch, ed., *British Humanitarianism: Essays Honoring Frank J. Klingberg* (Philadelphia: Church Historical Society, 1950).

16. See *Memorial of the Semi-Centennial Anniversary of the American Colonization Society* (Washington: Colonization Society, 1867), especially pp. 61–72, 191.

17. Nelson R. Burr, *A Critical Bibliography of American Religion* (Religion in American Life, 4, Princeton: Princeton University Press, 1961), p. 353; W. E. B. DuBois, *The Negro* (1915), as quoted by Gunnar Myrdal, Richard Sterner, and Arnold Rose, *An American Dilemma, The Negro Problem and Modern Democracy* (New York: Harper & Brothers, 1944), p. 860 n.

18. William A. Clebsch, ed., *Journals of the Protestant Episcopal Church in the Confederate States of America* (Austin: Church Historical Society, 1962), p. xiii.

19. Burr, pp. 359–360.

20. See David M. Reimers, "Negro Bishops and Diocesan Segregation in the Protestant Episcopal Church: 1870–1954," *Historical Magazine of the Protestant Episcopal Church*, 31 (Sept. 1962), 231–254. The situation changed in 1962 when John M. Burgess became suffragan bishop of the Diocese of Massachusetts. For details of attitudes and actions of major white Protestant denominations toward Negroes, see David M. Reimers, *White Protestantism and the Negro* (New York: Oxford University Press, 1965).

21. Horace Muzzy, San Francisco, Feb. 7–19, 1858, to Fidelia Muzzy, Huntington Manuscripts, no. 19327, Huntington Library. By permission.

22. James Edward Glazier, New Bern, N. C., June 24, 1862, to Annie G. Monroe, Glazier Collection, no. 58, Huntington Library. By permission. His war letters are full of passages substantiating these conclusions.

23. Lyman Abbott, New York, Oct. 12, 1865, to Jacob R. Shipherd, Brock Collection, box 120, Huntington Library. By permission.

24. William Walker Morrison, Maryville, Tenn., July 25, 1876, to William Brown, Brock Collection, box 181, Huntington Library. By permission.

25. Myrdal, p. 868.

26. Burr, p. 366.

27. Gideon Hawley, Mashpee, Mass., Jan. 8, 1776, to Samuel Cooper, Samuel Cooper Papers, no. 31, Huntington Library. By permission.

28. Orville A. Nixon, Journal, entries for July 23 and 9, 1855 (punctuation added), Huntington Manuscripts, no. 17012, Huntington Library. By permission.

CHAPTER FOUR: A LITTLE LEARNING

1. *New England's First Fruits* (London: for Henry Overton, 1643), p. 12; also Louis B. Wright, *Culture on the Moving Frontier* (New York:

Harper Torchbooks, 1961), p. 34; concerning Virginia schools, see *ibid.*, pp. 17 ff.

2. Increase Mather, *et al.*, Boston, May 13, 1718, To the Inhabit[ant]s of Boston at their publick Meeting . . . [Recommendations concerning the two grammar free schools], Mather File, no. 123, Huntington Manuscripts, no. 1452, Huntington Library. By permission.

3. Morris R. Cohen, *American Thought: A Critical Sketch*, ed. Felix S. Cohen (New York: Collier Books, 1962), pp. 52–53.

4. Anonymous, The Fathers of the Presbyterian Church in Virginia, pp. 21–22, Brock Manuscripts, no. 645, Huntington Library. By permission.

5. Jefferson, Monticello, Va., Apr. 13, 1820, to William Short, *Writings*, 15, 246. See Richard Hofstadter and Walter P. Metzger, *The Development of Academic Freedom in the United States* (New York: Columbia University Press, 1955), p. 240.

6. Jefferson, "Systematic Plan of General Education," in Adrienne Koch, ed., *The American Enlightenment* (New York: George Braziller, 1965), p. 298.

7. Koch, p. 281.

8. See William A. R. Goodwin, ed., *History of the Theological Seminary in Virginia and Its Historical Background* (2 vols., New York: Edwin S. Gorham, 1923).

9. Jefferson, Washington, Mar. 23, 1801, to Moses Robinson, *Writings*, 10, 236–237. The famous slogan appears in Jefferson, Monticello, Va., Sept. 23, 1800, to Benjamin Rush, *ibid.*, p. 175. See Fred C. Luebke, "The Origins of Thomas Jefferson's Anti-Clericalism," *Church History*, 32 (Sept. 1963), 350.

10. See *Am. Chr.*, 2, 16.

11. Horace Muzzy, San Francisco, Mar. 27–Apr. 4, 1858, to Fidelia Muzzy, Huntington Manuscripts, no. 19330, Huntington Library. By permission.

12. Jacob Smith Boreman, Reminiscences of my life in Utah, on and off the bench, p. 30, Huntington Manuscripts, no. 16917, Huntington Library. By permission.

13. George S. Phillips, Journal, Dec. 17 [16], 1844, Phillips Collection, box 2, Huntington Library. By permission. See also Miyakawa, *Protestants and Pioneers*, p. 109.

14. See David E. Blaine and Catherine Paine Blaine, Letters . . . written 1853 to 1862 from Oregon and Washington to relatives in New York, typescript compiled by Thomas W. Prosch, pp. 12–13 *et passim*, Huntington Manuscripts, no. 16776, Hungtinton Library. By permission.

15. Truman Marcellus Post, *The First Report of the Society for the Promotion of Collegiate and Theological Education at the West* (New York, 1844), pp. 25–28, as quoted by *Am. Chr.*, 2, 50–51.

16. E. Harris Harbison, *Christianity and History* (Princeton: Princeton University Press, 1964), p. 90. The essay containing these phrases, entitled "Liberal Education and Christian Education," was printed in *The Christian Idea of Education*, ed. Edmund Fuller (New Haven: Yale University Press, 1957).

17. Hofstadter and Metzger, p. 279.

226   NOTES FOR PAGES 118-133

18. For a summary of the character and effects of McGuffey's work, see Wright, pp. 215–222.
19. Charles Maclay, Article on the subject of lending aid to Dickinson Seminary at Williamsport, Pa., Apr. 4, 1849, Maclay Papers, no. 150(B), Huntington Library. By permission.
20. Wright, pp. 175, 223.
21. Catherine P. Blaine, Seattle, Aug. 4, 1854, Letters . . ., p. 77, Huntington Library. By permission.
22. George Henry Atkinson, Oregon City, Ore., June 28, 1853, to Thomas Hale, Atkinson Collection, Huntington Manuscripts, no. 4470, Huntington Library. By permission.
23. George Henry Atkinson, Oregon City, Ore., Mar. 6, 1855, to Josiah Little and Sophronia Little, Atkinson Collection, Huntington Manuscripts, no. 4475, Huntington Library. By permission.
24. See George P. Schmidt, *The Liberal Arts College, A Chapter in American Cultural History* (New Brunswick, N. J.: Rutgers University Press, 1957), p. 35. The quotation is from Henry Steele Commager, *The American Mind* (New Haven: Yale University Press, 1950), p. 167.
25. Horace Bushnell, *Movement for a University in California. A Statement to the Public, by the Trustees of the College of California, and an Appeal, by Dr. Bushnell* (San Francisco: Pacific Publishing Co., 1857), pp. 19, 14, 13 respectively.
26. See Schmidt, p. 41.
27. Quoted by David Mead, *Yankee Eloquence in the Middle West; the Ohio Lyceum 1850–1870* (East Lansing: Michigan State College Press, 1951), pp. 145–146.
28. For a summary, see Hudson, *Religion in America*, pp. 234 ff., where standard monographs are cited.
29. Adam H. Erwin, Salisbury, N. C., Apr. 10, 1867, to George L. Shearer, Brock Collection, box 154, Huntington Library. By permission.
30. R. N. Shedd, Lynchburg, Va., Feb. 2, 1869, to T. L. D. Walford, *ibid.* By permission.
31. William C. Mosher, Journal of a Presbyterian Missionary, 1854–1906, p. 194, Huntington Manuscripts, no. 16297, Huntington Library. By permission.
32. Robert T. Jones, Flat Rock, N. C., July 31, 1867, to George L. Shearer, Brock Collection, box 154, Huntington Library. By permission.
33. William E. Boggs, Memphis, Tenn., Apr. 27, 1875, to William Brown, Brock Collection, box 182, Huntington Library. By permission.
34. See Mosher, pp. 167–169. By permission.
35. William Henry Ruffner, Lexington, Va., Dec. 22, 1869, to William Brown, Brock Collection, box 181, Huntington Library. By permission .
36. Peter Tinsley Penick, Mebaneville, N. C., Nov. 11, 1875, to William Brown, Brock Collection, box 182, Huntington Library. By permission.
37. Benjamin Mosby Smith, Hampden Sidney, Va., Sept. 29, 1873, to William Brown, Brock Collection, box 180, Huntington Library. By permission.
38. Rush Nutt, near Natchez, Miss., *ca.* 1830–1835, Remarks upon

Education, fol. 5a, Nutt Collection, no. 363(19), Huntington Library. By permission. Nutt was as good as his word; in a much earlier letter to his wife on the occasion of the death of her brother, he invoked "christian fortitude," "the help of God," and the hope that Mrs. Nutt would be so "resigned to the will of God that you will put your trust in him—he is ready & willing to receive us—he will soften your afflictions & enable you to bear with your losses." Rush Nutt, Wicomico Church, Va., Feb. 6, 1818, to Eliza Nutt, Nutt Collection, no. 262, Huntington Library. By permission.

39. "History is necessary to the living man in three ways: in relation to his action and struggle, his conservatism and reverence, his suffering and his desire for deliverance. These three relations answer to the three kinds of history—so far as they can be distinguished—the *monumental*, the *antiquarian*, and the *critical*." Friedrich Nietzsche, *The Use and Abuse of History* (1874; trans. Adrian Collins, New York: Liberal Arts Press, 1957), p. 12. For a brief analysis of religious employment of these uses of history, see William A. Clebsch, "Anglican *Anamnesis*," *Anglican Theological Review*, 47 (Apr. 1965), 227–232.

40. See Hofstadter and Metzger, p. 115.

41. *Ibid.*, pp. 302–303, 315.

42. *Ibid.*, p. 211.

CHAPTER FIVE: "LET MEN BE GOOD"

1. A. N. Kaul, *The American Vision; Actual and Ideal Society in Nineteenth-Century Fiction* (Yale Publications in American Studies, 7, New Haven: Yale University Press, 1963), p. 14.

2. Williston Walker, *The Creeds and Platforms of Congregationalism* (New York: Scribner's, 1893), p. 203.

3. Daniel Boorstin, *The Americans, The Colonial Experience* (New York: Random House, 1958), p. 22.

4. *The Laws and Liberties of Massachusetts* (Cambridge, Mass.: Harvard University Press, 1929), sig. A2 verso; Boorstin comments, p. 24, "They were trying, for the most part, to demonstrate the coincidence between what the scriptures required and what English law had already provided."

5. See the excellent new edition of *Bonifacius*, ed. David Levin (The John Harvard Library, Cambridge, Mass.: The Belknap Press of Harvard University Press, 1966). For a revealing excerpt from Hopkins, see *Am. Chr.*, 1, 540–545.

6. Boorstin, p. 97.

7. Richard Coote, *His Excellency, the Earl of Bellomont His Speech To the Representatives of his Majesties Province of New-York, the 21th of March, 1699* (New York: William Bradford, 1699), p. 2. The three-page folio address is in the Ellesmere Collection, no. 9776, vol. 138, Huntington Library. By permission.

8. William Penn, *Primitive Christianity Revived, in the Faith and Practice of the People Called Quakers* (London: T. Sowle, 1696), pp. 1–2; see *Am. Chr.*, 1, 238, 241.

9. Sydney E. Ahlstrom, "Thomas Hooker—Puritanism and Democratic

Citizenship; A Preliminary Inquiry into Some Relationships of Religion and American Civic Responsibility," *Church History*, 32 (Dec. 1963), 428–429.

10. *Ibid.*, p. 427. On Lawrence and Carnegie, see Mead, *The Lively Experiment*, p. 147 *et passim*, and the sources there cited.

11. *The Works of John Witherspoon* (4 vols., Philadelphia: William W. Woodward, 1802), 3, 447–448; see James L. McAllister, "John Witherspoon: Academic Advocate for American Freedom," *A Miscellany of American Christianity*, ed. Stuart C. Henry (Durham, N. C.: Duke University Press, 1963).

12. John Moncure, sermon on I Kings 21:29, July 28, 1756, pp. 16–17, 19, Brock Collection, box 120, Huntington Library. By permission. For a survey of the genre of jeremiads and its function see Perry Miller, "From the Covenant to the Revival," pp. 322–368.

13. Author unknown, sermon on Psalm 147:12–14, *ca.* 1795?, pp. 25, 26, Brock Collection, box 120, Huntington Library. By permission.

14. See Luebke, "Origins of Thomas Jefferson's Anti-Clericalism."

15. Rush Nutt, Remarks upon Education, p. 3 recto-verso, Nutt Collection, no. 363(19), Huntington Library. By permission.

16. John Dewey, *A Common Faith* (New Haven: Yale University Press, 1934), p. 28.

17. Miller, *Life of the Mind in America*, p. 10. McIlvaine is erroneously made a Methodist by Miller on pp. 10, 54, 61, but is properly identified on pp. 92, 93.

18. Wright, *Culture on the Moving Frontier*, p. 97.

19. Schermerhorn and Mills, *A Correct View*, *passim*.

20. Joseph Augustine Benton, *The California Pilgrim* (Sacramento: Solomon Alter, 1853; San Francisco: Marvin & Hitchcock, 1853), p. 181.

21. Sermons, tracts, and articles abound. McIlvaine's "Address to the Young Men of the United States on Temperance" as quoted by *Am. Chr.*, 2, 41.

22. G. A. Cassil, Middle Fork, American River, Calif., May 5, 1850, to Hannah Cassil Kinkade and James Kinkade, Kinkade Correspondence, no. 4; John Thompson Kinkade, Secret Ravine, Calif., Mar. 31, 1858, to James Kinkade, *ibid.*, no. 71; Huntington Library. By permission.

23. William Byrd II, *The Prose Work of William Byrd of Westover, Narratives of a Colonial Virginian*, ed. Louis B. Wright (Cambridge, Mass.: Belknap Press of Harvard University Press, 1966), pp. 134–135, 283–284.

24. Schermerhorn and Mills, p. 15.

25. J. T. Edgar, Samuel Steel, and Robert Jefferson Breckinridge, commissioners of West Lexington, Ky., Presbytery, Cincinnati, 1831, Report to the [Presbyterian] General Assembly, Huntington Manuscripts, no. 25575, Janes Collection, Huntington Library. By permission.

26. See, in order: Stanislaus Laselle, Diary of an overland journey . . . by way of Ft. Smith, Ark., to Santa Fe, N. M., and the Spanish Trail . . . 1849, Feb. 6–Aug. 21, typescript (of original in Indiana State Library), Huntington Manuscripts, no. 16759; Charles G. Gray, An overland passage, June 17, 1849, Huntington Manuscripts, no. 16520, 1, 47; Huntington Library. By permission. The guarantee is by Joseph E. Ware, *The Emigrant's*

Guide to California (St. Louis: J. Halsell, 1849), p. 10. See Irene D. Parden, ed., *The Journal of Madison Berryman Moorman 1850–1851* (San Francisco: California Historical Society, 1948), pp. 94–95.

27. William Heath Davis, The Habits of the Miners on Sundays, typescript, Davis Papers, 2(256), Huntington Library. By permission.

28. Ray Allen Billington, *The Far Western Frontier 1830–1860* (New American Nation Series, New York: Harper & Brothers, 1956; Harper Torchbooks, 1962), p. 237. See also William A. Clebsch, ed., "Goodness, Gold, and God, The California Mining Career of Peter Y. Cool, 1851–52," *The Pacific Historian*, 10, 3 (Summer 1966), 19–42.

29. Horace Muzzy, San Francisco, Sept. 6–20, 1857, to Fidelia Muzzy, Huntington Manuscripts, no. 19318, Huntington Library. By permission.

30. Charles Maclay, Speech to the California assembly, 1862, first draft, p. 8, Maclay Papers, no. 165(1), Huntington Library. By permission.

31. Laurentine Hamilton, The Duty of the Chtn Ch in relation to the Religious Wants of the World, sermon preached in Oakland, Calif., Jan. 10, 1869, pp. [19, 22], Hamilton Collection, box 1, Huntington Library. By permission.

32. Hamilton, Salvation, individual & national by Knowledge, sermon preached in Oakland, Calif., May 8, 1870, p. [13], *ibid.* By permission.

33. Hamilton, What the True Manhood requires us to do, sermon preached in Oakland, Calif., Feb. 13, 1870, p. [1], *ibid.* By permission.

34. Horace Bushnell, *Society and Religion: a Sermon for California . . .* (Hartford: L. E. Hunt, 1856), in order, pp. 6, 6, 10, 11, 16, 22, 24, 25.

35. Kaul, pp. 37–44.

36. *Ibid.*, p. 34.

37. Excerpted in *Am. Chr.*, 2, 369–372.

38. Robert R. Roberts, "The Social Gospel and the Trust-Busters," *Church History*, 25 (Sept. 1956), 239.

39. Kohn, *American Nationalism*, p. 83. Herbert G. Gutman, "Protestantism and the American Labor Movement: The Christian Spirit in the Gilded Age," *American Historical Review*, 72 (Oct. 1966), 74–101; the discussion of this topic relies heavily upon Gutman's article and contains quotations, in order, from pp. 80, 82, 83, 84, 90, 95, 101.

40. Burr, *A Critical Bibliography*, p. 695.

41. Mead, p. 187.

CHAPTER SIX: "THIS NATION, UNDER GOD"

1. John Winthrop, *Winthrop's Journal*, ed. James K. Hosmer (Original Narratives of Early American History, 2 vols., New York: Scribner's, 1908), 2, 83–84.

2. Miller, *Errand into the Wilderness*, p. 6.

3. Congregational Churches of Massachusetts, Elders, Jan. 4, 1680/81, The Answer of the Elders to the Question propounded to them by ye Honrd. Genll. Court, Blathwayt Collection, no. 226, Huntington Library. By permission.

4. Congregational Churches of Massachusetts, Delegates of Associations,

What further steps are to be taken . . ., Sept. 13, 1705, Huntington Manuscripts, no. 1262 (Mather file), Huntington Library. By permission. Cf. Walker, *Creeds and Platforms of Congregationalism*, pp. 486–490.

5. The "Account" and Keith's *Journal* were edited by Edgar Legare Pennington and published in *Historical Magazine of the Protestant Episcopal Church*, 20 (Dec. 1951).

6. Miyakawa, *Protestants and Pioneers*, p. 46. See also L. C. Rudolph, *Francis Asbury* (Nashville: Abingdon Press, 1966).

7. Samuel Hopkins, *The System of Doctrines Contained in Divine Revelation* (2 vols., Boston: Isaiah Thomas and Ebenezer T. Andrews, 1793), *1*, 545, 556; see *Am. Chr.*, *1*, 540, 543.

8. Author unknown, sermon on Psalm 147:12–14, *ca.* 1795?, pp. 20, 28–29, Brock Collection, box 120, Huntington Library. By permission. Punctuation modernized.

9. Francis Grund, *The Americans in Their Moral, Social, and Political Relations* (1837), in Henry Steele Commager, ed., *America in Perspective* (New York: Random House, 1947), p. 87.

10. Miller, *Life of the Mind in America*, in order, pp. 165, 5–6, 11.

11. *Ibid.*, p. 55.

12. Phillips, *The American Republic*, pp. 130, 153.

13. *Ibid.*, pp. 62, 156–157.

14. *Ibid.*, pp. 174, 217, 232, 236.

15. *Work and Play* (New York: Scribner's, 1881), p. 360. Not all of Bushnell's essays can be neatly dated, and accurate dating of his writings would provide faint clues to the development of his thought, for he continually set leading ideas in changing juxtapositions. He was preoccupied with the motif of nationality at least as early as his Phi Beta Kappa oration given on "The True Wealth and Weal of Nations" during the economic crisis of 1837, and the achievement of American nationality through the Civil War provided a historic paradigm for the richly modern doctrine of the atonement which he propounded in his great work, *The Vicarious Sacrifice, Grounded in Principles of Universal Obligation* (1866), and its sequel, *Forgiveness and Law, Grounded in Principles Interpreted by Human Analogies* (1874); the very titles eloquently indicate his theological method. For a longer discussion of Bushnell's conception of American nationality, see William A. Clebsch, "Baptism of Blood: A Study of Christian Contributions to the Interpretation of the Civil War in American History," unpublished dissertation, Union Theological Seminary, New York, 1957 (University Microfilms), Ch. 3.

16. "The Founders Great in Their Unconsciousness," *Work and Play*, p. 141.

17. "Popular Government by Divine Right," *Building Eras in Religion* (New York: Scribner's, 1881), p. 311.

18. "Our Obligations to the Dead," *ibid.*, p. 329.

19. Schaff, *Der Buergerkrieg*, pp. 22, 25; trans. C. C. S[tarbuck], "Dr. Schaff's Lectures on America Delivered in Europe, 1865," *The Christian Intelligencer*, ed. Elbert S. Porter, 37, 9 (Apr. 26, 1886), 3, and 37, 10 (May 2, 1866), 21.

20. See Clebsch, "Baptism of Blood," pp. 136–189.

21. Robert Lewis Dabney, "Wilson's Slave Power in America," and "The New South," *Discussions*, ed. C. R. Vaughan (4 vols., Mexico, Mo.: Crescent Book House, 1897), 4, 249, 4. Dabney's review of Henry Wilson, *History of the Rise and Fall of the Slave Power in America* (Boston, 1872–1877), originally appeared in *Southern Planter and Farmer*, July 1897.

22. Abraham Lincoln, "Address to the New Jersey Senate at Trenton, New Jersey," Feb. 21, 1861, *The Collected Works of Abraham Lincoln*, ed. Roy P. Basler (9 vols., New Brunswick, N. J.: Rutgers University Press, 1953), 4, 236.

23. Lincoln, Washington, D. C., Aug. 22, 1862, to Horace Greeley, *Collected Works*, 5, 388–389.

24. *Ibid.*, 7, 23.

25. Robert Frost, "The Black Cottage," *Complete Poems of Robert Frost 1949* (New York: Henry Holt, n. d.), p. 75.

26. *Am. Chr.*, 2, 178.

27. E.g., *ibid.*, 2, 367–368.

28. The most important literature on the Maryknoll Fathers is discussed by Burr, *A Critical Bibliography*, pp. 413–415.

29. Hudson, *Religion in America*, p. 319.

30. Levine, *Defender of the Faith*, p. 27, citing several of Bryan's writings in which the phrase, or a variant of it, occurs.

31. Rufus M. Jones, "The Quaker Peace Position," *The Survey*, 34 (1915), 22–23, as quoted by *Am. Chr.*, 2, 398, 399, 401; emphasis added.

32. Mead, *The Lively Experiment*, pp. 134, 135.

CHAPTER SEVEN: A "POLYPOLITAN" CULTURE

1. The economic city has been touched upon in connection with public morality. The Princeton series on Religion in American Life promises as its third volume "a permanent—indeed classic—contribution to comprehension of the European background of religion and economics in America" by Jacob Viner; that volume had not appeared by mid-1967 and it seemed wise to attempt no systematic treatment of its theme in this study. See Smith and Jamison, eds., *The Shaping of American Religion*, p. 16.

2. See John E. Smith, *The Spirit of American Philosophy* (New York: Oxford University Press, 1963), especially pp. 103, 106.

3. William James, *A Pluralistic Universe* (London: Longmans, Green, 1912), pp. 321–322.

4. Mark DeWolfe Howe, *The Garden and the Wilderness, Religion and Government in American Constitutional History* (Chicago: University of Chicago Press, 1965), pp. 5–9.

5. Sidney E. Mead, "The Post-Protestant Concept and America's Two Religions," *Religion in Life*, 33 (Spring 1964), 204.

6. Herbert J. Muller, *Religion and Freedom in the Modern World* (Chicago: University of Chicago Press, 1963), p. 82.

7. Wilber G. Katz and Harold P. Southerland, "Religious Pluralism and the Supreme Court," *Daedalus*, Winter 1967, p. 191.

8. Leo Pfeffer, *Creeds in Competition; A Creative Force in American Culture* (New York: Harper & Brothers, 1958), p. 18.

9. Katz and Southerland, p. 180.

10. David E. Blaine, Oregon City, Ore., Dec. 23, 1856, Letters . . ., ed. Prosch, p. 197, Huntington Manuscripts, no. 16776, Huntington Library. By permission.

11. See Charles Y. Glock and Rodney Stark, *Religion and Society in Tension* (Rand McNally Sociology Series, Chicago: Rand McNally, 1965), pp. 134-135.

12. Fredrika Bremer, *The Homes of the New World*, trans. Mary Howitt (2 vols., New York: Harper & Brothers, 1853), 1, 625-626.

13. Strong, *Our Country, passim,* especially Ch. 10.

14. *Testem benevolentiae, Am. Chr.,* 2, 340.

15. R. Kemp Morton, *God in the Constitution* (Nashville: Cokesbury Press, 1933), p. 182.

16. William Lee Miller, "American Religion and American Political Attitudes," *Religious Perspectives in American Culture,* p. 84.

INDEX

233